THE RUSSIAN REVOLUTION OF 1917

DIMITRI VON MOHRENSCHILDT

The Russiar

Revolution of 1917

CONTEMPORARY ACCOUNTS

EW YORK

OXFORD UNIVERSITY PRESS

LONDON — TORONTO — 1971

082793-4491H/2

PREFACE

This volume consists of accounts by participants and eyewitnesses of the great Russian upheaval of 1917. Several selections are by makers of history, those who stood at the very center of revolutionary action; other selections, though not by the top leaders, are by active participants in the events described; still others are by ordinary citizens caught up in the whirlpool of revolutionary Russia.

A wide political spectrum of the contending parties and forces is represented here: Bolsheviks, Mensheviks, Socialist Revolutionaries, Cadets, Octobrists, and loyal monarchists. Whatever the nature of a specific contribution, whether it is—strictly speaking—a memoir, a commentary, or an analysis of a specific event or a revolutionary phase, most of the accounts in this volume can be considered as primary sources, the raw material of history.

It is hoped that the selections presented will give the student of history and the general reader a feeling for the atmosphere of the period and a better understanding of the complexity, the drama, and the passionate controversy of the year 1917.

The book is divided into three parts. Part I, "Russia on the Eve of the Revolution," deals with the background of the Revolution and contains articles on some of the major problems confronting Russia in the two decades preceding the Revolution. Part II, "Revolution and Civil War," comprises the bulk of the book. It covers rather extensively the crucial period from the fall of the monarchy to the Bolshevik seizure of power in October. Part III, "Epilogue," consists of R. Ivanov-Razumnik's reminiscences of his prison experiences under Lenin and Stalin. It provides a vivid account of one of the immediate consequences of the Bolshevik Revolution—the tragic

v

plight of the prerevolutionary intelligentsia—and can be considered as a fitting epilogue to 1917.

The reader should bear in mind that some of the accounts were written many years after the Revolution, largely from memory, which varies widely with each individual. He must also be aware that although more than half a century has elapsed since the Revolution, some of the accounts presented here still reflect the original emotions and the conflict of ideas that characterized the fateful year 1917. It will thus fall upon the reader to evaluate for himself the testimonies presented. The editorial comment was kept to a minimum, since the accounts should speak for themselves. However, in order to facilitate the task of interpretation, short identifications of the contributors, establishing their relationships to the events concerned, precede each of the selections.

The material for this anthology is drawn largely from *The Russian Review,* an interdisciplinary quarterly devoted to Russia past and present, which holds the copyrights to the articles reprinted from it. Material drawn from other sources, like that from *The Russian Review,* is acknowledged in a note following the introductory comments to each selection.

The transliteration of Russian names follows the usually accepted practice based on a simplified Library of Congress system of transliteration. Unless otherwise indicated, the dates are in the "old style" (Julian calendar), which, in this century, is thirteen days behind the Western (Gregorian) calendar. Footnotes supplied by the editor of this book are marked [Ed.].

Finally, I would like to express my appreciation to my colleagues Professors Warren B. Walsh, Nicholas V. Riasanovsky, Ralph Fisher, Jr., and Albert Parry for their encouragement in the preparation of this volume. Special thanks are due to the individual contributors, many of whom are now dead, whose contributions made this anthology possible.

Stanford, California   Dimitri von Mohrenschildt
June 1970

CONTENTS

Contents

PART I

RUSSIA ON THE EVE OF THE REVOLUTION

V. MAKLAKOV

The Agrarian Problem in Russia
Before the Revolution

V. A. Maklakov (1870–1957) was a Moscow and St. Petersburg attorney. Member of the Constitutional Democratic Party and delegate to the Second, Third, and Fourth Dumas, he was a lucid and sober orator and took special interest in the agrarian problem. After the February/March Revolution he was the Provisional Government's ambassador to Paris. In emigration, Maklakov was engaged in polemics with Miliukov concerning tactics and program of the Cadets and reasons for the failure of Russian liberalism. He is the author of several books on the Dumas, including *Vlast i obshchestvennost na zakate staroi Rossii (Government and Society in the Last Years of Old Russia)*, Paris, 1932.

The following authoritative analysis of the agrarian problem and Stolypin's reform can be considered a primary source, since the author reported agrarian reform bills in 1916 to the Fourth Duma.

The agrarian problem in Russia presented several paradoxes. A country of boundless territorial expanse, with a sparse population, suffered from a *shortage of land*. And the peasant class, elsewhere usually a bulwark of order, in Russia, evidenced in 1917 a revolutionary temper.

These peculiarities are rooted in history. I can deal here only briefly with their historic causes.

From *The Russian Review,* vol. 9, no. 1 (January 1950), pp. 3–15.

By the beginning of the nineteenth century, Russia had evolved a social order based upon serfdom. The landed class owned not only the land upon which the peasants were settled, but the peasants themselves. This crucial fact was reflected in the whole political system. The usual functions of the state — police, jurisdiction, collection of taxes, recruiting of the army — in rural Russia were performed by the landlords through the medium of their serfs, and the landlords were answerable for them to the state.

In 1861, with the emancipation of the serfs, the axis which supported the whole body politic disappeared. Other reforms became unavoidable; and the agrarian, judiciary, military reorganization filled the following years, known in history as the Era of the Great Reforms.

Serfdom became a thing of the past, but in its stead there arose the "peasant problem." Remnants of the old feudal relationships survived into the new era. In 1861, the emancipated peasants had been endowed with land bought for them by the state from their former owners and had to pay off their debt to the state in instalments. In order to protect the peasants against the loss of their land, these "allotted lands," as they were called, were declared by law "inalienable" and made the joint property of the whole village commune composed of former serfs of the same master. This commune was given the right of periodical re-allotment of the land among the individual homesteads. In this way the threat of "landlessness" was mitigated; but on the other hand, the peasant was made dependent on his commune in a manner unknown to the other social classes and alien to Russian law. It must be admitted that as a transitional phase from "slavery" to "freedom" this was a bold concept. Rural self-government going so far as to include the distribution of common lands, judges and officials elected by the peasants themselves, the application to rural life of "customary law" instead of the general Code — all this represented a democratic solution of the chief problem posed by the historic situation: that of finding a substitute for the authority of the landlords over their serfs.

However, this provisional solution should not have hampered the process of the gradual extension of general civil legislation to the peasantry. After all, the transformation of the serfs into full-fledged citizens had been the chief purpose of the reforms. The reform of the judicial system and that of local self-government (*zemstvo*) expressly recognized this goal. The same principle of "equalization" should have been applied to the problem of the "allotted lands" and the relationship between the individual peasant and the village commune. Autocracy, which in 1861 had used its absolute power to liberate the slaves and to endow them with land, surely would have been able to complete the process of "equalization." However, all great reforms have a tendency to change their pace—to slow up at times and even to give way to backward movements. "Revolution" and "reaction" are closely interlocked and feed each other. . . . So it happened in Russia in the late sixties. The reforms of Alexander II came to a standstill; and the seventies became a decade of intense revolutionary action directed against the person of the Sovereign. On March 1, 1881—the very day when Alexander II signed the decree introducing a kind of "popular representation"—which might have developed into a genuine constitutional system—he was killed by a terrorist's bomb. The reign of Alexander III began.

It is understandable that the new Tsar, who succeeded to the throne under such tragic circumstances, felt no inclination to give up absolute power, and declared in his Manifesto of April 29 that he would "preserve autocracy for the good of the people."* The great mistake of Alexander III, to which he was driven by his new advisers, was not the preservation of absolute monarchy, which only a short while ago had fully justified itself, but that for its sake he repudiated the great reforms of his father and initiated reactionary legislation in the fields of education (1884), local self-government (1889), and the judiciary. The same thing happened to the peasant problem. A backward movement set in, and the peculiar features which had been considered temporary, now came to be regarded as the groundwork of the state.

It was this attitude that lent its unusual character to the peasant problem in Russia. Everywhere the peasantry forms a social class of small landowners. In Russia it became a kind of *caste*. Since it possessed the exclusive right to the lands allotted in 1861, and these lands had been made "inalienable" and inaccessible to the other classes, few outsiders could enter this "caste."

---

* The revolutionary party made public a letter to Alexander III upon his accession, promising to stop terrorism if autocracy were replaced by a constitution. Nothing could have been more compromising for all advocates of liberal reforms. As to the revolutionary party, it was soon crushed.

That was not all. Whenever a peasant was able to make his way
up the social ladder, to obtain a university education, to achieve
rank and position in government or military service, he was auto-
matically raised into the higher social group of "honorary citizens"
and ceased to be a "peasant"—losing as a result his right to the
allotted land. This system inevitably influenced the status of the
peasant class. The elite of the peasantry, those who ought to have
been the champions of its interests, withdrew from their class, and
this kept alive the antiquated tendency to regard the peasants as
an inferior social group. The state subjected them to all kinds of
special impositions. Before the emancipation, these might have
been justified by their status as serfs (so long as the system itself
was not questioned). The peasants themselves, their time, and
their labor belonged to the landlord. The civic duties actually
performed by the serfs were imposed by the state upon the landlord
who was responsible for their execution. The routine of local administration—the repair of roads and bridges, the fight against
floods and fires, the maintenance of the lower police—all this was
the obligation of the landowners within the boundaries of their
estates, and it was carried out by their serfs. After the emancipation, these services became the responsibility of the peasants' elective authorities—who, in addition to looking after the needs of the
peasants, were thus compelled to carry out the orders of the general
administration. The heavy load of these impositions—which served
the interests of the whole population—was borne *exclusively by the
peasants,* who provided both the labor and the necessary funds.

This was not only a crying injustice but also a technically in-
efficient system. The obligation of the peasant class to "run er-
rands" for the general administration was an intolerable burden
which distracted them from their real work, the cultivation of the
land. The "elections" no longer were a matter of choosing the best
men, but became a system of rotation. Some official attempts were
made to correct the ensuing chaotic conditions in the villages.
In 1889, the institution of "rural superintendents" *(zemsky nachal-
nik)* was created—officers appointed by the government from
among the local landowners. They not only replaced the former
justices of peace elected by the organs of the local self-government
(representing all classes), but were put in control of the peasants'
elective authorities. Their decisions could be appealed only to their
own District Assembly, presided over by the District Marshal of the

Nobility. This innovation, which was meant to introduce some order into rural life, reminded the peasants of their recent subjection to the landlords.*

Thus originated the "peasant problem" in Russia. Their legal status alone would have explained the peasants' discontent. But to this was added the economic burden. The land allotted to them in 1861 may have been sufficient to support them at that time, but the population increased, and the load of taxes and duties grew from year to year, while the land area at the peasants' disposal remained the same. The system of communal land tenure kept farming on the lowest level. To leave the village in order to seek supplementary work, one needed the permission of the commune, which was not given without compensation. The average peasant could obtain additional earnings only through renting some land from a big landowner, or hiring himself out to work on a big estate. The peasants were fully justified in resenting their conditions; and it so happened that all the measures of the government directed their discontent against the landowners.

This had important consequences for the land problem proper. The peasants became convinced that they had a rightful claim to the land of their former masters. Under the system of serfdom, the master had the obligation either to provide his serfs with land or else to support them as his house servants. After 1861, if the emancipation had been completed, there would no longer have been any foundation for such a conception. But the government itself had turned the situation into a "class problem," with peasants and landowners in opposite camps. The subjection of the peasants to the landowners and their right to the latter's land were inextricably linked in the peasants' consciousness. The keener the peasant was made to feel his inequality with regard to the landowner, the stronger grew his conviction that he was entitled to the latter's land. (It is significant that the peasants, as was shown in 1917, usually claimed only the land of their own former masters.) The idea that land was God's gift, and as such should not be the object of private ownership, had little to do with the peasants' conviction. That was a fond illusion of many Russian idealists. The Russian peasant,

---

* In addressing a delegation of village elders at his coronation, Alexander III said: "Obey the orders of your Marshals of the Nobility!" There could have been no clearer reminder that things had not changed very much.

like any other peasant, was a believer in private property. He wanted the gentry's land for his very own.

One of the consequences of the peasants' attitude was the artificial aggravation of the land shortage. Russia had enough land for all who wished to cultivate it; but this presupposed an organized redistribution of the population and the settlement of vacant areas. It was not only the inertia of the government and the selfishness of the landowners—who profited from the availability of cheap labor near their estates—which prevented this redistribution: the peasants themselves resisted it, reluctant to abandon their right to the allotted lands and to give up the hope of coming into possession of the remaining lands of their former masters. In this way an artifical land shortage was created in the vicinity of the big estates.

The men at the helm of the state should have realized the danger that threatened Russia from this source; but under Alexander III they were in the grip of a violent reaction against the Great Reforms and blinded by their successful suppression of all revolutionary attempts. They believed in the necessity of upholding the old order. Their agrarian policy, accordingly, was based upon the preservation of some of the most outdated features of the traditional era: class division, isolation of the peasantry, its subjection to special laws and special authorities; in a word, the perpetuation of its inequality. The statesmen who shaped the agrarian policy of that reign were nurtured on these ideas. Witte alone of all the prominent men of that time understood that absolute monarchy could be saved only through a further development of the great reforms of the sixties. In charge of Russia's financial policy, he was determined to promote the industrialization of the country; and he realized that this presupposed a vast domestic market—a well-to-do farmer class instead of an underprivileged and pauperized peasantry. Witte's ideas were taken up under the successor of Alexander III, when the whole problem was posed in a different way.

It is impossible here to go into details, but it is generally known that under Tsar Nicholas II the question of the fundamental transformation of Russia's political system—of the replacement of autocracy by a constitutional monarchy—definitely came to the fore. The public had reached the conclusion that no real improvement of conditions was possible under absolute monarchy and what was needed was a thorough "Reform" instead of partial "reforms." The movement which called itself "liberating" steadily grew. Its slogan was: "Down with Autocracy!" Any concrete amelioration of conditions was appraised by this movement only as another stepping-stone in the struggle for a new order.

This did not come about all at once. The regime still could have gone back to the Great Reforms—with the full support of public opinion. Witte actually attempted to approach the problem in such a way. In 1897, in his report on the national budget, he stressed for the first time the necessity of *equalizing the status of the peasantry* with that of the other classes. In the eyes of the conservatives this smacked of revolution. Witte sought the support of the wider public. A special conference on agricultural economy was convoked under his personal chairmanship and with the participation of prominent public leaders. This led to a conflict between Witte and the diehards of the old order; the conference was finally dissolved and Witte resigned. Only then did the "liberating movement" gain momentum. Now the illegal "Liberation League" (*Soyuz Osvobozhdeniya*), as well as the revolutionary parties, came to the fore. What solutions did they offer for the agrarian problem?

Let us begin with the Social-Democratic party. A minority of this party, known as "Bolsheviks," has won power in Russia at the price of giving up not only the name but the very ideals of social democracy. The SD party had been an outgrowth of world capitalism, and in the fight against it favored *universal methods.* In Russia, industrial capitalism was still in the embryonic stage; the party, nevertheless, was determined to apply the tactics tested in Western Europe. Here, as elsewhere, it appealed to the factory workers and regarded the capitalists as the chief enemies. The Social Democrats realized that the class struggle could take a normal course only under a system of "rule by the people"; their program, therefore, called for the establishment of a Republic, with all power residing in a parliament elected by universal suffrage. Even then, however, a minority of the party, the future Bolsheviks, insisted that democracy should be preceded by a *dictatorship* that would achieve the total destruction of the existing order without interference—and thus clear the way for socialism.

The Social Democrats' treatment of the peasant problem was ambiguous. Owing to the government's mistakes, the peasantry was in a revolutionary mood, and the SDs were willing to take advantage of this. They were aware that the elemental destructive force of the peasantry was far beyond that of the urban working class, but they had little real sympathy with the peasantry, which was, after all, a class enemy of the proletariat. Hence the party's equivocations with regard to the problem.

At first the party was true to its ideology. In 1903, at its second convention, its platform included the abolition of all laws restricting the peasants' right to dispose of their land. As a result of this, the economically weakest members of the peasant class would have lost their plots. The SDs would have welcomed this as a *step forward*—a strengthening of capitalism, but at the same time the growth of the social-democratic army. What the peasants themselves wanted, however, was *more land;* and to gratify them, the party was willing to give them the so-called "segments"—those strips of land indispensable to the peasants, which in 1861 had been left in the hands of the landlords, and had become a source of the peasantry's economic dependence. This was better than nothing, but it was so little that the SDs themselves felt embarrassed. And so, when the other parties, including the Socialist Revolutionaries (SRs) and the Constitutional Democrats ("Cadets") made public their agrarian program, the SDs, at their Stockholm convention in 1906, amended their own program, and began to advocate the confiscation of *all* lands belonging to the landlords. In conformity with their socialist ideology, they recommended that the confiscated lands be made the property not of individual peasants but of their organs of self-government—an idea that had not been advanced by the peasants themselves. History failed to give the SDs a chance to show how they would have actually solved the problem and reconciled the "rule of the people" with the ideology of the "proletariat." Events outran them and left them behind. Only the Bolshevik section of the party has been able to put its ideas into practice. Under its dictatorship, the confiscated estates, instead of being turned over to the peasants, remained in the hands of the state and became the *sovkhozy*—state farms. As to the "allotted lands," which had belonged to the peasants since 1861, the Communists did everything to crush the individual peasants settled on them and to replace them with compulsory collective farms—the *kolkhozy.* Collective farming represented a technical advance and might have proved an advantage, but the Soviet government insisted on doing everything with a high hand, using violence and coercion. The peasantry as a social class of small landowners was destroyed. The official slogan was "liquidation of the kulaks" (well-to-do peasants), but every individual owner of a plot was branded a "kulak" and treated accordingly. As a result of the Soviet agrarian reform, all the land came under state control and the peasants were compelled to work for the state—which was in face a restoration of serfdom, but with a new ruthless master, the all-powerful state. As in 1861, the situation today cries for the emancipation of the peasants. Since technical progress has made the small individual farm unprofitable, it is difficult to foretell the future pattern of agriculture, but first of all, the peasant must be "liberated" once again.

The other socialist party—the Socialist Revolutionary—based itself upon the peasantry. The interests of that class were the constant concern of the trend known under the generic name of "populism." It held no menace for the state; the improvement of the peasants' lot was possible within the framework of the then existing political and social system.

Unfortunately, the government followed a different course. And so it came about that in the beginning of the twentieth century, when the "liberating movement" got under way, the peasant class could be readily incited to revolutionary action. The peasants regarded the landowners as their chief enemies. Frictions that grew out of petty local causes could be easily turned by agitators into mass movements directed against the landowners. Such revolts, whenever they happened, would be ruthlessly put down by the government, with the result that the interference of the authorities undermined the people's faith in the Tsar as the protector of the common people against the "masters."

The Socialist Revolutionary party was an outgrowth of this frame of mind. Its agrarian program had two sides.

On the one hand, the party demanded the requisition of *all privately owned land.* In this it went farther than the peasants themselves who claimed only the land of their own former masters. The land problem was thus severed from the Russian past and considered on the plane of an *international* ideology.

On the other hand, the SRs as a socialist party were opposed to the principle of private property, and the idea of turning over the confiscated estates to the peasants as their individual property, was repugnant to them. Their program, therefore, called for the transfer of the land to the "democratically organized rural communes for use on an equalitarian basis." The party was convinced that this was in harmony with the peasants' own conception of the land as the property of all. Only he who tills the land should be allowed to use it—but it should not belong to him as his property.

This idea has been often attributed to the Russian peasantry; and indeed, history had not taught the peasants to stand up for their individual rights, nor had it accustomed them to individual owner- ship of land. They had never enjoyed it, neither under the system of serfdom, or after their emancipation. Nevertheless, to assume that the Russian peasant did not aspire to become the rightful owner of his plot would be a rash conclusion. The opposite is prob- ably true. The peasants submitted to the periodical re-allotment of land by the communes as required by the law; but as time went on it became less frequent, the peasants managed to withdraw their homesteads from redistribution, despite all exhortations they failed to adopt "communal farming," and every single agricultural task was divided in such a way that everyone worked *on his plot for him- self.* It cannot be determined whether the agrarian program of the SRs was true to the peasants' own ideas or did violence to them. Today the question is academic: the party was not given the op- portunity to convert its program into reality, although it won the majority in the elections to the Constituent Assembly. The As- sembly was forcibly dispersed by the Communists after its first meeting. Later, the Communists boasted of having put into effect the whole agrarian program of the SRs. The latter would have disclaimed this. What the Communists did was to restore the forced labor of peasants upon land that was not theirs—something very different from the dream of the SRs.

Now let us consider the "liberal parties"—those who wanted to carry out their ideas within the framework of the constitutional system. Their influence varied in the course of time. The era of constitutional monarchy in Russia can be roughly divided into two periods: the first lasting from the introduction of the constitution (February 23, 1906) to the "coup d'etat" of June 3, 1907; and the second, from the latter date to the Revolution in February, 1917.

During the first period, the Constitutional Democratic party ("Cadets") played the dominant part. It originated within the circle of seasoned zemstvo workers and had participated in the "Liberation League"; it possessed an elaborate legislative program, as well as cadres of faithful supporters, long before the Revolution. It was victorious in the elections to the First Duma and assumed leadership in that assembly. What solution of the peasant problem did it offer at the height of its influence?

This problem had two aspects: the legal status of the peasantry on the one hand; and its provision with land on the other. Progressive public opinion had advocated "equal rights" for peasants for a long time. The Cadet party in the First Duma immediately introduced an "equal rights" bill. A special commission was charged to prepare four groups of laws based upon the principle that "all citizens of both sexes are equal before the law." It was assumed that this would incidentally solve the peasant problem. Such an assumption was obviously superficial. Next to the laws restricting the peasants' civil rights — which could be annulled without difficulty — there existed vast "special" legislation protecting their interests: the laws governing land tenure, the inalienability of the "allotted land," communal property, the right of the village commune to re-allot the land among the individual homesteads. The general code ignored all these relationships. It would have been impossible to determine the respective rights of the commune and the individual member on the basis of the "equal rights" bill. The Cadet party gave no clear answer to these concrete questions.

The party's agrarian bill also failed to provide the answers. The party was very proud of it, complacently asserting that its adoption would have prevented the revolution. Its main feature was the "compulsory alienation of all private lands with compensation of the owners at a fair rate." "Compulsory alienation" doubtless conformed to the wishes of the peasantry. The Cadet party tried hard to lend it an appearance of legality. Confiscation with compensation is admitted by all legislations in *exceptional* cases. The party, admittedly, did not deny the right of ownership to the land; why then did it have to turn the "exception" into a general rule? The gradual transfer of the landowners' estates to the peasants was already under way; it could have been accelerated by fiscal pressure and other *legal* means. There was no need for such an extraordinary measure. The bill calling for "compulsory alienation" undermined the very foundations of the principle of private property which, after all, at that time was still the basis of the whole social order. Moreover, so long as the technique of peasant farming remained unchanged, it was economically harmful, because it lowered the profitability of the land; in restoring the "class" approach, it ran counter to the principle of "equality"; and it was incompatible with the "protection of individual rights" to which liberalism was pledged. To rob the landlords of their property in order to give it to the peasants was a prefiguration in 1906 of the brutal and violent measures applied in 1928 by the Communist state to the "individual peasants."

Insofar as the demand for "compulsory alienation" was intended to win the support of the peasants, it was successful. But what were the party's plans regarding the tenure of the confiscated lands? It proposed to create a "state fund for allotment of land to the people who cultivate the soil by means of individual labor." The most urgent task—that of bringing order into the conditions of communal tenure and of protecting the rights of the individual member against the encroachments of the community—was ignored by the bill. Rural life was still to be governed by the principle described by the Duma member N. N. Lvov as "a rightless individual against a tyrannical crowd." The Cadet program, moreover, concentrated such an immense land fund in the hands of the state that the dependence of the peasantry upon the state and its organs would have been nothing less than a new slavery. This, too, anticipated on a small scale what was witnessed later, in 1917. Since the Duma insisted on that point, and its discussions kept the public in a state of excitement, the government finally dismissed the Duma (July, 1906) and attempted an agrarian reform itself.

Under Alexander III, the government's agrarian policy had taken a wrong turn. Now, after the dissolution of the Duma, the head of the government, P. A. Stolypin, put forth a "progressive program." Liberal parties still nurse a bitter memory of Stolypin's policies. This is understandable: in his merciless fight against the revolutionary surge he respected neither the constitution, nor the law, nor justice itself. Many were his sins—and yet in his agrarian policy he was on the right track. It was *his* course, and not the agrarian bill of the Cadets, which might have stopped the revolution.

Without waiting for the Second Duma to assemble, Stolypin put into effect two measures under Article 87 of the *Fundamental Laws* which enabled the government to carry out necessary measures in the absence of the two Houses (Duma and State Council), provided a corresponding bill be introduced during the first two months of their next session. A rejection of such a bill would nullify the measures already taken. The attempt to transform the whole system of land tenure under such a proviso was indeed a bold undertaking;

but the reforms in question were so important and so long overdue that Stolypin consciously disregarded the formal irregularity of his steps.

Stolypin's first decree (October 5, 1906) abolished the most notorious legal restrictions of the peasant class in the matter of freedom of movement, of education, etc. The necessity of this was so indisputable that the Duma—when the corresponding bill was brought in—didn't even take the trouble to consider it. Only ten years later, in 1916, was it taken up by the Duma then in session; not to reject it, but to broaden its scope. Article 87 in this respect offered certain advantages: the Upper House could not reject the amendments approved by the Duma without abrogating the whole measure. I reported the bill to the Duma, and I remember that after the adoption of various amendments the reporter of the same bill to the State Council conferred with me regarding a possible compromise. The February Revolution put an end to these conciliatory moves.

The second decree under Article 87 (November 9, 1906) concerned the system of land tenure. It allowed the rural commune to divide the common land among the homesteads for good, to be owned privately; and it enabled those who so desired to withdraw their share from common ownership even without the approval of the commune. Such a delicate matter could not be settled without a special law. Only a law could define the share every homesteader could rightfully claim for his own, and how it should be apportioned. Stolypin's decree settled these questions, although not always fairly. Anyway, it liberated the peasant from the stranglehold of the commune.

The respective bill was introduced in the Second Duma. The socialist parties could be hardly expected to support it—for didn't it actually promote bourgeois private property? The Constitutional Democrats, although not socialists and avowed supporters of law and order, also opposed the bill, on the ground that it failed to mention "compulsory alienation of the land," which the party considered essential. Before any agreement with them could be reached, the Duma was dismissed once again. In violation of the constitution, the electoral law was changed in such a way as to ensure a majority of representatives of the landed class in the next Duma ("coup d'état" of June 3, 1907).

When in November, 1907, the Third Duma convened, the Cadets had lost their leadership to a party farther to the right—the Octobrists. The passage of Stolypin's bill was now a certainty, since the Octobrists were in full agreement with it. On the other hand, the opposition of the left was joined by the extreme right, which wanted to preserve the special status of the peasants and their dependence on the village commune. For the same reason the passage of the bill was threatened in the State Council, where it was finally adopted in a very close vote.

The opponents of the bill maintained that the peasantry would repudiate it, because private ownership of land was contrary to its sense of equity. Nevertheless, during the seven years that the law remained in force, 27 million *dessiatins*—nearly 80 million acres— were divided up among individual farmers, and 1613 thousand new homesteads were created. This result could not have been achieved through coercion alone: after all, the methods of government were not yet those of the Bolsheviks. The success of the reform was the best proof that the government had taken the right course.

Russia's evolution, however, was arrested first by World War I and then by the Revolution—which now threatens to become universal. What new order will be born out of it, how in the end the agrarian problem will be solved, how the interests of the "toilers" will be reconciled with the industrialization of agriculture and the necessity of large-scale farming—cannot yet be foreseen. This is not only a Russian, but a general problem. But in backward Russia, history has posed the problem under special conditions—as a survival of serfdom and feudal relationships. Within these limits it could have been settled without a revolution. If this was not done, and the social revolution broke out, of all places, in agricultural Russia, the responsibility for it rests on the one hand, upon the government, which in its fight to retain power was afraid of reforms, and on the other hand, upon the inexperience of our political parties, who strove to solve world problems for which the time had not yet come in Russia. The history of the agrarian problem in Russia serves to illustrate this.

MARY STOLYPIN BOCK

Stolypin in Saratov

Mary Stolypin Bock (1885–   ) is the daughter of P. A. Stolypin, chairman of the Council of Ministers, and Minister of the Interior, 1906–11. Stolypin's agrarian reform sought to replace the traditional Russian village communes by individual peasant farms. The author's book of reminiscences about her father was published in 1953 in Russian by the Chekhov Publishing House in New York.

In the following article, the author describes her father's courageous behavior during the revolutionary uprising of 1905, when he was governor of the Saratov province on the Volga.

The Saratov province, and especially its Balashov district, had long been known for their violent revolutionary elements. Apparently Stenka Razin's spirit did not disappear from the fertile banks of the Volga. Liberal representatives of the zemstvo began coming forward openly against the administrative and legislative measures of the government. My father used much of his strength in preventing a feeling of bitterness and animosity, which was taking possession of the zemstvo workers and their adherents, from expanding and preventing any possibility of joint action. With all the force of his intellect and energy he fought the weakening of the social structure from the influence of demoralizing forces generated by the prolonged war. Differences of opinion began to show not only in the political life of the country, but also in the social life. The leftist elements began to show extreme defiance and hostility.

I remember a concert at which, before the program started,

From *The Russian Review,* vol. 12, no. 3 (July 1953), pp. 187–93.

several leftist members of the zemstvo, together with their families, noisily pushed aside their chairs and left the hall when my father entered. During social balls, it very often happened that young men and girls from the leftist circles, when passing by my mother or me, not only did not step aside, but knocked against us and even pushed us. In line with these insignificant facts, more serious signs of the brewing revolution brought a gloomy turn into our life. Strikes became more frequent, there were no electric lights, shops were closed.

In his endeavor to unite the conflicting elements, my father arranged that winter a banquet for about sixty zemstvo workers. This was a very interesting gathering; the irreproachable dress coats of the representatives of the highest land aristocracy mingled with peasants' coats and peasants' dresses. The minds, moods, and political convictions of those present were as varied as their external appearance. Although speeches flowed unrestrainedly, although political adversaries talked amicably to each other and it seemed possible to find a common language and to agree on common ideals, as soon as the same men met in zemstvo meetings, it became clear to everybody that the differences were too deep and would be still deeper in the future.

In May, 1905, news came of the defeat of our Navy at the Tsushima strait. It is impossible to express in words how young and old people alike were appalled by this tragedy. In the summer alarming letters began to come to Koloberje [Stolypin's family estate in Lithuania] from my father. Failures on the front fomented discontent in the rear, people became more and more excited, and we who lived so far from father and followed the course of events only through his letters and newspapers, worried terribly about him. Soon our premonitions were confirmed; we came to know, thank God from his own letter, that there had been an attempt upon his life. During the inspection tour of his province, two shots were fired at him somewhere in a village, and father, as well as the officials accompanying him, saw the fleeing criminal. My father rushed to catch him but was stopped by his functionary on special duty, Prince Obolensky, who forcibly held him by the arm. Father, when describing the occurrence, strove to calm my mother, saying that this was only a solitary instance, that everything was more quiet than the newspapers were reporting, and that most important of all, he would soon be with us.

By order of His Imperial Majesty . . . General Sakharov was dispatched for the suppression of disorders to the Saratov province, which was strongly infected with a rebellious spirit. On father's invitation, he stayed at our house. We knew of his coming from the letters of my father who, although he was not pleased with the interference of a stranger in the affairs of the province, spoke well of him. It was natural that it was painful to my father, who always spoke so disdainfully of persons afraid of responsibility, to share with somebody else the running of provincial affairs, however complicated they might be.

When we left Koloberje for Saratov, Sakharov was already there. On the third day, when we were nearing Saratov and only a few stations from the final stop, a functionary on special duty unexpectedly entered our railway car and declared that he was sent by father to meet us. Very surprised by this, mother invited him into our compartment and a few minutes later she came out pale and very agitated. It turned out that the day before General Sakharov was killed in our house, and father sent this gentleman to notify mother in advance, before she could read of this tragedy in the newspaper, and to reassure her that he himself was safe and sound. One can imagine the feeling with which we drove to the house, from which only two hours before the body of the General had been carried out, and in whose rooms the scent of incense eloquently reminded one of funeral services.

We learned of the circumstances of this assassination. The office of the General was arranged on the second floor, in the smoking room on the left of the reception room, which separated it from father's study. During the morning reception, a young, modest-looking woman appeared and expressed a wish to see the General. She held a petition in her hands. The functionary on duty brought her into the smoking room. When closing the door, he noticed how the petitioner put the paper before Sakharov and then stepped behind him. Two or three seconds thereafter a shot resounded, and Sakharov, bleeding profusely and staggering, ran out through another door and dropped dead on the floor. The assassin, who hastened to flee, was seized on the staircase by the functionary on special duty, Prince Obolensky. The paper brought by her, the "petition," was the death sentence for the General.

The following shows how bad was the work of the gendarmerie guard in Saratov. On the night before the assassination of General

Sakharov, some workingmen came to my father with the warning
that terrorists had arrived from Penza with the intention of killing
Sakharov. However, the Colonel of gendarmerie, summoned by my
father, declared with aplomb: "I know what these men want. The
General has nothing to fear from them." And to what degree the
frame of mind of a part of society was revolutionary is shown in the
case of the attorney-at-law Maslenikov, who sent flowers to the
imprisoned assassin of General Sakharov.

When we all became a little quieter after the assassination of the
General, father told us all about what he had had to live through
from the time of his departure from Koloberje. The trip to Saratov
was very frightening. Having reached Moscow, father learned to
his dismay that all the railroads were on strike. Extremely concerned for the well-being of the Saratov province, he began to search
for the course to adopt and luckily succeeded somehow in finding
his way to the Volga, where regular steamer traffic was not interrupted. During his journey he heard nothing but news of disorders
throughout Russia. Tidings of peace, however profitable the terms
seemed in the beginning, were received with great suspicion by the
people of Russia who saw in them a sign of our defeat. This gave a
chance to the notorious "dark forces" to avail themselves of the
favorable opportunity of inciting the people against the ruling
power.

The closer he came to Saratov the more ominous were the rumors
of what was going on there. Popular revolts were springing up in
villages, peasants burned the estates of the landowners, destroying
everything they chanced to set their hands upon — very valuable
libraries incomprehensible to them, pictures, porcelain, antique
furniture, and even cattle and crops so close to the peasants' hearts.
Almost never did the peasants steal, but with a bright flame they
burned magnificent manors, cattle-sheds, barns, and granaries.
They hewed to splinters, trampled under their feet, broke and tore
everything that the owners carried out of the burning houses with
the hope of saving some remnants of their property. And many
landowners fled, without even having time to look back at their
beloved homes, on which former generations had lavished so much
labor and love.

Until my father's return to Saratov the situation in the city was
threatening. Troops stayed quietly in their barracks not taking any

part in the suppression of the sedition. However, the following happened, according to my father's report. Two days before his return to the city a large crowd of people gathered in the theater square and bloody fighting was to be expected any minute. The city's Mayor, Nemirovsky, hid himself in the Archbishop's house. The crowd proceeded on its way to batter this house, but stopped before the closed doors of the high wall surrounding it. Before these doors stood a lonely policeman as white as a sheet. The rightists, though numerically weak at that time, were able to organize themselves quickly and began to demolish lodgings of the prominent leftist leaders who hastened to exhibit ikons in their windows to demonstrate their loyal feelings. . . .

Straight from the steamer, accompanied by the police, my father walked into the center of the disorders on the theater square. As he approached the old part of the city, more and more excited and hostile clusters of people began to gather. With measured steps he passed calmly through the crowd. A bomb fell directly at his feet from a third story window. Several men were killed but he remained unharmed, and a few moments after the explosion the crowd heard the calm voice of the Governor: "Move on to your houses and have confidence in the authority protecting you!" Thanks to his composure and presence of mind, the excitement subsided, the crowd dispersed, and the city once again assumed a peaceful appearance.

Of course, this calm did not last long. The revolutionaries were quite aware of how propitious the moment was for them and did everything in their power to encourage insurrection in the Saratov and Penza provinces. With the view of maintaining a rebellious spirit in the people, they were busy arranging one demonstration after another, one meeting after another.

With my father's arrival in Saratov, the adherents of law and order recovered their spirits, thanks to his calmness and assurance. The rightist groups understood that it was not good to await events with folded hands and began to organize. Soon they collected about 80,000 rubles for the fight with the leftists. A systematic plan was drawn up. Saratov was divided into three sections in which were opened popular clubs with libraries, stages for theatrical performances, mutual benefit clubs with free medical help. All the work of the rightist organizations was directed by these clubs. Father soon acquired some talented and energetic assistants, good public speakers who took great pains in this work, such as Count D. A. Olsufiev, Count Uvarov, and a representative of the Nobel firm, Ivanov.

At the head of the church administration at that time was the able, well-educated Hermogenes, acting always without mercenary motive and knowing how to attract the poor. People filled the Cathedral and seemed never to tire of hearing divine services for three or four hours without interruption. In the hall of the conservatory the lectures of the distinguished clergyman, Father Chetverikov, attracted large audiences, which consisted of representatives of not only the rightist groups, but also of the leftist. After one of these lectures, a prominent Socialist Revolutionary, Arkhangelsky, told Prince Kropotkin: "If all your priests were like this Chetverikov, then there would be no need for our existence."

Now, when revolutionaries arranged demonstrations and marching processions, they met with organized resistance. A throng of demonstrating revolutionaries, each holding a pole in one hand and a revolver in the other, would meet a rightist group marching toward them. The latter moved in orderly rows, the strongest and most daring in front. In the second row, each rightist had a basket with cobblestones which the marchers in the last row picked up from the pavement. The men in the rear passed them into the baskets of the men ahead, who threw them at the adversary. Under the volley of stones the revolutionaries would usually start disorderly shooting, but in the end would disperse. Gradually the city became more quiet. The governmental and private organizations worked well together. Father did his best not to call out the troops.

But in the countryside the situation was different. The peasantry was divided. The patriotically disposed peasants had no energetic leadership, while the leftist elements had an abundance of disciplined and energetic leaders. Pogroms of estates continued. While travelling by railroad through the province of Saratov, one could see through the windows of the car the steppe illuminated by estates set on fire by flaming torches. As fate would have it, one of the first of the estates to be devastated was the country seat of a liberal landowner who had contributed large sums of money to subsidize leftist newspapers! When misfortune struck, this idealistic liberal asked my father to send troops for the restoration of order. My father, however, did not send military detachments to the villages, but preferred to exercise his civilian powers as governor. He thought it aimless and unreasonable to tire the troops by constantly shifting them from one place to another, and he knew also that this might lead only to the weakening of the central power. Father thought that the main issue was the preservation of the state administrative apparatus in its entirety and that only this could save Russia. The strength of Russia was not in large estates which had outlived their time and were already being sold by their owners to the peasants through the Peasant Land Bank. The reconstruction of Russia, he thought, should proceed in the direction of eradicating the vestiges of serfdom and in replacing the communal land proprietorship by individual ownership of land.

Uprisings in the villages often took such an ugly form that those peasants who had not gone out of their minds were often repelled by revolutionary excesses. Often a peasant's heart must have bled at the sight of cows, horses, or sheep roaming in the fields with ripped stomachs, mooing or bellowing from pain and dying in agony. Some revolutionary manifestations must have appeared ridiculous to them. Once, for example, a revolutionary, a veterinary by profession, while leading his adherents to destroy the estate of a landowner, dressed himself up in a costume of the time of John the Terrible, a short shoulder mantle and a Monomach's cap on his head. In many places peasants came to their senses very quickly and began to ask the rightists to help them and to come to their gatherings.

On his part, my father began more and more often to undertake trips through the province, appearing in person and unexpectedly in places where dissatisfaction was the strongest and where the leaders of the leftist groups worked most energetically. Unarmed, he entered into the bellowing crowd, and nearly always his mere appearance, his calm and stern air, caused passions to subside, and the mob which has been excited and brawling a minute before, would quietly disperse. His speeches were short and easily understood by every simple worker and peasant, and usually had an instantly sobering effect. Few people knew, I think, what this expenditure of energy and will power cost my father. I remember that after one of his dangerous trips into a center of sedition, he wrote to my mother: "Now I have come to know the meaning of 'the hysterical lump in the throat,' which constricts it and prevents speech, and I know what concentration of will is needed not to allow a single muscle of the face to tremble and not to raise the voice above the desired range."

Once a man standing in front of father suddenly drew a revolver out of his pocket and pointed it straight at his chest. My father threw open his overcoat and facing the mutinous crowd said loudly, "Shoot!" The revolutionary dropped his hand and the revolver fell.

I had a snapshot which showed father riding into a crowd which had been rioting a moment before, but now all, to the last man, were kneeling. This throng of several thousand people fell on their knees at the first words father pronounced.

Sometimes rioters, after listening to father, asked for a priest and religious banners and listened to the Te Deum. During one of his trips, father walked directly from the train to a village where people had been waiting for him. A fellow with an excited and malevolent air stepped out of the crowd and went straight towards father. At first he walked indecisively, but when he saw that father walked alone, without accompanying policemen, he insolently raised his head and, looking straight into father's face, was about to say something, when suddenly he heard my father's calm and imperious voice: "Hold my overcoat!" The man obediently took the overcoat and stood holding it in his hands all the time my father was making his speech.

In those troubled times, my father knew that it was better for him to go alone to the people whom he loved and esteemed, that it was necessary to speak to the masses without intermediaries, and that only then would the people, feeling instinctively the sincerity of his words, understand and trust him. And peasants listened attentively and benevolently to his sometimes stern, but always truthful words. Father obtained results not by shouts, eloquent phrases, or threats, but mostly by his courage and uprightness, and by the firmness of his belief in the ideals which guided him and which he served.

A. TYRKOVA-WILLIAMS

The Cadet Party

A. Tyrkova-Williams (1869–1962), Russian writer and publicist, was one of the founders of the Constitutional Democratic Party (Cadet) and a member of its Central Committee from its foundation to 1917. Soon after the Bolshevik *coup d'état,* she left Russia with her British journalist husband, Dr. Harold Williams, going first to England where, for a number of years, she was active in emigré politics. A vital and creative woman, she is the author of eleven books in Russian and English, including her two-volume memoirs, published in Russian in New York. She came to the United States at the age of eighty and died in Washington, D.C.

In the article printed here, the author, on the basis of her active association with the Constitutional Democratic Party, describes the origin, composition, program, tactics, and the role of the Cadets in the Dumas and in the Provisional Government.

Political parties first appeared in Russia when the Tsar, on October 17, 1905, issued the Manifesto granting civil liberties and popular representation. Prior to this, the government had jealously suppressed every attempt to form parties, convinced that they would ultimately destroy autocracy. Actually one of the causes of the downfall of the Tsarist regime was the fact that during the brief lifespan of Russian parliamentarism the forces supporting the new constitutional system had had no time to organize effectively or to establish a working relationship with the government. The socialist secret organizations, which had arisen at the end of

From *The Russian Review,* vol. 12, no. 3 (July 1953), pp. 173–86.

the nineteenth century and were active underground, were neither willing nor able to achieve this. Their conspiratorial nature deprived them of the chief characteristic of political parties—they were not responsible to public opinion. Liberal public opinion found a partial outlet in the organs of rural and municipal self-government. Periodically these organs would summon conventions to discuss their immediate economic and financial problems; but local self-government was so closely bound up with the general political situation that broader political issues could not be avoided. Many participants of the zemstvo conventions joined the secret Liberation League formed in 1903 with the purpose of fighting for political freedom and popular representation.

The Liberation League could by no means be termed a political party. It was rather a kind of war coalition of diverse groups, monarchists and republicans, liberals and socialists, temporarily united to carry on a guerilla fight against the common enemy—autocracy. Of the League's open activities the most important was the publication abroad, first at Stuttgart and then in Paris, of the weekly *Osvobozhdenie* ("Liberation"). Next to outspoken criticism of the government it contained a positive program and detailed projects for the most urgently needed reforms. The white paper-covered issues of *Osvobozhdenie* were smuggled into Russia where they were widely circulated and eagerly read, preparing the minds for the inevitable and long overdue constitutional reform. Inside Russia, the League worked underground, secretly recruiting members and sympathizers; it also arranged meetings of learned societies, banquets, and conventions of a seemingly non-political character. Doctors, engineers, educators, all kinds of professional people from every part of the country would come together, and in these crowded gatherings political issues were at first indirectly but, as time went on, ever more boldly discussed. Public opinion was at last ready for a front assault on the Tsarist regime, weakened by the general unrest and the disastrous war with Japan. Labor strikes and peasant riots lent strength to the theoretical demands of the intelligentsia. A new mass psychology was emerging. New voices made themselves heard. It was felt that the goal of popular representation was at long last in sight and that the time had come to prepare for parliamentary work and to unite people of similar views in political parties. In September, 1905, the liberals held a convention in Moscow attended by twenty zemstvo workers and forty

members of the Liberation League, with the purpose of drawing up
the program of the first liberal party. Their task consisted in the
codification of the various reform projects elaborated and discussed
for three years on the pages of *Osvobozhdenie*. The time had come
to translate theoretical essays into items of a party program.

In October this program was submitted to a constituent convention foregathered again in Moscow and was adopted almost without
objections. The assembly was unable to finish its work—it was
interrupted by the all-Russian general strike. Nevertheless, before
separating, the participants declared the new Constitutional-
Democratic Party in existence. The party received its definite shape
in January, 1906, in St. Petersburg, at a congress attended by a
multitude of new members. It displayed great unanimity, since
the political ideals and reform plans of the new party had been
known and accepted by liberals for a long time. The name of the
party was abbreviated to the initials C.D. (pronounced in Russian
"Ka-Day," which soon became Cadet; under this name the party
was known throughout its short history). It was also called the
Party of Popular Freedom.

Less than three months separated the two conventions, yet, in
the meantime, the situation had drastically changed. The peaceful
and bloodless general strike, whose slogan was "popular representation," at last convinced the government that reform could no
longer be postponed. On October 17/30, 1905, the Tsar signed the
Manifesto granting political rights and establishing the Duma. The
new party had every reason to hope that its program, so long a
purely academic issue, would at last enter the field of political
reality.

The program affirmed the right of the people to take part, through
its elected representatives, in directing the political life of the nation.
Paragraph 13 read: "Russia must become a constitutional and
parliamentary monarchy. The political system is to be determined
by fundamental laws."

Later, in the Duma, this latter point led to heated arguments
between the Tsar's ministers and the opposition. Who was to establish the fundamental laws, where did the privileges of the sovereign
end and the rights and duties of the people's representatives begin?
This and similar problems remained unsolved until the very downfall of the monarchy.

The drafters of the party program found it much easier to define the legal norms necessary to protect civil rights, such as freedom of speech, of worship, of the press. Nor was it very difficult to formulate the articles dealing with labor. The social legislation advocated by the Cadets approximated the minimum demands of the socialist parties: it included the right to organize in unions, the right to strike, freedom of assembly, participation of labor deputies in factory inspection, an eight-hour working day, strict control of child and female labor, arbitration of labor disputes, insurance against accidents, disease, and old age.

In his widely read pamphlet "What is the Party of Popular Freedom?" (1917), A. A. Kornilov, a well-known historian and the permanent secretary of the party, wrote: "All the articles of our labor program have the sole purpose of improving the lot of the workers within the framework of the capitalist system and facilitating the conditions of the fight they are waging against capitalism. We differ sharply from the Social Democrats in that we take our stand above classes, since we believe that we must pursue the interests of all social classes. While we recognize the existence of class antagonisms and the obligation to help the weaker side in the class struggle, we yet believe that to aggravate these antagonisms and to make them the cornerstone of social policy would contradict our basic principles."

Much more troublesome and complex proved the task of deciding on a correct agrarian policy. The peasants made up eighty percent of the population and formed the foundation upon which rested not only the national economy but the whole life of the country. The overwhelming majority of the peasantry owned their own land. In 1861, with the abolition of serfdom, the peasants were given permanent possession of their homesteads with gardens and orchards as well as arable land, fields, and pastures. This was, however, a peculiar form of land tenure, connected with the *obshchina,* the village commune. Russia had no entailed estates, no family ownership of inalienable lands. Actually, only the peasant lands were inalienable; yet they were owned not by the individual peasant family but collectively by the whole village commune. The common lands were divided into lots and distributed among the households roughly according to the number of family members, that is, the number of workers and consumers. Re-allotment was not frequent, and in practice every family enjoyed permanent use of the same lots. From time to time the village commune, guided by immemorial custom, would allot additional strips of land to needy households. No doubt this system had its defects, both economic and legal, but it cannot be denied that it greatly contributed to rural stability. The peasants lived in their own houses and owned, albeit on a communal basis, the land they tilled and which fed them, gave them a measure of security, and made them independent.

Conditions, however, varied widely throughout the country. In the central, densely populated provinces with less fertile soil, the lots were of insufficient size and the peasants very poor. The problem of how to improve their condition and to increase their holdings had been a subject of public discussion and government study for decades. The official approach was naturally more cautious, and the improvement achieved by governmental measures was rather slow. The Ministry of Agriculture worked out the sensible and constructive policy of encouraging the migration of peasants from European Russia to the fertile areas of Siberia, Central Asia, and the Caucasus. It goes without saying that this migration was not compulsory but voluntary. Another policy was to grant generous loans, through the State Peasant's Bank, to village communities seeking to purchase new lands. The Ministry of Agriculture also did much to raise the level of rural economy through small loans, encouragement of cooperatives, establishment of agricultural schools, and model experimental farms. Left-wing public opinion considered all these measures inadequate. For decades, in books, magazines, academic lectures, conventions of learned societies, various plans had been offered for the solution of the agrarian problem, some going so far as to propose the nationalization of all land and its redistribution among the peasants. As usual in politics, especially in times of impending change, arguments and statistics were colored with emotion. Feelings of compassion and a strong sense of collective class guilt determined the approach to the agrarian problem no less than the practical interests of the peasants themselves.

Up to the middle of the nineteenth century, the Russian intelligentsia consisted chiefly of members of the nobility and gentry, the class of landlords and slave-owners. Pushkin, Lermontov, Nekrasov, Turgenev, Tolstoy, and in part, Dostoevsky, all came from this class. The literature they created was saturated with compassion for the unfortunate and underprivileged and produced the type of the "penitent nobleman" tormented by the sense of his responsibility for the abuses of his feudal forefathers. He was filled with the ardent desire to atone and to make up to the emancipated serfs for all they had suffered in the past as slaves. This peculiar penitent psychology was responsible for the tendency to sacrifice upper-class privileges for the benefit of the lower classes. This mood dominated the socialists and was also reflected in liberal public opinion.

The leading majority of the new Cadet party belonged to the landlord class. All the more characteristic of progressive opinion of the time was paragraph 36 of the Cadet program. It recommended "the increase of the land area held by the tillers of the soil, such as landless and landpoor peasants and other categories of small landholders, out of State, Crown, and Church lands, as well as through alienation of landed estates, their present owners to be compensated by the state according to a fair valuation." Paragraph 37 read: "The alienated lands are to be incorporated into the national land fund."

The agrarian program was to play a fateful part in the history of the party. It aroused the hostility of the government and the resentment of a part of liberal opinion—those landlords who shared the constitutional aspirations of the party, yet believed that efficient landowners were making an important contribution to the productivity of the country and that the manor houses were the cultural centers of rural Russia.

However, the chief difficulties encountered by the Cadets were connected not with their program but with their tactics. To work effectively in the Duma, it was necessary to establish some kind of relationship with the government. This proved impossible for both sides. The electoral campaign had already demonstrated the intransigence both of the government and the opposition. The first elections of the people's representatives in Russia took place under the most abnormal conditions, in the midst of terror, labor strikes, peasant uprisings. The situation was close to anarchy. Again and again the revolutionaries assassinated government officials of every rank, from policemen to powerful provincial governors. In retaliation the authorities declared one province after another under martial law and carried out mass arrests and executions. Little was left of the great judicial ideas proclaimed by Alexander II in the sixties.

Meanwhile the socialists, not satisfied with the October Manifesto, clamored for a Constituent Assembly elected by universal, equal, and secret suffrage. They boycotted the Duma before it was born. The Cadets did not join in the boycott, and for this suffered much abuse from the Left at the electoral meetings. On the other hand, the administration, especially in the provinces, violated electoral freedom through wanton chicanery. *The Herald of the Party of Popular Freedom* which the party began publishing in January, 1906, in St. Petersburg, was swamped with indignant reports from every part of the Empire. The correspondents told of attempts by local administrators to intimidate voters suspected of sympathy with the Cadets; campaign literature of the party, already passed by the censor, would be confiscated; electors would be arrested to prevent them from attending meetings and taking part in the elections. As often as not the officials were just confused and did not know which restrictions were still in force and which had been abrogated by the October Manifesto.

The newborn liberal party had to wage a fight on two fronts. On the Left, the socialists branded them as traitors to the national cause for their willingness to take part in the Duma. On the Right, the authorities did everything they could to intimidate the voters. In the press and at the political meetings, the Cadets denounced the government for unlawful interference in the elections and pressure upon the voters. They hoped to bring the administration to reason through stern resolutions: "The Central Committee of the C.D. party demands that the government forbid the local administration to interfere with the electoral campaign of the parties. The government must make a definite choice between an autocratic and a constitutional Russia. . . . Of all the important political parties, the C.D. party alone is consistently and steadfastly constitutional. . . . " But the government did not heed the demands of the liberals and persisted in obstructing electoral freedom.

At the beginning of the constitutional regime, the government was disconcerted by the wave of enthusiasm for the new parliament that swept the nation. For the first time the long-cherished dream of freedom was coming true, and all the secret hopes could be voiced aloud. People grown up in a free country are hardly able to imagine the festive exaltation and fervor which seized the nation during the elections to the First Duma and the few weeks of its existence. The chief exponents and interpreters of the general mood were the Cadets; not only because the other parties, instead of supporting the Duma, were attacking it but also because the party counted

among its members many prominent scholars and jurists qualified
to deal with political problems and able to give eloquent expression
to their deep-rooted convictions. Even their opponents admitted
their great oratorical gifts. Their speeches constantly fed the mass
enthusiasm stirred up in the nation by its first representative assembly.

The intellectual eminence of its leaders increased the responsibility of the liberal party. Between the birth of the party and the opening of the Duma there was an interval of hardly more than four
months. During that brief period the party had to prepare itself
for parliamentary work, to create the party machinery, to explain
the principles of a liberal policy and the meaning and necessity of
the reforms it advocated. And all this had to be done in an atmosphere of unrest, strikes, terroristic acts repaid by the government
with terror from above. One cannot help wondering how in the
midst of all this turmoil the foundations of society remained un-
shaken. This was not yet the revolution that stunned the country
in 1917, but it was anarchy, and it had a fateful influence on the
first two Dumas and, in particular, on the activities of the Cadet
party.

The composition of the First Duma was significant: out of 478
seats the Cadets had won 179. The two vaguely circumscribed
groups that called themselves "moderates" and "non-partisans" included many "fellow-travellers" of the Cadets. They often voted
with the Cadets, sometimes with the Laborites, (*Trudoviki*). The
latter group consisted of about one hundred people, mostly peasants, without party affiliation, but with socialist leanings. Whenever the vote was directed against the government, which happened
nearly always, the Laborites also voted with the Cadets. The Polish
group with its 45 deputies kept apart. The Poles repeated the tactics of the Irish in the British Parliament, emphasizing that Russian
affairs of state did not concern them and often abstaining from the
vote. But it goes without saying that they were, like the rest of the
Duma, in opposition to the government.

Only a tiny group of deputies led by Count Heyden considered
themselves not "in opposition to His Majesty" but "His Majesty's
opposition." They tried hard to restrain the denunciatory zeal of
the rest of the deputies and to direct their energies into the channel
of constructive legislation. Count Heyden and his followers were
wise, respected, outstanding men, but their voices were drowned in

the storm. Ministers and deputies faced each other in the Tauride Palace not as partners in the conduct of affairs of state but as mortal enemies. The opposition was attacking, the government—until the emergence of Stolypin—was on the defensive, clumsily and reluctantly dodging the arrows thrust at it from every bench of the Duma. It was ceaselessly assailed for all its failings and mistakes— the outdated administrative methods, the court-martials, the undemocratic electoral law, the discrimination against Jews. All this had been condemned by public opinion long ago; now at last all the resentment and all the grievances, big and small, accumulated during a century of struggle for a constitution, were brought into the open on the rostrum of the Duma. To judge from the press and from the declarations submitted to the Duma by an endless stream of delegations from every corner of the land, the whole nation seemed to support the opposition. The government's reply to all this impassioned eloquence was an embarrassed silence. From time to time the senile Prime Minister Goremykin would slowly ascend the steps of the rostrum and read some vapid statement from a paper. It was a voice from a far-away world.

The First Duma lasted 72 days and was dismissed on July 8. As a pretext for the dissolution, the government seized upon a public declaration of the Cadet party expounding the agrarian plank of its program, considered by the party of the utmost and immediate importance. The dissolution decree, however, provided for elections to another Duma. The Second Duma convened in March, 1907. Like the First, it proved shortlived. This time the pretext for the dismissal was provided not by the Cadets but by the Social Democrats. Stolypin, the new young and energetic Prime Minister, had the entire Duma deputation of Social Democrats arrested and brought to trial on the charge that they were organizing an armed uprising. There was little factual proof for the charge, yet all the defendants were found guilty and deported to Siberia.

Thus, popular representation in Russia for which so many generations of the finest Russian men and women had fought and made sacrifices had a difficult start. The goal, to be sure, had been reached at long last, but the normal functioning of the new parliament met obstacles at every step. The Cadet party, which regarded the consolidation of constitutional monarchy in Russia as its primary objective, was weakened and disheartened by the contempt of popular representation displayed both by the socialists and the government. The *Osvobozhdenie* group, who had become the Duma leaders, had hoped for an opportunity to carry out far-reaching reforms, instead, they were compelled to devote their efforts to the political education of the public in order to rally it to the support of the most elementary principles of freedom and law. This task was a familiar one to the professors within the party. One of the first issues of *The Herald* contained the following instructions: "What every party member should do: He should forget his former lack of civil rights and behave like a free citizen. He should fight against all those who exploit the people's ignorance to further their own interests. He should exercise a moral and intellectual influence upon those around him. He should circulate the party program, pamphlets and leaflets, but never in a clandestine way: every recipient of party literature should know who supplied it so as to know where to turn for explanations of what he fails to understand."*

The party had a deep faith in the power of the vital and honest word and somewhat naïvely expected that its literature would bring to reason the terrorists of Right and Left. While all over the country the conflict between terrorists and authorities was being fought out on the plane of naked force, the·party adopted the following resolution at its first convention: "The party does not recognize violence as a means of political overturn. The ruling power will be unable to withstand the pressure of public opinion. The party's strongest weapon is therefore the organization of public opinion through agitation and propaganda. . . . The party supports all methods of direct action upon the government except armed revolt. Not revolt, but unity among all opposition groups is regarded by the party as its chief tactical instrument."

This characteristic resolution faithfully reflects the missionary spirit of the Cadet party. While striving for reforms through legislation, it yet considered the development of public ethics and the training in citizenship no less important as a basis for a constitutional system. The party carried out this task of enlightment through its local committees set up in most cities of any importance. All party activities were directed by the Central Committee and the Duma deputation.

The Dumas that followed the first two, prematurely dissolved assemblies, gradually settled down to practical work, with the

The Herald, November 22, 1906.

Cadets taking an active part in it. They never again won as many seats as in the First Duma. The party had 98 in the Second and only 53 in the Third Duma, partly as a result of the altered electoral law and of administrative pressure. In the Fourth Duma, elected in 1912, there were 59 Cadet deputies. Nevertheless, the nation listened to the voices of the Cadet deputies as intently as ever. The speeches of Rodichev, Miliukov, Shingarev, Maklakov, were eagerly read and discussed all over the country. Debates in the Duma had become more business-like. The government at long last submitted the national budget to the Duma for consideration. For the first time in Russian history, the budget was publicly debated, and the discussion of it filled the pages of the press. During the spring of 1908, the literate part of the nation absorbed a whole course in political science. The public became aware of the immense complexity of the national economy in the vast Empire with its rapidly growing wealth. It was the discussion of the budget that brought about some intercourse between Duma deputies and officialdom. In the open sessions in which both sides took part clashes were still frequent, but in the committees, where the items of revenue and expenditure were examined one by one by both sides, the exchange of opinions assumed a more dispassionate character. And in response to the quieter rhythm of parliamentary life, the pulse of the nation slowly returned to normal. Revolutionary excesses became rare. Administrative reprisals relaxed. Martial law, which had rightly caused so much bad feeling, was called off. At the same time the vigorous growth in every field of the national economy — industry, commerce, agriculture — created a feeling of contentment and stability. The public energy, which only a short while before had found an outlet in abstract theories and the clamor for extreme reforms, now was turning toward constructive practical tasks. Schools sprang up like mushrooms. A plan for universal education was in preparation. The publishing houses and the press were unable to satisfy the growing demand for books and knowledge. In all these educational and constructive activities, the Cadets, both individually and as a party, were playing a dynamic part. They were gaining in stature and authority. Gradually, their ideas were winning some recognition even in those official circles which the Cadets had long regarded as a stronghold of incurable reaction. The Duma was becoming an organic part of the state structure, and the Cadets largely contributed to this process.

The war of 1914 demanded of the party a swift and decisive reconsideration of its former position. The political and social energies accumulated during the last eight years suddenly had to be turned from domestic problems to the defense of the country. During the Russo-Japanese war, the opposition had been defeatist. That war was generally regarded as thrust upon the nation by the Tsarist regime and of no vital concern to the national interest. There were many who welcomed the military disasters. Some of the revolutionaries actually collaborated with the Japanese. In Paris an unsuccessful attempt was made by the Japanese to bribe even the liberals into collaboration with them. An emissary was sent to P. B. Struve, then Editor-in-Chief of *Osvobozhdenie*. I was an eyewitness of the ensuing scene and watched Struve throw out the messenger of the enemy power with quite unacademic fury. This happened in 1905. Since then the nation had come a long way. Now the most advanced political views and aspirations found open expression in the Duma. The Duma had brought the public into closer contact with the machinery of the state. A vigorous and healthy civic consciousness was developing. And when the storm broke out, the nation arose to defend the country.

This patriotic spirit penetrated even into the ranks of the most determined political opposition. While some of the socialists remained defeatists, others took a "defensist" position, being ready to postpone the revolution until the foreign enemy was repulsed. This was a most unpleasant surprise for the Kaiser, who had counted on the defeatism of the Russian intelligentsia. But the defeatists among the Russian socialists, for their part, had miscalculated: they had been convinced that the German Social Democrats would refuse to support their belligerent government. The feelings of the Russian defeatists were deeply hurt when their German comrades proclaimed "internal peace" and put a stop to their struggle against the Kaiser's government. In Russia, the liberals took a similar stand. The day after the declaration of war, the Cadet party issued a proclamation containing the following passage: "Whatever our attitude with regard to the government's domestic policies, it is our first duty to preserve our country, one and indivisible, and to maintain its position among the great powers, which is being disputed by our enemies. Let us lay aside our internal differences, and let us firmly keep in mind that in this hour our first and only task is to support our front fighters, with faith in the righteousness of our cause, with calm fortitude and with hope for the success of our armed forces."

The Cadets made good their new policy both in words and in deeds. Some of the younger party members voluntarily joined the armed forces. Others engaged in the vast and multiform war effort behind the front: care of the wounded, care of the soldiers' families, and later on the complex task of supplying the front. But the Cadet party's chief contribution to the unification of the country was made in the Duma. In August, 1915, on the initiative of Miliukov, the Progressive Bloc was formed. It comprised, next to the Cadets, the Octobrists, Nationalists, and Progressives. The ultra-monarchists and the socialists did not join the Bloc. For a while, the struggle between government and opposition came to a standstill. From enemies, the Cadets were prepared to turn into partners of the government. The Duma deputies anxiously watched the developments at the front and in the country. They did not try to hush up the deficiencies uncovered in the army by the war. As early as January, 1915, barely six months after the start of the war, two prominent Cadet leaders, Miliukov and Shingarev, exposed the ominous shortcomings of the supply organization in a closed session of the Duma. The army was short of guns, ammunition, machine guns, even rifles. There was no question yet of aircraft—even in Germany aviation was still in the embryonic stage.

The Duma became the center of the patriotic effort. The nation, in its determination to defeat the enemy, rallied to the support of the army. Special industrial committees were formed which helped to convert peacetime industry to war production. No credit for this is due to this or that party—it was an all-out national effort. Still, the influence of the Cadets was immense. They used their talents and experience to arouse public opinion and to rally it to the task of defense. It was Russia's misfortune that the healthy impulse to defend one's country had to contend with destructive forces. At the top, they were responsible for the deplorable choice of ministers who refused to cooperate with the Progressive Bloc and other public forces. These men undermined the confidence of the nation and the army in the Tsar and his advisers. Revolutionary propaganda found easy access to minds and hearts weary of four years of war. Sinister rumors of treachery in high places spread through the nation and, most alarmingly, through the army.

Even the sober, level-headed Miliukov fell a prey to this provocation and on November 1, 1916, denounced in the Duma the sinister influence of Rasputin on the Tsar and his ministers. This speech of the leader of the Cadets sounded the signal for the revolutionary landslide which for many decades delivered Russia into slavery to the Marxist dictators and relegated political freedom, the goal of the Cadets, to a remote future. . . . From then on all the efforts of the party, from participation in the Provisional Government to the armed fight and the underground struggle against Bolshevism, were no more than impotent attempts to stem the onrushing flood. It is true that after Miliukov's speech the cadres of the party swelled through the enrollment of thousands of new members and that the patriotic prestige of the Cadets increased. Nevertheless, they as well as the moderate socialists were powerless to put up a dam against Communism. The Bolsheviks promised peace, while the Cadets, regardless of the revolutionary storm shaking the country and the Bolshevik propaganda demoralizing the war-weary army, persisted in calling the nation to carry on the war "side by side with our Allies until the victorious end."

In the first Provisional Government the Cadet ministers and their allies, supported by the "Committee of the Duma," were in the majority. But before long the majority in the cabinet passed over to the socialists, who had the support of the Soviets (Councils of Soldiers' and Peasants' Deputies). From the outset, these two organizations — the Duma Committee and the Soviets — were struggling for power. The Soviet Encyclopedia, which cannot be suspected of wishing to exaggerate the importance of the Cadet party, thus described its role in 1917: "During the period March–July, 1917, the Cadet party carries on an active fight for the liquidation of the diarchy and for the exclusive rule of the bourgeoisie. The Cadet party becomes a rallying center for all the counter-revolutionary forces struggling against Bolshevism and the revolutionary masses."

After the seizure of power by the Bolsheviks, the Cadet party, for two months longer, went on openly denouncing them in the press, at political meetings, in the Petrograd Municipal Council, as usurpers and traitors charged by the Germans with the task of disorganizing the Russian army. Lenin retaliated to these virulent attacks with a special decree (December 11, 1917) which read: "The members of the leading organs of the Cadet party, as a party of enemies of the people, are to be arrested and brought to trial before the revolutionary tribunal."

Shortly after this decree, two prominent Cadet ministers in the Provisional Government that had just been overthrown, Shingarev and Kokoshkin, were brutally assassinated at the Mariinsky Hospital in Petrograd. In January, 1918, the Constituent Assembly, elected on the basis of the most democratic electoral law, was forcibly dispersed by Lenin's order. The political game was over. The long dark era of the dictatorship of the proletariat, actually the dictatorship of Lenin and then of Stalin, had started. The liberal movement represented by the Cadets was crushed. Stalin in his *Problems of Leninism* has given the following appraisal of the Cadet party: "During the struggle against Tsarism, when the bourgeois-democratic revolution of 1905–1916 was in preparation, the liberal-monarchist Cadet party represented the most dangerous social cement of the Tsarist regime. It was a party of conciliators, set upon conciliation between Tsarism and the majority of the people, that is, the peasantry as a whole."

As an orderly purposeful political organization created to help establish a constitutional system in Russia, the party had been destroyed by Lenin's decree. Individual members took part in the armed fight and the underground struggle against the Bolsheviks, but these idealists were no match for the Cheka. Many perished in the cellars of the Cheka, others went into exile with the forlorn hope of making world opinion realize what a frightful menace to all mankind the Soviet regime represented. But this was a task for individuals. The party as such had ceased to exist. Yet the humanitarian ideals of right and justice that inspired it will surely rise again in Russia, once the country frees itself from Communism. The whole world will breathe easier then.

ALEXANDER KERENSKY

Russia on the Eve of
World War I

A. F. Kerensky (1881–1970), a central figure in the revolutionary
upheaval of 1917, became known as a young lawyer, acting as coun-
sel for the defense in political trials. He was a member of the Tru-
dovik (Labor) group in the Third and Fourth Dumas but later adhered
openly to the SR party. After the February/March Revolution he became, at the age of 36, Minister of Justice, Minister of War (May–
July 1917), and Prime Minister (July–November 1917). Soon after
the seizure of power by the Bolsheviks, he fled from Petrograd to
Paris and later came to the United States. He is the author of a number of books on the Provisional Government and on the Bolsheviks
of which the latest is *Russia and History's Turning Point,* New York,
1965. He is also co-editor, with Professor Robert Browder, of a three-
volume collection of documents on the Provisional Government published by the Hoover Institution at Stanford in 1961.

The article below, although controversial in some respects, gives
a broad, first-hand account of the social, political, and economic
conditions in Russia on the eve of World War I, from the point of
view of an active opponent of Stolypin's policies and of the Imperial
regime.

From *The Russian Review,* vol. 5, no. 1 (Autumn 1945), pp. 10–30.

The brief period of Russian history from the revolution of 1905 to the war of 1914 was a time of great importance for Russia's internal development.

Foreign public opinion has a very imperfect idea of this period. It is generally believed that the attempt to "Europeanize" Russia by the establishment of a constitutional regime ended in complete failure. Due to the innate attachment of the Russian people to tyranny, so runs the argument, tsarist absolutism easily triumphed over the liberal intelligentsia's "absurd dream." It is believed that after the revolutionary outburst of 1905–1906, the autocrat and his "boyars" became once more Russia's all-powerful masters. They resumed the exploitation of their "slaves," deprived of all civil rights. Serious historical studies devoted to Russia call this period "quasi-constitutional." When, after an exhausting war, totalitarian dictatorship was established in Russia, Western public opinion considered this regime of violence as a normal return of the old tyranny—a Red instead of a White, tsarism.

The last short years before the war—the beginning of Russia's great catastrophe—were marked by a dynamic development of economic, cultural, and political forces.

Already at the time of the First Duma (in the spring of 1906), a bitter strife broke out in court and government circles between two tendencies. One group shared the sovereign's hatred of the constitution which had been granted in October of 1905, under the pressure of the revolutionary movement, and insisted on a return to absolutism. The "Union of the Russian People," an extreme reactionary organization, impersonated "the indignant population." From all parts of Russia, its members sent addresses demanding the suppression of the Duma and the abrogation of the October Manifesto.

The other group, whose representatives had not entirely lost the sense of reality, declared that the return of absolutism would be sheer madness; the suppression of popular representation would incite even the most moderate and loyal elements to side with revolution. Moreover, Russia's international situation did not permit a reactionary course.

It was the second group that triumphed. Instead of suppressing popular representation and constitution, it was decided to modify the electoral law. The latter was to create in the Duma an efficient governmental majority formed by the gentry and the moderately progressive bourgeoisie. At the same time it was decided to proceed to a hasty land reform. A "Third Estate" of French or German pattern was to be created; this new class of well-to-do farmers was to replace the gentry, whose influence was on the wane. The reform was to be accompanied by drastic repressive measures against the revolutionary movement, though the latter was obviously declining.

On the eve of the summoning of the First Duma, P. A. Stolypin, Governor of Saratov, had been appointed Minister of the Interior. He was a "new man," almost unknown to St. Petersburg bureaucratic circles. Less than three months later, simultaneously with the dissolution of the First Duma (July 21, 1906), he was appointed Premier with the mission of applying the plan I have just described.

Stolypin's meteoric rise was a symptom of the times. This landowner of old provincial stock was not a courtier and had never filled high official functions in St. Petersburg. He had spent his life in the provinces and had many connections among the zemstvo* leaders and social workers. He knew the zemstvo's activity well and held it in high esteem. In Saratov, where I was elected in 1912 to the Fourth Duma, he was considered a "liberal" governor.

Stolypin was a man of strong will and an eloquent speaker, well fitted for a big political career. He did not care to govern Russia in the dull silence of bureaucratic offices. He did not look upon the Duma as a silly, useless "cackle-shop," as his predecessor, the soulless bureaucrat Goremykin, had called it. On the contrary, Stolypin was attracted by the role of a constitutional premier, making speeches in parliament, waging an oratorical battle with the opposition, and leading his own majority. The St. Petersburg officials lacked a fighting temperament. Stolypin had plenty of it. This was to decide his future.

The Tsar liked the new Premier because he was young, fearless, devoted to the throne, and firmly decided to apply the program of state reform. The leaders of the Council of United Gentry saw in him a man of their own; he was to save the country gentry from decimation. The Octobrists and the other moderate conservative

---

* Local self-government institutions in imperial Russia.

constitutionalists, scared by the revolution, clung to him as to an anchor of salvation. His program — the union of the government and of the conservative forces for the consolidation of the constitutional monarchy and the final liquidation of unrest — was their own program. They hailed him as the Russian Thiers who would create a strong bourgeoisie, like the French statesman who, after the Commune, consolidated for many years the bourgeois Third Republic. But Thiers was backed by the strong French peasantry, profoundly imbued with the instinct of private property. In Russia, such a peasant class was still to be created. And many scores of years were required for its formation.

I was a confirmed adversary of Stolypin and of the social circles which supported him. I believed, as did all the Russian opposition, that Stolypin's tactical slogan: "First the pacification of the country, then reforms," was dangerous for Russia's future. Even Count Benckendorff, Russian Ambassador to London, warned St. Petersburg that only reforms, accomplished in time, could bring pacification.

But whatever the errors, and even the crimes, committed by the Stolypin government, the fact remains: it did not aim at the restoration of absolutism and the suppression of popular representation. It sought the establishment of a conservative, bourgeois-aristocratic, constitutional monarchy.

Stolypin's tragedy consisted in the fact that he felt obliged to fight not only socialism but also democratic liberalism. What was far more unfortunate for the fate of his program was that Russia lacked the social basis for the creation of a bourgeois constitutional regime of European pattern. For, as we have seen, there was no politically strong "Third Estate" in the country which could have served as an intermediary between the upper classes and the labor classes. This "Third Estate" was still in the making.

True, following the rapid development of towns and industry, the urban bourgeoisie acquired a certain influence in social and political life. But there was no such class in the villages. The First Duma elections proved already that the peasants, who mostly represented labor economy and not capitalist economy, could not play the part of a conservative class.

As to the non-peasant landownership, it was obviously declining. Economically it was so much weakened, that its participation in production did not even attain 10 per cent. The government and the leading conservative circles had accepted the fact of the gradual liquidation of the gentry landownership. They only sought to preserve certain of its more vital elements, by offering them the support of a strong peasant group of well-to-do farmers.

It must be recalled that a large part of Russian peasantry was submitted to the regime of communal landownership (the *obshchina* or the *mir* system). This system was hailed first by the Slavophiles, and later by the Populists. Both groups believed that the Russian peasants' feebly developed instinct of private property would protect Russia against the inroads of Western capitalism, and that the Russian people could adopt more easily the more perfect and more equitable forms of public economy. The Populists demanded the "nationalization" or "socialization" of land. They were convinced that the peasant would easily pass from the communal to the collective agricultural regime.

Actually the peasant commune, such as it existed in Russia, had very little in common with the ideal commune of the Slavophiles or the Populists. For the administration, it was simply a convenient police apparatus, permitting it to "keep the peasants under tutelage and to treat them like children," in Witte's words. Until 1903, when the principle of joint liability finally was abolished, it was especially a convenient institution for tax-collecting as the arrears due by a member of the commune had to be paid by all the other members. Thus, the *obshchina* in the hands of the administration was corrupted and turned into a source of economic regression. And the peasants themselves were irritated by the fact, that, according to the existing system, they were compelled to remain in the commune whether they liked it or not.

After the agrarian disorders of 1905–1906, many people realized that the compulsory police commune must be suppressed. As to the future of the liberated communes, this had to be left to the peasants' own decision. In accordance with their wishes, the communal lands would have to be partly split into privately owned holdings, and partly turned into agricultural cooperatives. This was the underlying principle of the agrarian bill of the First Duma which provided for a partial expropriation of private lands with due compensation to the owners. The land of some private estates was to be distributed among the peasants, who then would determine themselves the fate of the communal regime. This plan offered a healthy, democratic solution of Russia's fundamental, political and economic problem. Had it been realized, the social differentiation of the rural population would have proceeded in a free and natural way. Doubtless, a "bourgeois minority" would have been formed among the peasant masses, and it would have created in Russia a farm economy of the West European or the American type. In Siberia and the Ukraine, this minority even could have been turned into a majority. But the government refused to accept the bill, and it was on this issue that the First Duma was dissolved.

After the dissolution of the First Duma, the land reform was taken in hand by Stolypin. On November 22, 1906, three months before the opening of the Second Duma, the new agrarian law was promulgated according to section 87 of the Fundamental Laws, which granted the Emperor the power to publish decrees in the interim between the sessions of the Duma, later to be ratified, however, by the legislative assemblies (*i.e.* the Duma and the State Council).

Stolypin's land reform proved that he had a fighting temperament, but no political wisdom. In his hands, the land reform, based on healthy principles, became a weapon of political and class struggle. Instead of suppressing the compulsory character of the commune, in the interests of free peasant economy, Stolypin abrogated the commune in the interests of the peasant "bourgeois" elements. The reform was applied with great energy; it brutally violated the elementary principles of justice and law. The government backed the strong against the weak. It encouraged the well-to-do peasants to separate themselves from the commune against the majority's will. These well-to-do peasants received the best portions of the land of the commune, infringing upon the latter's rights. Moreover, they were granted loans equaling 90 per cent of the value of the land received.

During a period of some five years,* the peasant agrarian regime in Russia was submitted to a drastic tranformation. And what were the results? Stolypin was very proud of his role of a land reformer. He even invited foreign specialists to survey his government's work. Speaking in the Fourth Duma, and severely criticizing the social and political consequences of the reform, I quoted the German

---

*The Stolypin agrarian law was not given a definitive form and put into operation until 1911. Shortly after the outbreak of the war, the new land settlement had to be suspended [Ed.].

scholar, Professor Aufhagen. Having visited the Russian countryside, on the government's special invitation, Professor Aufhagen
subsequently wrote that "Stolypin's reform had thrown the torch of
civil war in the Russian villages." And P. Miliukov recalls the words
of another foreign observer, Professor Preyer, who was favorable to
Stolypin's plans. Returning from his survey of Russian rural life, he
correctly stated that "the aim of the reform had not been achieved."

Indeed, by January 1915, in spite of all the persuasion and all the
privileges granted, only 2,729,000 peasants demanded the conver-
sion of their plots of land into private property (about 33 per cent of
all the households in the communes). The rural population showed
coldness and even hostility towards the reform for two reasons.
First, they condemned the methods. The average peasant did not
want to go against the commune. The "backing of the strong" idea
was something against which he naturally revolted. He did not want
to become a "half landlord" at the cost of his neighbors. Secondly,
the conditions of freedom granted by the October Manifesto opened
to the rural population a new path of economic progress which was
in tune with his aspirations. This path was cooperation, encouraged
both by the zemstvo and the leftist intelligentsia. The Slavophiles
and Populists were partly right: the social spirit of the average
Russian peasant was not a mere fancy. Stolypin's reform was a
failure because it went against the peasants' will.

Stolypin had pledged himself to suppress the revolutionary movement and to pacify Russia. But here again, as in his agrarian policy,
he showed a fighting spirit, but a lack of political wisdom.

Russia was truly ready for pacification. The revolutionary movement was dying out of itself. For the October Manifesto had opened
the way to freedom, to a creative social and political work. The so-
called "excesses of the revolution"—"expropriations" (looting of
banks "for the needs of the revolution"), murder of subaltern officials, etc.—awakened first perplexity and then irritation on the part
of the population at large, which frankly condemned them. Stolpyin
could have taken advantage of this mood and "finished off" the
revolution, by restoring true peaceful conditions. Instead, he "finished off" the already disarmed revolutionaries. The defense of the
state against unbridled popular instincts very soon became the revenge of a victorious class. Stolypin believed that the very firmness
of his "pacifying policy" would gain the population's support. But
he obtained the opposite results. The sterner his attitude, the louder
grew the people's protest.

The first two or three years following the dissolution of the First Duma had been called the age of "White Terror." Today, this definition may sound strange indeed. After the experiment of totalitarian dictatorship in Russia and Western Europe, it is as absurd to call Stolypin a terrorist ruler as to compare the art of an amateur singer to the genius of a Chaliapin. Suffice it to say that following the unsuccessful assault on Lenin, the number of hostages shot in one day (5000) was far greater than that of the persons (1144)* executed by Stolypin's courts-martial during the whole period of their existence. In those days, ruthless repression was directed against a very small part of the population, that which actively struggled against the government. Today, the entire population lives in a perpetual state of fear and trembling. Moreover, after each act of governmental terror, the most prominent representatives of literature, science and art, are compelled to send enthusiastic congratulations to the totalitarian leaders. In Stolypin's days, nobody, except the "Black Hundred," dared to openly express their sympathies with governmental executions. And all cultured society, headed by Leo Tolstoy, voiced its indignation after each new execution. Russian society protested, not because it sided with revolutionary terror which had degenerated into absurd excesses, but because it was inspired by one of the deepest traditions of Russian spiritual culture—repulsion for capital punishment. Russia, let it be remembered, was the only country in the world where capital punishment was not applied to ordinary criminal offenders. And Russia did not want the government to adopt the ways of vengeance, bloodshed, and violence in its struggle against political opponents. This is why, after Stolypin had created his courts-martial, Leo Tolstoy wrote his sensational appeal to the government, beginning with the words: "I cannot be silent. . . . "

This is why one of our most brilliant orators of the Duma, the moderate liberal, Rodichev, publicly branded the minister, by calling the gallows' noose "Stolypin's neck-tie." After the fall of the monarchy in 1917, the government of the democratic revolution immediately abrogated capital punishment for all offences. This measure, fulfilling one of the most sacred pledges of the emancipation movement, awakened general enthusiasm. Russia's spiritual

---

* Some Soviet sources estimate the number of executed by Stolypin courts-martial as over two thousand [Ed.].

atmosphere before 1914 condemned Stolypin's "pacifying" policy
to certain failure, as well as his land reform.

Stolypin's own end was tragic. In 1911, during a gala performance at the Kiev theater, Stolypin was attacked as he sat a few feet
away from the box occupied by the Tsar and his daughters. The
minister was mortally wounded by a revolver shot of a former
anarchist and secret police agent, a man called Bagrov. At that
time, the Tsar could no longer endure his favorite of yesterday. The
special investigation ascertained that, during his stay in Kiev,
Stolypin was not guarded by the police, as was usually the case.
Kurlov, the undersecretary of the Minister of the Interior who directed the police, was to be put to trial. But the Emperor personally
stopped the investigation. There was a mystery about the minister's
death. The assassin was executed without delay and held incom-
municado until his death. People well informed of the secret conflict between the premier and Rasputin believed that the police had
permitted the assassin to strike, in order to please the minister's
powerful opponents. Stolypin himself once said to A. I. Guchkov:
"I have the feeling that I shall be murdered by the police."

Thus, Russia's all-powerful "pacificator" was powerless to chain
the "dark forces" supported by the young Empress. Stloypin was
too honest, independent, and progressive a man to please Rasputin.
But the Premier had also lost the sympathies of the Octobrists. The
latter were the leading party of the Third Duma, created by Stolypin's own conservative electoral law of June 16, 1907. Sir Bernard
Pares, the prominent English author who is an authority on Russia,
has stated quite correctly that, given the spirit then existing in
Russia, even a Duma exclusively composed of former ministers
would have been in opposition to the government. But the Third
Duma did not consist only of "former ministers." Of course, it was
neither a leftist nor a democratic body. The new electoral law had
reduced to a bare minimum the participation of peasants, workers,
and of the urban democracy. In the provinces, the elections were
actually in the hands of the declining gentry. And the almost general
suffrage previously existing in the cities was revoked. The number
of deputies was reduced, and half of the seats were given over to an
insignificant minority of bourgeois capitalists, by means of an in-
genious "curial" system. The representation of non-Russian nationalities likewise was drastically curtailed. Poland, for instance,
was given 18 seats in the Third (and Fourth) Duma, instead of the
previous 53.

Popular representation, chosen according to Stolypin's electoral law, was rightly called "Russia's crooked mirror." The leftist and socialist parties, which played the leading role in the first two Dumas, nearly disappeared from the Third Duma (1907–1911). Only 13 peasants of the so-called Labor Group retained their seats, and there were only 20 Social Democrats. The Socialist Revolutionary Party resumed its earlier boycott tactics. The party of the liberal intelligentsia (the Cadets), which formerly led the floor, now became the party of "His Majesty's opposition," with 56 deputies. The reactionaries were much in evidence. The extreme rightists and the instigators of pogroms had no organic link with the nation (when monarchy was overthrown, they faded away in twenty-four hours); but they were subsidized by the champions of absolutism and the Police Department. Fifty seats were held by the so-called "popular representatives" of these chauvinist groups. The reactionary deputies, led by some gifted demagogues, undermined the Duma from within, continually provoking violent incidents. Next to them sat 96 members of the newly formed Nationalist Party. They represented mostly the Western and South-Western regions where a centuries-old struggle was waged between the Russian, Polish, Lithuanian, and Jewish population. The entire space between the Cadets and the right wing was filled by 154 Octobrists whose number had been insignificant in the First Duma; now they formed over one-third of the elected body.

I have stressed the composition of the Third Duma, for it was about the same as that of the Fourth Duma, of 1912–1917. And yet, the Fourth Duma played an important part in the people's struggle against the last monarch and his entourage. The Third Duma, in spite of its conservative majority and its influential reactionary wing, was also active. Indeed, it proved to be a no less zealous champion of the constitutional regime than the First Duma. The difference was only in methods and temperament.

The First Duma reflected the soul of popular Russia. It was the Duma of "the people's wrath." It uncovered all the dark sides of the old regime. It was irreconcilable and would tolerate no compromise. It demanded the capitulation of supreme authority: the transfer of the plenitude of power into the people's hands. Its fundamental aspiration was expressed by V. D. Nabokov, the son of the Minister of Justice under Alexander II and Alexander III: "Let the executive power submit to the legislative." But the First Duma bestowed no laws on the country, because it was di. solved before it had been able to begin its organic parliamentary work. The Second Duma was considerably more to the left than the First Duma, and it was dissolved after less than three months (in April 1907).

The Third Duma began its existence without glamor. Its majority aimed at a compromise: loyal collaboration with the government on the basis of the October Manifesto. The latter, which inspired the leading Octobrist Party's program, granted popular representation legislative powers, the right to examine the budget and the right of interpellation. Having modified by a *coup d'état* the original electoral law, the government solemnly proclaimed the Duma's immutability. And the Octobrists were firmly decided to take advantage of their parliamentary rights; they wanted to consolidate popular representation and to transform the Duma into a decisive factor in Russia's political system.

But neither the Tsar and his entourage nor the democratic public opinion understood these tactics. At first, after the stormy days of the first two Dumas, the Tsar was well pleased with the newly elected house. He believed that it was composed of men informed of local affairs and local needs; men whose advice would help the ministers to prepare good laws while not interfering with the sovereign's prerogatives. The loyal attitude of the Third Duma was interpreted in the same way by the public opinion. It was hostile to the Duma's conservative majority and called its leaders "the servants of reaction."

In reality, the Duma's leaders were not reactionaries. The Octobrist Party was formed by the members of the middle and upper classes of the Russian society. It comprised zemstvo and gentry elements, as well as industrialists and merchants, representatives of liberal professions and of St. Petersburg and provincial bureaucracy. There were few theorists among them, but many men possessing practical experience gained in the administrative, municipal, or zemstvo work. And this experience led them to the firm conviction that Russia had come of age and needed bureaucratic tutelage no longer. The Russo-Japanese war had definitely proved that bureaucracy was unable to cope with the needs of a growing empire.

N. A. Khomyakov, the President of the Third Duma, was a former high official and a wealthy landowner who belonged to ancient aristocratic stock. He was the son of Alexis Khomyakov, one of the founders of Slavophilism. As to A. I. Guchkov, the crea-

tor of the Octobrist Party, he belonged to quite a different milieu.
He was the grandson of a serf and belonged to the Moscow mer-
chant intelligentsia. He was proud of his origin, despised social
privilege, and did not trust bureaucracy. In spite of these differences, Khomyakov and Guchkov were members of the same party.
Both believed that the consolidation of the constitutional regime
was to be the fundamental aim of their activity. Both were aware
that without popular representation and a deep reconstruction of
the Russian political system, their country was threatened by a
catastrophe which the first exterior conflict would bring about.

Europe was on the brink of a volcano. The question was not
whether a general European war would break out, but *when* it
would break out. The experience of Port Arthur and Tsushima had
opened the eyes of all Russian patriots. . . . And the entire process
(which lasted seven to eight years) of turning a loyal conservative
majority into opposition and finally into a revolutionary body, took
place under the pressure of patriotic anxiety, which soon became
patriotic indignation.

I knew Guchkov well. In 1917, we were for a time together in the
Provisional Government. Later we often met abroad, in exile. He
assured me that the Octobrist leaders did all they could to hasten
the consolidation of Russia's internal situtation and to prepare her
for the inevitable international conflict. Germany's industrial development followed a dynamic rhythm; she was feverishly building
her fleet; her army's technical power grew from day to day. All
those who were better informed of the international situation than
the man in the street clearly understood the danger: Russia's temporary weakness caused by the Japanese war and revolutionary
chaos was considered by Germany as a trump card in her struggle
for hegemony.

Guchkov, Khomyakov, and the other Octobrist leaders were
aware of another danger: the abnormal, neurotic atmosphere which
surrounded the Tsar. They knew that they could not trust the sovereign's feeble will. Therefore, they refused all of Stolypin's tempting offers to enter the cabinet. They preferred to control the government's activity, thanks to the Duma's right to examine the budget;
to back the cabinet in its struggle against Rasputin; and to consolidate Russia's economic and military power through organic legislation.

The Tsar's idyll with the Third Duma did not last long. According to the fundamental laws of the Russian Empire, the army and navy remained under the emperor's direct control. Formally, the Duma could not interfere with the corresponding ministers and with their activity. But the budgets of these departments were examined by a Duma committee. As in all parliaments, the budget committee became the leading and most influential organ of the house. All ministers treated it with due consideration. Before the budgets of separate ministries were examined by the committee, they were carefully studied by special sub-committees. Thus the Ministry of War and Ministry of the Navy were actually controlled by the Duma. After the Russo-Japanese war, the fleet was to be reconstructed, increased, and rearmed, according to modern technical demands, and many urgent reforms were needed in the army. But the army and navy lacked efficient direction. Higher military and naval boards were continually constructed and reconstructed. A number of highly important administrative posts were entrusted to entirely irresponsible grand dukes, who pursued their own personal or political aims, taking no one into account. Both in the army and navy, energetic military technicians feverishly drafted the necessary reforms, but they had not the power to apply them.

A. Guchkov was made chairman of the Duma Defense Committee. He was in touch with the boldest champions of reorganization in the War and Navy Ministries. Thus the Duma* became the leading center in the reconstruction of national defense. It played a prominent role in Russia's preparation of the war of 1914. This was due both to the work it directly accomplished and to the fact that the healthy forces of the army and navy felt its support. And popular representatives knew that they were backed by the leaders of the armed forces. In the spring of 1908, when the budget of the War Ministry was examined by the Duma, Guchkov made a speech demanding that the Grand Dukes should consent to a "patriotic sacrifice": they were to give up their prominent role in the miliatry administration. This statement was made with the full consent of the army and navy leaders; the interference on the part of completely irresponsible persons gravely hindered their work. The speech stirred the indignation of court circles. To Empress Alexandra, Guchkov's activity was an assault against the prerogatives of su-

---

* This applies both to the Third and the Fourth Dumas.

preme power. Guchkov was nick-named the "Young Turk" by his reactionary opponents and became their enemy number one.

The Empress rightly considered the leader of conservative constitutionalism as the most dangerous adversary of her own political plan: the reestablishment of unlimited absolutism. "Octobrism" and all the moderate groups following in its wake formed but the rear-guard of democratic forces. But it was the vanguard of the more enlightened members of the higher military, bureaucratic, and court circles. It waged a progressive battle against reaction, and it led the way, against its own will, towards the revival of a widespread democratic movement. The Octobrists did not desire Russia's further democratization. But they sought to place her at a political, cultural, and economic level which befitted a great power. They were encouraged by the moderate opposition and by the more cultured elements of high administration. This is why the Third Duma, and the Fourth Duma which succeeded it, in spite of their "counter-revolutionary" origins, played a progressive role in Russian history. Some of their laws and the very fact of their existence, hastened Russia's remarkable development, which marked the last years preceding the war.

First of all, public education rapidly improved. When war broke out, Russia was on the eve of achieving general compulsory education. The absurd and criminal opposition to public education pursued by reactionary ministers at the end of the nineteenth century ceased in the early twentieth century. At the time of the First Duma, the Minister of Public Education Kaufman-Turkestansky (the son of the famous organizer of Russian Turkestan), prepared a bill providing for a system of general education which eventually was accepted by the Third Duma. The State Council,* however, rejected the bill and returned it to the Duma for further examination. It was finally passed, in a modified form, by the Fourth Duma, with full support of the new Minister of Public Education, Count Ignatiev, who was firmly convinced that conditions in Russia made general education both necessary and possible. Had it not been for the war, this system would have been completely established by 1922.

In 1929, Yale University Press published for the Carnegie Endowment a book entitled *Russian Schools and Universities in the*

---

* The State Council played the role of the upper chamber. Half of its members were elected by certain public bodies while the other half were appointed by the Emperor.

World War. It was written by two prominent authorities on Russian education, Professors P. Novgorodtsev and D. Odinets, with a preface by the former minister, Count Ignatiev. This excellent work should put a stop to the absurd legend concerning Russia's "complete illiteracy" in pre-revolutionary times. It has been stated, for instance, that there were only "ten per cent of literates in Russia," and that the ruling class tried to close the access to public education to children of peasants and workers. As a matter of fact, even before the constitutional period, the zemstvos were spending 25 per cent of their budget on popular schools. During the Duma period they were spending one third of their budget for this purpose. In the space of ten years (1900–1910), government subsidies to the zemstvo schools increased twelve times. At the beginning of the present century, there were 76 thousand primary schools in Russia with 4 million pupils. In 1915, there were over 122 thousand schools with 8 million pupils. The school term was lengthened and the program enlarged, in order to give the more gifted peasant children the possibility to pass directly from primary to secondary school. Primary schools did not only teach children; they also became centers for the instruction of adult peasants. They organized libraries, lectures, Sunday and evening classes, and theatrical performances for adults. Special courses for teachers were started by the zemstvo and cooperatives. Every year cheap excursions abroad were organized for teachers; before the war, thousands of them visited Italy, France, Germany, and other Western countries. To quote the authors of the work just mentioned: "The conclusion to be drawn from the general state of primary and secondary education in Russia in the years preceding the war is that throughout the history of Russian civilization never was the spread of education so rapid as during the period in question."

At the same time, the zemstvo and the cooperatives attained remarkable results in the field of agricultural technique. From 1906 to 1913, the surface of cultivated land increased by 16 per cent and crop production by 41 per cent. The budget of the zemstvo's agronomical aid to peasants increased six times. The government also made large expenditures on agronomical aid. With the zemstvo, the government encouraged mechanized peasant agriculture. The governmental Peasant Land Bank bought millions of acres of land from the gentry and resold them to the peasants. Loan cooperatives and the zemstvo furnished the live-stock and the implements. By 1914 over 75 per cent of lands suitable for agriculture in European Russia were held by the peasants. During the brief years of Russia's economic prosperity before the war, the agricultural export increased one and a half times. And the role of peasant economy on the domestic and foreign markets was predominant. Three quarters of grain and hemp, nearly all the butter and eggs, vegetables and meat, were furnished by the peasants and peasant cooperatives.

Simultaneously with the transfer of land into peasant hands and the dynamic growth of peasant economy, a large-scale colonization movement—from European Russia into the Asiatic parts of the Empire—was started during that period. It was sponsored by the government, the zemstvo and the cooperatives. Siberia achieved a typically "American" rate of development. Between the Russo-Japanese war and the First World War, its population doubled. The surface of cultivated land nearly trebled. Agricultural production increased more than three times. By 1914, most of the market of Russian butter exported to England was held by Siberian peasant cooperatives. In 1899, the export of butter was non-existent in Siberia. In 1915, the cooperatives exported 100,000 tons of butter.

Thanks to the constitutional regime, the cooperative movement attained its full development. And it was precisely in cooperation that the Russian people, and especially the Russian peasants, revealed their democratic spirit and their talent for organization. By 1914, nearly half of the peasant households in Russia joined the cooperative movement. In his book *Russia under Soviet Rule,* N. A. Basily gives an exhaustive outline of Russia's development at that time. He quotes extremely significant figures concerning peasant loan cooperatives. In 1905, they had 729,000 members; in 1916, 10,500,000 members. In 1905, their total investments amounted to 37½ million gold rubles; in 1916, to 682⅓ million. The urban cooperative movement grew in the same proportion. The federation of consumers' cooperatives, headed by the Moscow Central Union, became one of the most influential economic, and even political, forces in Russia. It organized wide strata of the population, consolidated the basis of their material welfare, and pursued cultural work. The cooperative leaders, mostly belonging to the leftist parties, fortified the healthy, creative, democratic aspirations of the labor masses. The growth of the cooperatives was encouraged by the increase of the general welfare of the working class. This development was revealed by the purchase of consumer's goods (sugar,

butter, kerosene, shoes, clothes, etc.). It was clearly illustrated by
the increase of public savings. According to the Soviet economist,
Professor Liashchenko, the deposits in state savings institutions
amounted in 1906 to 831.2 million gold rubles; and on July 1, 1914,
to 1704.2 millions.

My readers may find these figures dull, but I want to show the
achievements of Russian public economy on the eve of the great
catastrophe which befell Russia, and which was ushered in by the
war of 1914. I wish it to be understood that during the brief period
of the "five year plan" of *political freedom,* immense economic results could be achieved. This could be done without returning the
population to slavery, without depriving it of all political rights,
and condemning the country to famine and misery unheard of in
the history of cultured nations.

According to the calculations of one of the most prominent authorities on Russia's economic development, Professor Prokopo-
vich, during the constitutional period, Russia's public income (in
spite of the depression caused by the Russo-Japanese war) increased 79.4 per cent in fifty provinces of European Russia.
The total turnover of foreign trade, as quoted by N. A. Basily,
amounted in 1906 to 1896 million gold rubles; in 1913, it was
equal to 2913 millions. The length of the railroad system in 1905
was 52.5 thousand *versts;* in 1915, 64.5 thousand *versts.* The
building of the famous "Turksib"* was started at that time. The
railroad revenue in 1908 equaled 169 million gold rubles; in 1912,
449 millions. Professor Liashchenko states that the number of
spindles in cotton mills in 1900 was 6646 thousands, and in 1913,
9200 thousands. In two years, 1910–12, machine building increased by one third: from 101.9 million gold rubles to 136.6
millions.

I shall add to these few data the following conclusions drawn by
Soviet party economists concerning the economic achievements of
Russia during the constitutional period. I am quoting from the
Outlines of the History of the October Revolution, published in
Moscow by the *Istpart:*

> Russia was rapidly moving ahead along the capitalist lines of devel-
> opment, overtaking the older capitalist countries. . . . The gross output

* A railroad connecting Turkestan with Siberia. It was completed after the
Revolution.

of industry increased by 44.9 per cent between the years 1900 and 1905, and by 1913 it had increased by 219 per cent. Individual industries showed even greater increase. Technically, industry as a whole was greatly extended and modernized. A very incomplete summary gives a total of 537.3 million gold rubles as the investment in industrial equipment for the years 1910–12. During this flourishing period the increase in the capital stock of our industry was three times as rapid as that of America. As regards the concentration of our industry, Russia became one of the foremost countries in the world: the concentration of its industry was greater than that of America, for instance.

The last point is of paramount importance. The excessive concentration of Russian industry had two far-reaching consequences. On the one hand, the presence in big urban centers of large masses of workers created extremely favorable conditions for their organization. On the other hand, the growth of concentrated industry strengthened not so much the middle classes as the forces of banking capital. Thus, in both rural districts and urban centers, Russia's economic development did not modify sufficiently her social structure to create a new solid foundation for a capitalist society.

Many public leaders of the period were of the opinion that, in the process of her political and economic growth, Russia was to follow the path of Western capitalism. They believed that the war broke off this evolution determined by economic laws. As for myself, I did not think so at the time, and still do not think so. My personal experience persuaded me that the "peculiar way" of Russia's political and social life was not an utopia imagined by the Slavophiles and the Populists, but an historical fact.

From the fall of 1906 and up to the Revolution of 1917, I frequently visited all parts of Russia, first as a "political defender,"* and later as a member of the Duma.

After the 1905 revolution, numerous trials started throughout Russia: in the two capitals, in the center and in the border-lands, in civil and military courts. People were tried for anti-governmental speeches delivered at public meetings, for "subversive" articles and proclamations. Sometimes several persons at a time, or even scores of persons were put on trial: party or revolutionary committees, organizers of local uprisings, deputies of the dissolved Dumas, mili-

* In pre-revolutionary Russia, this name was given those lawyers who, as an act of civic duty, offered their services free of charge to the defendants in political trials [Ed.].

tary organizations, unions of railroad employees, teachers, workers and peasants, organizers of political "expropriations," leaders of strikes and peasant rebellions. In a word, Russian life with all its aspirations, hopes, and intimate moods was reproduced in the courtroom as in a film. But while this film went on, Russia's real life continued. In every town, I talked not only to the accused and their relatives, to judges, prosecutors, local officials, but also to the representatives of the local intelligentsia, political leaders, and cultural workers. All of them did their best to explain "local conditions" to the attorney from St. Petersburg. In those days, political defenders enjoyed special consideration. There were no secrets from them. They could, if they liked, see things exactly as they were. In the courtroom, the defender was not, as in totalitarian countries, a governmental official, struggling not so much against the government, as against the accused. In the darkest days of reaction, facing the most cynical judges (though it must be said that they were a minority), we could still be the independent defenders of right. No one dared to interfere with us. And no one was afraid to testify in behalf of the accused, the political enemies of the regime, or against the agents of the secret police.

When I described all this to a Soviet citizen of the younger generation, he listened to my story as to a fairy-tale. And yet, there were cases, which would appear even more fantastic to the subjects of a totalitarian state.

I witnessed such a case in the Lena gold-fields. In this God-forsaken region of Siberia, workers in those days suffered great hardships. In 1912, a strike broke out. The workers, with their women and children, marched towards the management's office. The local gendarme chief ordered the shooting of the strikers. There were many killed and wounded. This savage act of repression awakened general indignation throughout the country. The Minister of Justice, Makarov, poured fat on the fire by declaring: "So it always has been, and so it will be." These cynical words led to a new outburst of indignation. A campaign of protest was launched, and, for the first time since 1905, the workers organized political strikes. In order to pacify public opinion, the government sent Senator Manukhin,* who enjoyed general respect, to investigate the Lena shoot-

---

* In imperial Russia, a senator was a member of the highest judicial body in the country.

ing. At the same time, the Duma opposition decided to conduct its own investigation.

I was entrusted with this mission, though at the time I was not a member of the Duma and did not enjoy parliamentary immunity. I left for the Lena region with two other political defenders. We were not at all sure that the administration would allow us to visit the gold-fields. But when we reached Irkutsk, both the Governor-General of Eastern Siberia and the Governor of the Irkutsk province, helped us in every possible way. Neither did Senator Manukhin hinder our work. Both committees began their investigation simultaneously. We questioned the victims, summoned witnesses, inspected the locality, wrote our reports. When in the fall of 1912, I was elected deputy from Saratov, I disclosed the results of our investigation in the Duma. My conclusions almost fully coincided with those of the government committee. Thanks to our combined efforts, the guilt of the Lena administration was clearly established.

Can we imagine anything of the kind happening in totalitarian Russia or Germany? Of course not! And why? Because in those days, the Russian government recognized the civil rights, and after the October Manifesto, the political rights of the population. There were many arbitrary acts, but those who committed them knew that they were *violating law*. And the people *understood their rights perfectly and struggled to defend them*. It was possible to *struggle for right* and against the officials who violated it. This is entirely impossible in totalitarian countries.

The normal life of every state is founded on the gentlemanly instinct of "fair play." Both the government and the people must obey the "rules of the game." When the government, invested with the plenitude of power, abrogates these rules on its own behalf, authority is transformed into organized violence. As to the people, they must choose between two alternatives: to blindly obey arbitrary power, or else to struggle against it using the most extreme methods.

When I was elected to the Duma, the field of my observations widened. I could observe in action the entire mechanism of the imperial government. I grasped all the tragic intricacy of the relations existing between the government and the Tsar's palace. The spirit of Russian ruling circles was revealed to me.

I clearly realized two facts. First, I did not so much see, as feel that a new conflict between the sovereign and the country was inevitable, because of the Tsar's personality and the tragic conditions prevailing in the palace. Second, I realized that following this conflict, power would not remain in the hands of conservative and liberal circles, which backed the Duma majority.

This latter conclusion was due to my direct knowledge of the real correlation of forces in Russia. This correlation of forces could not manifest itself in the Duma, because of Stolypin's electoral law. The members of the liberal opposition were not aware of the inevitable issue: due to Russia's social structure and to her spiritual traditions, *universal suffrage* (like that, for instance, in Western Europe or in America) *would fail to consolidate the old edifice.* Russia was the only great power where universal suffrage would thoroughly democratize the nation without "armed rebellion" or "social revolution."

And this democratization would not only be political, but also social. An overwhelming majority of peasants among the population; a country gentry which was dying out; a rapidly increasing industrial proletariat concentrated in the cities, feebly developed middle classes; an immense bureaucratic army, mostly formed of cultured elements belonging to the lower classes not interested in the preservation of capitalism; and an intelligentsia, historically educated in the tradition of Russian spiritual culture, in the non-class principles of social justice and the inviolability of the individual—all this predetermined the issue of the struggle, waged between the palace and the "bourgeois" majority of the Duma.

Having learned in the Third Duma the methods of struggle in behalf of popular representation, the Octobrist Party became in 1912, in the Fourth Duma, a party of opposition.

Before the opening of the newly elected body's session, Guchkov launched his slogan: "*Against* the participation of irresponsible men in state affairs. *For* a government responsible to the nation's representatives."

Thus, in the fall of 1912, Guchkov repeated the demands, which P. Miliukov and the Cadets expressed in 1906, at the time of the First Duma. A new critical hour of Russian history was drawing near, and the rapprochement of two previously irreconcilable political enemies—the Cadets and the Octobrists—was inevitable.

The salvation of the monarchy, as symbol of the Empire, through the transfer of the plenitude of power into the hands of a government enjoying the confidence of popular representation, was the aim of both these parties. But such an aim could no longer be realized. All the delays granted by history had expired.

Today, this is obvious to everybody. But to certain Russian political leaders of liberal and socialist circles, the fact was already
apparent in those days, because of the considerations stated above.

At least five years before the fall of the monarchy, some of us
began preparing for the inevitable.

The main points of the program of the future republican government were settled, and the work of organizing the leading democratic forces throughout Russia was begun. A federal democratic
republic on the basis of radical social reforms — such briefly was the
stand we took.

This was in no way in conflict with the individual socialist, radical, or liberal party programs. It was only a way of "carrying outside the common bracket" such factors as those public men who felt
the heart-beats of the country considered to be indisputable for
democracy as a whole; such points as they held would have to be
fulfilled immediately after a revolutionary *coup* or the election of a
representative assembly by universal suffrage. During the last few
years before the war, my political friends and myself considered as
our most urgent aim the selection of a skeleton staff of men of all
parties who would be capable of political work in harmony with
every party, group, and organization of the Left for the furtherance
of this indispensable common democratic program. In a word, our
task was to prepare a coalition of all the democratic parties, not
with a view of fulfilling the program of any one section, but to carry
out a common national policy. This marshaling of the democratic
forces was already in progress when the Fourth Duma met. After
that it proceeded even more rapidly, both because public opinion
became more favorable, and because there were enough people of
every opposition party in the new Duma itself who were convinced
that an early end of the monarchy was inevitable, now that it had
degenerated into Rasputinism.

The course of Russia's internal events was brutally interrupted
by war. It profoundly modified the country's spirit and created a
new political atmosphere.

The Tsar faced once more, and for the last time, the possibility of
making peace with his people, united in a patriotic impulse — in the
name of the Fatherland's salvation. The country was ready for this
reconciliation. But the "woman with perverted ideas," as the Empress Dowager called the Tsarina, closed this path to the Tsar.

MARK ALDANOV

P. N. Durnovo—
Prophet of War and Revolution

M. A. Aldanov (pseudonym of M. A. Landau, 1889–1957), a Russian historical novelist and publicist, is best known for his novels dealing with the French Revolution and the Russian revolutionary movement. In these novels he analyzes the part played by chance in history. He has also written extensively historical and political essays, which are aften considered superior to his novels. A moderate socialist, he emigrated to France in 1919, spent a few years in the United States during the 'forties, and then returned to France, where he died.

The following article is a personality sketch of P. N. Durnovo, Director of the Police Department and Minister of Interior in 1905–6. It analyzes the famous memorandum that Durnovo presented to Nicholas II in February 1914, in which he opposed Russia's entry into an alliance against Germany and accurately predicted the consequences for Russia and the dynasty of a major war. This article is based on Aldanov's interviews with both revolutionaries and former government officials who had dealings with Durnovo.

The most striking of all predictions, known to me in history, was made by a man—not famous, and now forgotten—who had never enjoyed popularity or even a good name. I have in mind a memorandum presented to Nicholas II, in February 1914, by a

From *The Russian Review,* vol. 2, no. 1 (Autumn 1942), pp. 31–45. Slightly abridged.

retired Russian statesman, Peter Nikolaevich Durnovo. This remarkable document was little known in Russia. In America and Western Europe, I think, hardly anyone has heard of it.

To begin with, I shall give a *curriculum vitae* of the author of this report, without, for the moment, touching on his personality. Peter Durnovo was born in 1844. He belonged to a family of old nobility—of one root with the Tolstoys*—but not rich or influential. He studied in the Naval Academy, spent nine years in far-sea cruises, then graduated from the Military-Law Academy and served in the Justice Department as Assistant Prosecutor in various parts of Russia. In 1881 Durnovo transferred to the Department of the Interior and in three years became Director of the Police Department. At this post, one at that time of great power, he remained ten years. Then, because of a very unpleasant incident (which I will expose further), he was removed from this position, by a resolution of the Emperor Alexander III, which contained a sharp rebuke. It was not until seven years later, during the reign of Nicholas II, that he was able to return to government service. From 1900 to 1905 he was Assistant Minister of the Interior consecutively under Sipyagin, Plehve, Svyatopolk-Mirsky and Bulygin. Count Witte, in spite of strong opposition, invited him to be Minister of the Interior in his cabinet. Together with the other members of this cabinet he resigned in 1906, before the opening of the State Duma, and was replaced by Stolypin. He was appointed to the Council of State, where he was one of the leaders of the rightist group, and never returned to power. He presented his memorandum six months before the start of World War I. It made no impression on the Tsar (at least we do not know that it did, and there were no visible results). In 1915 Durnovo died a natural death. This was rather unusual for a man holding so long in Russia the posts of Director of the Police Department, Assistant Minister of the Interior and Minister of the Interior. The Socialist Revolutionary Party had "condemned him to death," but did not succeed in carrying out this verdict.

Durnovo's memorandum is based on the following premise: a war in Europe will break out in the near future, the chief reason for which will be Anglo-German economic rivalry.

*Vasily Yulevich Tolstoy was nicknamed "durnoi" (one meaning of which in Russian is "ugly). From his son Vikula stemmed the Durnovo family, one of whom, Konstantin, took part in the election of the first Romanov to the throne.

There is as yet nothing remarkable in this prediction: war at that time was "in the air," and many were speaking and writing about its possibility, some with horror, others, much more rarely, with elation. Durnovo spoke of the coming war objectively and realistically, from the point of view of common sense and practical advantage; he considered war to be senseless and extremely un-profitable for Russia.

To begin with, Durnovo indicates the alignment of the chief powers in the war: on the one side Germany and Austria, on the other Russia, England, and France. This also, in itself, was not a proof of special foresight on the part of the author of the memo-randum, as such was at that time the most probable alignment. It is true that in Germany, between August 1 and August 4, 1914, many statesmen hoped that England would remain neutral and that the participants of the war would be Russia and France on the one side and Germany, Austro-Hungary, and Italy on the other. But such a belief was rather naïve. Durnovo had no doubts on the subject, as he believed that the basic reason for the war was the British-German rivalry. Under these conditions England obviously could not remain neutral.

Durnovo's extraordinary foresight becomes evident in his anal-ysis of the position of the other powers. Without any hesitation he states at once that Turkey will enter the war on the side of the Ger-man coalition. It is well known that at that time this was not by any means the opinion generally accepted by diplomats: the British and French had great hopes of keeping Turkey in her traditional posi-tion within the Anglo-French orbit.

Just as confidently and unreservedly Durnovo predicts quite correctly the role of the small Slavonic countries: Serbia, Monte-negro, and Bulgaria (Poland and Czechoslovakia were not yet in-dependent states at that time). He writes to the Tsar that Serbia and Montenegro will enter the war on the side of Russia, but that Bul-garia will go against her. This latter prediction was extremely un-orthodox. Even after the war had begun, and up to the last moment, it was not believed in Petersburg that Bulgaria would decide to go to war against Russia, her former liberator.

Still more remarkable, in my opinion, was the prognosis regard-ing Japan. Durnovo writes that Japanese aspirations in general are directed towards the Philippines, Indo-China, Java, Sumatra, and Borneo. He believes, nevertheless, that Japan in the existing situation will not venture to challenge the Anglo-Russian coalition. On the contrary, he does not exclude the possibility that Japan will come out against Germany. Here we find a prediction not only of events to come within six months or a year, but for twenty-five years ahead. At the time not a single important European statesman wrote or even thought of Japan's desire to seize the Philippines, Indo-China, Java, Sumatra, and Borneo. The more daring and brilliant then was this distinction between the general and temporary orientation of Japan's policy. Both were discerned quite correctly by Durnovo.

No less remarkable was the prediction concerning Italy. Durnovo maintains that Italy will not come out on the side of Germany as this is not to her advantage. Much more probable is her adherence to the coalition of England, France and Russia. But, in any case, at first Italy will wait. Durnovo meant that Italy would bargain (though he does not use the word) and would come out (on the side of the Allies) after having stipulated for herself the most profitable terms of participation in the future division of the spoils. The position of Rumania, he says, will be practically the same. Rumania will remain neutral for a time, and then will throw her weight on the side of the winner.

These predictions would still be imcomplete if Durnovo had not raised in his memorandum the question of the United States. He was apparently the first politician of that time to do so. He makes the surmise that the United States will fight on the side of the Allies and underlines the basic difference between the United States and Japan. The United States is *essentially* hostile to Germany, while Japan is not essentially so, but only in certain specific political situations.

Thus the whole alignment of powers in the coming war was forecast by Durnovo with complete and absolute accuracy. Everything happened as if to order.

The memorandum goes on to the question of the course the war will take. Here he deals almost exclusively with Russia.

Durnovo asserts that Germany's war preparation will exceed all expectations. He has the highest opinion of Germany's military strength. Is Russia, he asks, ready for war? His answer is in the negative. This can be taken as a proof of civic courage. Durnovo's memorandum was written for the Tsar and perhaps for two or three of the most important members of the government. He could not have failed to understand that this part of the memorandum would not please either the Tsar or the Ministers. If Russia was not prepared for war, whose fault was it if not theirs? Nevertheless, he did not fear to express all he thought, all that eventually proved to be the bitter truth. Russia was *not ready* for war. "She has," says Durnovo, "an insufficiently developed industry, an insufficient railroad system, too little heavy artillery, too few machine guns, too few fortified positions." Moreover, "every war has invariably, up to now, been accompanied by a last word in military technique," and technical backwardness is an unfavorable condition for such a "last word." At the same time, the brunt of the war will fall on Russia, as England has no army, and France has an insufficient population.

What will then happen, asks Durnovo, on the Russian front? Military reverses will come. The responsibility for them will be placed on the government, on the tsarist regime. A smouldering discontent, the ground for which in Russia is extremely favorable, will begin to spread. Preparations for a revolutionary outburst will be set in motion. Furthermore, in the fighting with the Germans the greater part of the regular officers of the army, who form the chief support of the tsarist regime, will, of course, perish. Without them, the army, consisting of peasant soldiers and war-time officers recruited from the intelligentsia, cannot be relied upon. Durnovo states outright that war will amost inevitably bring Russia to revolution.

He predicts also the course of the revolution. I consider this part of his prediction the most remarkable, as at that time absolutely no one else in Russia, except perhaps Lenin, thought as did Durnovo. He asserts that the liberal and moderate parties in Russia have no support in the masses, that neither the peasants nor the workers will follow them. "There is no one behind our opposition, it has no support in the people, who see no difference between a government of bureaucrats or intellectuals." Therefore, the moderate parties will be swept aside at the beginning of the revolution, just as the tsarist government which they will have overthrown. What will then happen? The army will be seized with the elemental peasant urge for the land. "The law-making institutions and the intelligentsia opposition parties, lacking any real authority in the eyes of the people, will be unable to stay the turbulent waves of popular uprising that they themselves will have raised and Russia will be hurled into darkest anarchy, the outcome of which it is impossible even to surmise."

Durnovo barely mentions other countries except Germany. And here, in spite of his high opinion of the military might of the Empire of Wilhelm II, he is as pessimistic concerning it as he is about Russia. In his opinion revolution will also follow the war in Germany, as ground for it also exists there, although not to the same extent as in the empire of Nicholas II. In the final part of the memorandum Durnovo invariably speaks of the defeat of Germany in the war with the Allied coalition. He does not give his reasons. I know (though not from his memorandum) that Durnovo had his own point of view on war in general. To Clemenceau are attributed the words: "War is too serious an undertaking to be left to the military." Apparently Durnovo, who had received a military education and served nine years in the navy, thought the same. This is to some degree apparent from his remarks, as cited above, that every war is accompanied by a new development in the field of military technique and that technical backwardness is an unfavorable factor for such new development. This statement, substantiated in 1916–18 by the example of tanks, shows that he considered military success as mainly contingent on the industrial potentiality of a country. My knowledge of his ideas confirms this in full. Durnovo placed the industrial potentiality of England and the United States very high. He was by no means an Anglophile or an Americanophile, but he foresaw the decisive role of English and American industry and was partly guided by it in his prognosis.

The conclusion to be drawn from his memorandum was simple. Russia will lose everything by the war. There will be a military defeat which will bring with it the destruction of the monarchic form of government and of the capitalistic regime. A social revolution will take place, the consequences of which cannot be appraised. The result of the war for Germany will not be much better. These two countries, however, are the chief bulwark of political and social conservatism and of the monarchic idea. Therefore, these two countries, and Russia, in particular, ought not in any case go to war. They must live in peace with each other.

This conclusion is of little interest. It is as elementary and flat as the political prognosis of Durnovo is complex, keen, and remarkable. To say "do not go to war" is to say practically nothing. An explanation should then have followed as to what to do with the

German military party, with the boundless ambition of Wilhelm II, with the centuries-old aggressive tendencies of German political literature, finally, with what was then called the "economic expansion" of Germany. I must note, that in his analysis of the reasons for war Durnovo used methods which might almost be called Marxist.* He was, in his way, an "economic materialist." But there is not a sign of this in his conclusion. He simply advises one monarch to talk it over and come to an agreement with another monarch. And then all will be well.

In the brilliancy of its prognosis, however, I know of no other document which can compare with Durnovo's memorandum. It consists wholly of predictions, and all these predictions have come true with astounding accuracy. And yet they were made by a man who had never been active in foreign policy. A plain police official who had dedicated nearly all his life to police duties foresaw that which the greatest minds and the most famous statesmen did not foresee!

Durnovo's memorandum was found by the Bolsheviks in the papers of Nicholas II and appeared in Soviet publications, first in excerpts, under the editorship of Professor Tarlé,† and then in full, edited by Michael Pavlovich.‡ Both the editors, in introductory notes, speak with great praise of the intellect and insight of the author of the memorandum. Professor Ţarlé calls it the "swan song of the conservative school."

I must confess that when I first read the document I had doubts as to its authenticity. It is true that the Bolsheviks, when the matter does not concern their own party or, more particularly, the roles

---

* Several other statesmen of the old Russian regime showed an amusing secret sympathy for the Marxist line of reasoning. As far back as in the eighties of the past century the extremely reactionary statesman Count Dmitry Tolstoy told the future German chancellor Bühlow, then attached to the German Embassy in Petersburg, that if monarchy fell in Russia, it would be replaced by communism: "le communisme de M. Karl Marx de Londres, qui vient de mourir et dont j'ai étudié attentivement et avec intérêt les théories." (Memoirs of Prince von Bühlow, I, 576.)

† E. V. Tarlé. "Germanskaya orientatsyya i P. N. Durnovo v 1914 godu." *Byloe,* *XIX,* 161–176.

‡ "Zapiska Durnovo," *Krasnaya Nov',* No. 10, 1922, pp. 178–199. English translation in F. A. Golder's *Documents of Russian History 1914–1917,* New York, 1927.

of Stalin and Trotsky in the history of the Russian Revolution and the Civil War, are usually honest in their publication of historical documents; they do not falsify them. Besides, the Bolsheviks could not have been in the least interested in falsely attributing remarkable political foresight to a reactionary dignitary of the old regime. Nevertheless, some doubts arose in my mind. Durnovo's predictions were really too successful, a hundred per cent correct. I therefore questioned several former statesmen, living in exile, who, because of their position in 1914 or from personal relationships, could have known of memoranda presented to Emperor Nicholas II. I received confirmation that the Durnovo memorandum was not apocryphal—the original was actually presented to the Tsar in February 1914, and copies of it were given to two, or perhaps three, of the most important ministers of that time. One of the men I interviewed had lived, in 1914, in the same house as Durnovo, and had often met him (although they were neither close associates nor held similar political opinions). He told me that Durnovo, as early as 1913, if not before, had talked to him in the same vein as the views expounded in his memorandum. There cannot, therefore, be any doubt as to the authenticity of the memorandum.

I took the opportunity to question the former statesmen as to the personality of P. N. Durnovo, as nothing has been written about him, except for casual mention in various volumes of reminiscences. In the newest Russian historical literature he is not touched upon at all. I also questioned some revolutionists, now in emigration, who due to their former activity had had dealings with Durnovo in his capacity of Director of the Police Department and of Assistant Minister and Minister of the Interior.

Both these groups agreed, in general, in their evaluation of Durnovo. "He was a clever man," said Count V. N. Kokovtsev, former President of the Council of Ministers under the old regime. "He was a clever chap," said a man who, in his time, while perhaps not himself planning to assassinate Durnovo, at least was in sympathy with those who had such an idea in mind. There are no two opinions about the great worldly wisdom of the author of the memorandum. Count Witte,* in whose cabinet Durnovo was a minister, and the well-known revolutionist A. I. Ivanchin-Pisarev,† who had dealings

---

* Graf S. Yu. Witte. *Vospominaniya,* Berlin, 1921, II, 64–66, 97 and 109.
† A. I. Ivanchin-Pesarev. *Vospominaniya o P. N. Durnovo. Katorga i Ssylka.* Moscow, 1930, Book 7, p. 68.

with Durnovo in connection with various arrests and deportations to which he was subjected during the regime, speak of the man in approximately the same terms.

In money matters he was honest, and no one had ever accused him of any form of corruption. He had a family, and very likely expenses outside the family, but no fortune, and he was always in need of money. He played the stock-market, but without much success. On one occasion, having lost heavily, he turned to the Tsar for help. There was nothing uncommon in this; at all times in tsarist Russia persons close to the throne, in emergencies, applied to the Tsar for help. Usually, such requests were made to the Tsar through the intermediary of a third person. Durnovo on this occasion asked the Minister of Finance, Witte, to obtain for him sixty thousand rubles (about 30,000 dollars), but Witte, who did not favor this custom, refused to do so. Durnovo then turned to the Minister of the Interior Sipyagin, who finally obtained this sum for him, despite the fact that the Emperor Nicholas II at that time was not too kindly disposed towards Durnovo. Much later, at the time of Durnovo's final retirement, the Tsar made him a present of two hundred thousand rubles.

Of the men from the revolutionary camp, whom I questioned about Durnovo, there was not one who said that he was harsh or cruel. On the contrary all admitted (in this regard agreeing with the statesmen of the old regime) that he was rather a well-disposed man with a slight, and perhaps even not so slight, leaning towards cynicism. When he could do someone a service, without much trouble, he did so. As an official he committed not a few illegalities. Among other things, as a firm believer in human corruptibility, he tried his utmost to influence green revolutionists to collaborate with the Police Department by giving "inside information" on the work of their organizations. This was something in between the idea of *agent provocateur* and the practice of police in most countries.

He had no hate for the revolutionaries. His attitude towards them was one of gentle irony, and to those whom he considered to be intelligent and gifted men (like the writers Korolenko and Annensky, and the scientist Klements) he even strove to be useful, in so far as this depended on him. If he was asked to do a small official favor he usually would not refuse, and in cases when the matter did not depend on him alone he would give helpful advice. He also had some eccentricities well known to his immediate subordinates.

These would, for instance, warn petitioners who sought an interview with Durnovo: "do not address him formally as 'Your Excellency,' he hates it; address him, as one intellectual to another, by the first name and patronymic—Petr Nikolaevich." Interviewing petitioners, he would grasp the essence of the matter at once, without lengthy explanations, and his replies were brief: "very well," or "I cannot do it," and his word could be firmly relied upon. He would willingly invite outstanding revolutionists to come into his study, and then enter with them into conversations on political topics, at times urging some of them to write their memoirs. I do not think that he cared very much for history, but revolution interested him as a significant psychological phenomenon. During the lull in the revolutionary movement, which followed the crushing of the revolutionary party Narodnaya Volya, he complained of "boring business." Before, that is during the peak of the terrorist activity of the Narodnaya Volya, at the time of the attempts on the lives of the Tsar and the Ministers "business" was "more interesting." As is known, one of the chief leaders of the above-mentioned party, Lev Tikhomirov, eventually sent from abroad a petition for pardon, stating that a complete change had taken place in his political views. Tikhomirov actually was pardoned (probably not without Durnovo's intervention) and returned to St. Petersburg. Durnovo arranged a dinner in his honor, although he knew perfectly well that only three or four years ago this revolutionist had plotted against the life of the Tsar. Durnovo was convinced that he would get from Tikhomirov valuable information on other revolutionists. However, he was mistaken, Tikhomirov categorically refused to give away his former comrades. This surprised Durnovo and even "aroused his indignation."

Let us, however, be fair to him. Against the background of present day political police and their methods . . . Durnovo stands out very favorably. He believed in pecuniary bribery, but the thought never entered his head that it was possible to draw information from a man by means of torture. He did not have a single case of this kind to his account; no one even ever accused him of it. As regards his intelligence it would, of course, be ridiculous even to make a comparison between him and the various European Himmlers.

I shall add one more feature which is to a certain extent an "intrusion" into Durnovo's personal life. Although he has now been dead more than a quarter of a century, I would not presume to touch upon it, were it not for the fact that it has already been referred to in print. The event which was the cause for Durnovo's dismissal in 1893, with an extremely sharp rebuke from Alexander III, is mentioned not only in the memoirs of the revolutionist Ivanchin-Pisarev, but also in those of Count Witte. The chief of the Russian political police was all his life a passionate admirer of women. He had many love affairs, during which he forgot everything. One of these love affairs cost him dearly. One day a young and very pretty petitioner came to see him to plead for her brother, an ensign, who had become involved in some apparently insignificant political affair. Durnovo fell violently in love with the fair petitioner. Her request was granted; her brother was "punished" only by being sent on a distant cruise. A correspondence sprang up between the all powerful chief of police and the lady, which at least on his side was of an extremely impassioned nature. He wrote in one of his letters that when she was kind, he felt such a surge of humanitarianism that he would like to free every political prisoner; her indifference, on the other hand, provoked him to such fury that he was ready to send scores of men to the gallows! His love was not returned. The lady bestowed her favors on one of the foreign ambassadors in St. Petersburg. Durnovo, beside himself with jealousy, committed an act which had no precedent. He ordered his agents (that is the agents of the police department) to secretly enter the building of the foreign embassy, to search the ambassador's papers and steal the lady's letters! This was done. The Ambassador, however, lodged a personal complaint with Alexander III against this act of the chief of the Russian police. The Emperor who did not mince words, even when addressing dignitaries, wrote the resolution: "Remove this swine within twenty-four hours." Durnovo was immediately dismissed. His career was interrupted for seven years. And after these years, even during the reign of Nicholas II, his friends had much difficulty in having him readmitted to government service. Count Witte writes that many years later the Dowager Empress Maria Feodorovna for a long time refused to appoint Durnovo's daughter as lady in waiting; she did not wish to extend a favor to the daughter of a man whom her husband had called a "swine."*

The relations between Witte . . . and Durnovo were peculiar.

---

* Witte, *op. cit.,* p. 64.

Each valued the other for his capacities but neither liked the other. In his memoirs Witte constantly refers to Durnovo's intelligence, experience, and energy. He also stresses his courage. At the height of the terrorist activity of the revolutionary parties, Durnovo, who was marked for death and who was constantly trailed by terrorists, defied danger. "He had a very dear friend, a lady, whom he visited daily, causing considerable worry to his body-guards."* At the same time Witte considered Durnovo to be totally unprincipled.

It must be noted that the entrance of Durnovo into Witte's cabinet, after the promulgation of the constitution, was the chief reason why even the moderate liberals refused to join this cabinet, although Witte urged them to do so. Guchkov, Shipov, and Prince Trubetskoi told Witte that they were ready to cooperate with him, but not with Durnovo. Witte immediately let the latter know of this attitude. "What have they against me?" asked Durnovo. "I answered," tells Witte, "that they gave no explanation, but that probably the reason was his affairs with women, of which there had been much talk in the past. He replied 'Yes, in that I am guilty.' On this we parted."†

In this "explanation" Count Witte was, of course, avoiding the issue, or just joking. The trouble was not in his "affairs with women," nor even the affair connected with the papers of a foreign ambassador. This had been to a large extent forgotten. The trouble was that the former head of the Department of Police was an odious figure to all of liberal Russia. He was regarded as a bitter reactionary. This reputation of his was extremely surprising to Witte, who knew, through his official contacts, that in conversations and in conferences Durnovo expressed liberal thoughts and, due to his great intelligence, was usually against reactionary measures and suggestions (in particular he was a defender of the Jews and an opponent of anti-semitic measures). Furthermore since Durnovo knew the police business thoroughly, a fact which seemed of paramount importance in revolutionary times, Witte sacrificed the participation of liberals and invited Durnovo to the post of Minister of the Interior. Later, he considered that in doing so he had made a serious mistake. According to Witte's own words, Durnovo,

* Witte, *ibid.,* p. 288.
† Witte, *ibid.,* p. 94.

having realized that the former was not popular in high places, began at once to intrigue against him!

This is highly probable. Witte's characterization of Durnovo is very nearly correct. But if the creator of the Russian constitution underestimated at the time Durnovo's readiness to serve any ideas, then, at the time he wrote his memoirs, he also underestimated the latter's mental capacities. Although he speaks highly of Durnovo's intellect, Witte never imagined that this cunning, experienced police official was a man of exceptional perspicacity and that he would leave as a legacy a historical prediction of such remarkable depth and power. Count Witte apparently had never heard of Durnovo's "memorandum." Both these men died at almost the same time. . . .

One can gamble on the best side of man's nature—and win. One can gamble on the worst—and also win. P. N. Durnovo did not believe in the good in human nature. One of his predecessors, Potapov, used to say: "I have never trusted a single man and I have never had to regret it." This was likewise the philosophy of Durnovo. For a certain period of time he won. History unfolded not as he would have wished, but exactly as he foresaw. . . .

SIR PETER BARK

The Last Days of the Russian Monarchy—Nicholas II at Army Headquarters

Sir Peter Bark (1869–1937) was Minister of Finance of the Russian Imperial Government during World War I. After the Bolshevik Revolution, he had a distinguished career in England as Director of the Anglo-International Bank and was primarily responsible for the financial reconstruction of central and southern Europe, following the war. He became a naturalized subject of Britain and was knighted by King George V.

The following article is a documented eye-witness account of the events at Army Headquarters, March 1–2/March 14–15, 1917, which decided the fate of the Imperial regime. The dates are according to the "new style."

During the tragic days of March 14–15, 1917, the destiny of the great Russian Empire was sealed by the army at its General Headquarters.

The month of March has often proved a fatal one in the history of Russia. On March 25, 1801, Emperor Paul I, who had become mad, was assassinated. On March 13, 1881, the unfortunate Emperor Alexander II, who had given his country great liberal reforms, was blown to pieces by a bomb. On March 15, 1917,

From *The Russian Review*, vol. 16, no. 3 (July 1957), pp. 35–44.

Emperor Nicholas II abdicated, and it is from that moment that the eclipse of a great country began.

The Emperor left Headquarters in Mogilev for Tsarskoe Selo during the night of March 12–13. By order of the revolutionaries, who had occupied the Ministry of Ways and Communications, his train was stopped en route and directed to Pskov, seat of the headquarters of the northern front, under the command of General Ruzsky. The General was in continuous communication by direct telegraphic line with the President of the Duma, Rodzyanko, who now headed the revolution, and with the Emperor's Chief-of-Staff, at Mogilev, General Alexeev.

The Emperor arrived in Pskov with his attendants on Wednesday, March 14, about 8:00 p.m. and received General Ruzsky in his private car. The Emperor had received the following telegram from General Alexeev:

> The imminent dangers which threaten us, namely the anarchy which can invade the whole country, demoralizing the troops and rendering impossible the continuation of the war in present circumstances, demand the publication by Your Majesty of a calming declaration. This would only be possible by constituting a government responsible to the Duma and by authorizing the President of the Imperial Duma to form it. The news which I have received still leaves hope that the deputies under the presidency of Rodzyanko will succeed in preventing the disaster and that it will be possible to work with them. But each hour that passes diminishes the chances of restoring order and increases the possibility of success of the extreme left. I implore Your Imperial Majesty to publish the following manifesto:
>
> "To all our loyal subjects:
>
> The terrible and ferocious enemy is making his last efforts to conquer us. The decisive hour is near. The destiny of Russia, the honor of our heroic army, the well-being of the people, the future of our country which is dear to all of us, requires at any price the continuation of the war to final victory. In the hope of gathering the living forces of the nation to achieve victory, I have decided to constitute a government responsible to the people's representatives and I have authorized the President of the Duma, Rodzyanko, to form it, choosing persons who hold the confidence of all Russia. I hope that all my loyal subjects will rally to the Throne and the representatives of the nation and will help our army to fulfill its supreme task.
>
> In the name of Russia, I appeal to all her children to fulfill their duty to their country, to prove that she is invincible and that not one effort of the enemy can inflict defeat."

Ruzsky remained in audience with the Emperor for a long time and only left him after 11:00 p.m. Then he had a conversation by direct telegraphic line with Rodzyanko. He told him that the Emperor had agreed that the President of the Duma should form a new government responsible to the Duma, and he also informed him of the manifesto telegraphed by General Alexeev. He added that the Emperor awaited Rodzyanko in Pskov. Rodzyanko answered that he could not leave the capital, as he feared that anarchy would increase in his absence. He had the impression that his own power was shaky and uncertain. He had been obliged to form a Provisional Government. Passions were breaking loose around him and, in those circumstances, he feared that the concessions announced by the Emperor would no longer suffice. People were now insisting that the Emperor should abdicate in favor of his son, who, during his minority, would have to remain under the regency of Grand Duke Michael.

General Ruzsky imparted the gist of this conversation to General Alexeev. Either personally, or through his aides, Alexeev informed all army commanders of the situation, inviting them to send a telegram to the Emperor, through General Ruzsky, imploring him to abdicate in favor of his heir, Grand Duke Alexis, with Grand Duke Michael as regent.

The following telephone conversation took place between General Klembovsky of Headquarters, and one of the army commanders, General Evert:

> General Alexeev has authorized me to communicate to you the following: His Majesty is in Pskov. He has consented to publish a manifesto which satisfies the desires of his people and to form a government responsible to the Duma. His Majesty has authorized the President of the Duma to form a new cabinet.

When the general commanding the northern front gave this communication to the President of the Duma, the latter replied, at 2:30 a.m., that the publication of the manifesto would have been opportune on March 12, but that it would now be useless. The revolution had broken out in all its fury, it was extremely difficult to check popular passions, the troops were demoralized. Until now, the President of the Duma possessed national confidence, but he feared that he would no longer be able to contain the revolutionary movement which was destroying everything in its way. The dynasty problem had been clearly spelled out by the revolutionaries. The war could not be brought to an end unless the Emperor abdicated in favor of his son. Existing circumstances did not admit of any other solution. Every minute of indecision could only increase popular demands. The army was on the side of the Provisional Government and the railway system was under its control. The army must be saved from demoralization, the war waged to the end, the independence of Russia and of the dynasty must be saved at the price of concessions, however bitter. General Klembovsky concluded:

> If you share these views, please telegraph your humble request to His Majesty urgently and by the intermediacy of General Ruzsky, at the same time sending a copy to General Alexeev. I repeat that the loss of a minute may be fatal to the existence of Russia. The commanders-in-chief of the army must be united on this point and act with the same purpose in mind, in order to protect the army from hesitations and defections which are probable. The army must continue to fight against the foreign enemy. Decisions concerning domestic policy must be taken in such a way that the army will not have to take part in revolutionary measures. It can be done if those decisions are taken by high authorities.
>
> March 15, 1917, 10:15 a.m.

General Evert asked whether he still had time to come to an agreement with the commanders-in-chief of the other armies, and whether these generals had received the same communication.

General Klembovsky replied:

> All commanders-in-chief have received the same communication. Time is pressing, every minute is precious. There is no other issue. The Emperor hesitates. The unanimity of opinion of the commanders-in-chief can move him to take the only decision which could save Russia and the dynasty. If there are any more delays, Rodzyanko fears that he will be unable to maintain order and that the whole country may sink into anarchy. The Tauride Palace and the Emperor's family are guarded by troops which are on the side of the revolt.

The conversation ended at 11:00 p.m.

General Brusilov received the same communication from General Alexeev, who also requested him to telegraph the Emperor. Brusilov immediately replied: "One must not hesitate. Time presses. I agree with you. I am telegraphing my humble request immediately to the Emperor through the intermediacy of General Ruzsky. I entirely share your views. There can be no other opinion on this subject."

On Thursday morning, March 15, General Ruzsky reported to the Emperor the conversation he had had with Rodzyanko during the night and submitted to His Majesty the telegrams which he had received from the commanders-in-chief of the armies. At 2:30 p. m., the Emperor received the following telegram from General Alexeev: "I take the liberty of submitting to Your Imperial Majesty the following telegrams which I have received:"

From Grand Duke Nicholas:

> General Alexeev has described to me the dangers of the situation and asks me to join him in confirming that one must take extraordinary measures to ensure victory which is necessary for the well-being and future of Russia and the safety of the dynasty. As a loyal subject, faithful to the oath which I have sworn, I make bold to implore your Imperial Majesty on my knees to save Russia and your heir, for whom I know that Your Imperial Majesty has the deepest love. After making the sign of the cross, do yield to him your inheritance! There is no other solution. I invoke the Almighty with more ardor than I have ever done and implore Him to grant you strength and to protect you.

From General Brusilov:

> I beg leave to transmit to His Majesty my humble request which is based on my loyal love for my country and for the throne. The only means of saving the situation and to continue the war, without which Russia will be lost, is to abdicate in favor of the Grand Duke, your heir, under the regency of Grand Duke Michael Alexandrovich. There is no other solution, but one must hasten, in order that the revolutionary fires be extinguished as soon as possible, otherwise innumerable catastrophes will follow. By that act of Your Majesty the dynasty will be saved and the crown will pass on to its legitimate heir.

From General Evert:

> The Chief of staff of Your Majesty has informed me of the situation in Petrograd, Tsarskoe Selo, in the Baltic Sea and in Moscow. I know also the conversations of General Ruzsky with the President of the Duma. Sir, one could not rely upon the army to check the revolt in Russia. The army will remain faithful to the authorities only to save Russia from an external attack. I am taking measures in order that the news of the revolt should not spread among the troops, and their morale would thus be safeguarded. Both capitals lack the means of quelling the disturbances. An immediate decision is needed to stop them in order that

they should not extend to the troops on the front. Considering the situation, and yet remaining loyally devoted to Your Majesty, I implore you, for the sake of our country and of the dynasty, to take the decision advised by the President of the Duma. That is the only way to put an end to the revolution and to save Russia from the anarchy which threatens her.

From General Alexeev:

In submitting these telegrams to Your Imperial Majesty, I implore you to take this decision. May the Savior guide Your Imperial Majesty! Any delay threatens the very existence of Russia. Until now we have succeeded in saving the army from the contagion which comes from Petrograd, Moscow, Kronstadt, and other towns. But we are not certain of being able to maintain discipline in the future. If the army gives its support to the revolt, it would mean the end of the war, the dishonor of Russia, and general disaster. Sir, you do ardently love your country, and for its good, for its independence, for winning the victory of its armies, I beg you to take the only decision which might ensure a favorable outcome from the present situation. I await the orders of your Majesty.

Thus, the army abandoned its chief. The Emperor had no choice but to sign the abdication act which had been imposed upon him.

He conferred at length with the court physician, Fedorov, who was treating the heir, and asked him to state sincerely what he thought of his son's health. Fedorov told the Emperor that hemophilia was incurable. It was possible that with much care the Grand Duke might live a relatively long time, but he could never be cured. The Emperor thanked Fedorov and thereupon abdicated for himself and for his son, passing the crown of Russia to his brother, Grand Duke Michael. He wrote out the manifesto of abdication himself, the text of which is as follows:

During the ceaseless struggle against the foreign enemy, who for nearly three years has been attempting to conquer our country, the Savior has submitted Russia to hard trials within the country. These troubles threaten to have a disastrous effect upon the continuation of the war. The destiny of Russia, the honor of our country demand that the war should be pursued at any price till complete victory.

Our cruel enemy makes his last efforts, and the hour when our brave armies and those of our fearless Allies will succeed in defeating him is not distant. During these days, which are decisive for Russia, we have concluded it to be our duty to our people to facilitate the rallying of all their forces so as to attain victory as soon as possible. Thus, in agreement with the Duma of the Empire, we have decided to abdicate, to leave the Imperial Throne of Russia, and to lay down the supreme power.

As we do not wish to separate from our beloved son, we have transferred our inheritance to our brother, Grand Duke Michael Alexandrovich. We are blessing his accession to the throne. We recommend that our brother govern in complete agreement with the representatives of the people at the legislative Assemblies, relying upon the principles which these Assemblies will proclaim, and, after taking his inviolable oath, endeavor to respect these principles for the good of our dear country.

I invite all the loyal sons of my country to fulfill their sacred duty which is to obey the Emperor in these difficult moments, and to help him, as well as the representatives of the nation, to lead Russia to victory, success, and glory. May God help Russia!

> Nicholas
> Pskov, March 15, 1917.
> 3:00 p.m..

In the evening, the delegates of the revolutionary Duma, Guchkov and Shulgin arrived in Pskov, bringing with them the draft of the abdication act in favor of the heir under the regency of Grand Duke Michael. They were immediately introduced to the Emperor who appeared to be calmer than anyone present. The two delegates seemed embarrassed and did not know how to begin their explanations. The Emperor put them at ease by saying that he had already made his decision. He did not want to hinder Russia from choosing the course traced by destiny. He handed over to the delegates the act of abdication he had already signed.

The delegates were perplexed. They did not know whether they could accept a decision other than the one which had been made by the Duma. However, yielding to the quiet and firm attitude of the Emperor, they accepted his act of abdication.

The only modification suggested by Shulgin was to add that Grand Duke Michael should take an oath to respect the constitution. Shulgin, who was a convinced monarchist, thought that an oath would strengthen the union between the sovereign and his people. He proposed the words, "solemn oath." The Emperor approved without hesitation, but suggested instead "inviolable oath," which was accepted.

Later, Shulgin gave an account of his mission. True to his genuine sincerity, he said that when the delegates received the manifesto written and signed by His Majesty, so full of dignity and marked with such nobility of soul, they felt ashamed of the absurd document they had brought with them.

It was also decided that Grand Duke Nicholas would replace the Emperor as Supreme Commander. A wire was sent to him at Tiflis to inform him of this. The Emperor approved the appointment of Prince Lvov as Prime Minister of the Provisional Government and also signed a ukase addressed to the Senate to confirm this appointment.

During the night of March 15–16, the Emperor left Pskov to return to Mogilev, arriving Friday evening. The following day, Saturday, March 17, at 9:00 a.m. he went to the study of General Alexeev to hear for the last time the latter's report on the military situation and to take leave of his staff. General Alexeev was deeply moved. He began his report hesitatingly. The Emperor put him at ease by his calmness and by the questions which he asked concerning the disposition of the troops. His Majesty had a remarkable memory and though the front extended over more than two thousand kilometers, he remembered the different units, the name of their commanders, and the particular circumstances under which they were operating.

When Alexeev had finished his report, the Emperor embraced him and thanked the other generals, shaking hands with them and wishing them success.

On the same day, the Dowager Empress Mariya Feodorovna arrived from Kiev. She was received at the station by the Emperor and his retinue, Grand Dukes Alexander Mikhailovich and Serge Mikhailovich, General Alexeev, and members of his staff. The quiet and composed attitude of the Empress and the Emperor made a deep impression on all those who were in attendance.

The Emperor went with the Dowager Empress to the house where he lived in Mogilev, and there mother and son had a poignant meeting. Both of them already knew that the revolutionary Duma had succumbed to the elements of the extreme left and that, under their pressure, Grand Duke Michael Alexandrovich had also signed an act of abdication. A specially convoked Constituent Assembly was to decide further what regime would be established in Russia. It was the end of the dynasty, and it was the last time that mother and son saw each other.

The Emperor remained several days more in Mogilev. On March 19, he took leave of his staff. At 11:00 a.m. it gathered in the study of their chief. The following were present: Grand Dukes Serge Mikhailovich, Alexander Mikhailovich and Boris Vladimirovich; the Emperor's retinue, and all the generals, officers, and civilian functionaries of the staff, headed by General Alexeev. Also present were men belonging to regiments which were stationed at Mogilev. The room was crowded; even the staircase and entrance hall were full of people. Conversation was in subdued tones and all eyes were turned towards the door through which the Emperor was to enter. Ten minutes passed, then rapid and light steps on the stairs were heard. There was complete silence, followed by the command: "On guard!" The Emperor, wearing a Cossack uniform, entered quietly and advanced to the center of the hall, General Alexeev beside him. The Emperor remained silent for some moments, then, amid perfect stillness, he spoke in his clear, sonorous voice. He said that he submitted to God's will and was laying down his post as Supreme Commander. He knew that all the members of his staff had loyally worked for the prosecution of the war against a powerful enemy during the year and a half he had been their Chief. He cordially thanked the whole staff for its work and expressed the conviction that Russia and her Allies would be victorious and that Russia's sacrifices had not been in vain.

General Alexeev began to answer in a moved and halting voice, but he could not continue because tears prevented him from talking. He only had time to say that His Majesty attributed too much value to the work of the Headquarters staff. Everyone had done what he could, but it was the Emperor himself who bestowed all his thought and all his soul to his work, while giving strength and confidence to the people who surrounded him and needed it to save Russia. The Emperor appraoched Alexeev and embraced him.

Since the first words were pronounced by the Emperor, tears had risen to the eyes of the listeners. Several officers fainted, and all those present felt the same emotion experienced when death brings final parting from a loved one.

The Emperor quickly recovered self-control, stepped towards the troops and saluted them. The men answered: "We salute Your Imperial Majesty!" Then broke out shouts, tears and prayers: "Do not abandon us!" He then left the hall and went down the stairs, surrounded by a crowd of soldiers and officers full of emotion and dismay.

On March 21, before leaving Mogilev, the Emperor signed his last appeal to the armies, the text of which he had written himself:

> Today, I am addressing for the last time my dearly loved armies. I have abdicated for myself and for my son, and I am leaving the throne of the Emperors of Russia. The supreme power has passed over to the Provisional Government formed by the Duma of the Empire. May the Savior help this government to lead Russia towards glory and success! May God help you also, my brave soldiers, to preserve our country from a cruel enemy! For two years and a half you have taken upon yourselves the heavy responsibilities of the struggle. Much blood has been shed, many efforts have been made, and the hour of victory is approaching when Russia and her Allies will crush, in a common effort, the last attempts of the enemy. This unprecedented war must be conducted to the final victory.
>
> Those who think of peace and wish it now are twice traitors to their country. Every honest soldier must think that way. I urge you to fulfill your duty and to valiantly defend your Russia. Obey the Provisional Government! Execute the orders of your commanders! Remember that the enemy is profiting by our indecision! I firmly believe that love for our glorious country is not extinguished in your hearts. May God protect you, and may St. George, martyr and conqueror, lead you to victory!

General Alexeev telegraphed this text to Guchkov, Minister of War in the Provisional Government. He received orders not to publish it and to take measures that it should not become known to the troops.

PART II

Revolution and Civil War

PAUL MILIUKOV

The Revolution of 1917

P. N. Miliukov (1859–1943), eminent historian and leader of the Constitutional Democratic Party, was near the center of events in 1905–6; in 1916, when he was the principal organizer of the so-called "progressive bloc" in the Duma; and immediately after the February/ March Revolution, as Minister of Foreign Affairs in the Provisional Government. After the October/November Revolution, he joined the anti-Bolshevik forces of General Kornilov and Denikin in the south of Russia. In November 1918, he left Russia first for the Balkans, later to permanent exile in western Europe. Miliukov's memoirs, covering the years 1905–17, were published in Russian in 1955 by the Chekhov Publishing House in New York. (English edition under the title *Political Memoirs,* Ann Arbor, The University of Michigan Press, 1967.)

The original source of the excerpts below is Miliukov's *History of the Second Russian Revolution* (in Russian, Sofia, 1921) and his *History of Russia,* vol. 3 (in French, Paris, 1933). Although these historical accounts were written shortly after the Revolution, in which Miliukov was deeply involved, they display considerable restraint and objectivity. All the dates are according to the "new style."

From *The Russian Revolution: Why Did the Bolsheviks Win?,* ed. by Robert H. McNeal, pp. 46–54. Copyright © 1959 by Robert H. McNeal. Reprinted by permission of Holt, Rinehart and Winston, Inc., New York.

Five Days of Revolution

Toward evening on March 12, when the full scope of the revolutionary movement had become clear, the temporary committee of the State Duma decided . . . to assume the power which had fallen from the hands of the government. This decision was taken after prolonged discussion and in full awareness of the responsibility it placed on those who took it. . . . For the first four or five days the newly created regime worked day and night amid the confusion and disorder of the Tauride Palace. The immediate task of the temporary committee and the government formed by it was to clarify its relations with the government formed alongside it by the socialist parties [the Soviet], which had claimed from the very outset to represent the democratic classes of the population—the workers, soldiers, and eventually even the peasantry. . . .

Even before it had completed these negotiations, the temporary committee undertook the abolition of the old regime as its main task of the moment. Everyone realized that Nicholas II could rule no longer. Even in his telegram of March 11 to the tsar, Rodzianko had demanded only "immediate instructions to a person enjoying the respect of the country to form a new government"; i.e., he had used the previous formula of the Progressive Bloc. He added that "delay is impossible" and that "any delay would be fatal," and "prayed to God that in this hour responsibility will not fall on the bearer of the crown. . . . "

[In this spirit] A. I. Guchkov and V. V. Shulgin left at three o'clock on March 15 and were in Pskov at ten in the evening. They were immediately invited to the private railroad car of Nicholas II. There, after Guchkov had stated the need for Nicholas II to abdicate in favor of his son, the former sovereign answered calmly and with his usually polite inscrutability: "I have been thinking the matter over yesterday and all day today and have decided to abdicate. Until three o'clock I was ready to abdicate in favor of my son. But then I realized that I was unable to part with him. I hope you will understand this. Therefore I have decided to abdicate in favor of my brother." The delegates were speechless at this expression of paternal feelings, though one may wonder whether there was some hidden political notion in the tsar's decision. Nicholas

II did not want to risk his son but preferred to sacrifice his brother and Russia to the unknown future. Thinking as always about himself and those closest to him first of all, even at this critical moment, and having refused to come to a decision which, though difficult, was to a certain extent the natural one, he again opened up the whole question of the monarchy at a time when this question could only be settled in the negative. Such was Nicholas II's last service to the homeland. . . .

During that day of March 15, however, the political situation in Petrograd changed once more. This change was first evident when at about three o'clock Miliukov delivered his speech on the newly formed government in the Catherine Hall of the Tauride Palace. This speech was enthusiastically received by the large audience which had filled the hall to overflowing, and the speaker was carried out on the shoulders of the audience when it was over. However, amid noisy shouts of approval there were also notes of discontent and even protest. "Who elected you?" the speaker was asked. The answer was, "We were elected by the Russian revolution," but "we will not retain this power a single moment after representatives freely elected by the people tell us that they want to see in our places people more deserving of their trust."

Finally, to the most vital question—the question as to the fate of the dynasty—the speaker answered as follows: "I know in advance that my reply will not satisfy all of you. However, I shall give it. The old despot who brought Russia to complete ruin will either abdicate voluntarily or he will be deposed. Power will pass to a regent, Grand Duke Michael Alexandrovich. The heir will be Alexis (Nicholas' son) (stir and shouts of 'That's the old dynasty'). . . . "

The excitement caused by Miliukov's announcement of the regency of Grand Duke Michael Alexandrovich increased considerably by the end of the day. Late in the evening a large crowd of extremely excited officers penetrated the building of the Tauride Palace, declaring that they would not return to their units unless Miliukov retracted what he had said.

At the very moment that this happened in Petrograd, Nicholas II in Pskov changed his original decision to abdicate in favor of his son and "decided to abdicate in favor of my brother." This change made defense of a constitutional monarchy even more difficult, for it was no longer possible to count on the minority of the new sovereign, which would have made a natural transition in consolidating a strictly constitutional system. Those who had already agreed to accept Alexis were not at all obliged to agree to accept Michael. . . .

Under these predawn impressions a preliminary conference of members of the government and temporary committee was held to determine what to say to Grand Duke Michael and how to say it. The evening before, Kerensky had declared himself for a republic in the Soviet of Workers' Deputies and had reported on his special status in the ministry as a representative of democracy and on the particular weight of all his opinions. . . .

N. V. Nekrasov had already managed to draft an abdication speech. Miliukov alone took the opposite view: that it was necessary to preserve a constitutional monarchy until the Constituent Assembly met. . . . After a passionate debate it was decided that both points of view should be placed before the Grand Duke, and he should make the decision on abdication. Around noon the Grand Duke met with the members of the government. After some speeches the Grand Duke, who had been silent the whole while, asked to have some time to think the matter over. He went into another room and called in Rodzianko to talk with him in private. When he came out to the waiting deputies he told them firmly that his final choice inclined toward the view championed by Rodzianko, the chairman of the Duma [i.e., abdication]. Kerensky then proclaimed, "Your Highness, you are a very noble man!" He added that he would say this everywhere from that time on. Kerensky's grand statement was not in harmony with the prosaic decision that had been made, for the Grand Duke did not convey a feeling of love and suffering for Russia but only one of fear for himself. . . .

This is how the first capitulation of the Russian revolution took place. The representatives of the State Duma in essence settled the question of the monarchy. They created a position which was weak from the very start, a position from which all the later mistakes of the revolution were to spring. In the general consciousness of the people involved in these early events the new regime created by the revolution inherited its position, not from the legal documents of March 15-16, but from the riots of March 12. Herein was its strength, which was felt at that time, and herein was its weakness, which became apparent later.

"Revolutionary Democracy" Takes the Offensive—the May Crisis

The Congress of Workers' and Soldiers' Deputies discussed the question of the war on April 11. It called on "all peoples to exert pressure on their governments to renounce programs of conquest" and "affirmed the necessity of negotiations between the Provisional Government and the Allies in order to work out a common agreement in this sense."

[The pressure of events forced the Provisional Government, too, to formulate its views on the war. The question was discussed by the ministers at the end of April. Miliukov, as minister of foreign affairs, led the discussion and proposed a note to be sent to the Allies. This note pointed out that] ". . . the general premises expressed by the Provisional Government are in complete accord with those high ideals which have constantly been expressed by many outstanding statesmen of the Allied countries, especially America. This not only cannot imply the idea of Russia's weakened role in the common struggle, but, on the contrary, intensify the desire of the entire people to wage the World War to a decisive conclusion. . . . The Provisional Government, defending the rights of our homeland, will fully observe the obligations assumed in regard to our Allies. . . ."

The note was dated May 1, the day of the first open celebration in Russia of the international workers' holiday, May Day. Public buildings were decorated that day with gigantic signs saying, "Long live the International." Lenin's followers had energetically prepared their posters and slogans for this holiday. . . .

May Day passed relatively quietly, and Lenin's propaganda was decidedly rebuffed by most of the street speakers and the public. However, the publication of the note two days later provided the Bolsheviks with a new pretext for the first armed street demonstration against the Provisional Government. At three or four in the afternoon the reserve battalion of the Finnish regiment approached the Marian Palace with posters saying, "Down with Miliukov" and "Miliukov must resign."

[Using this pretext,] Kerensky decided to bring up the ministerial crisis openly and thus strengthen the position of those who favored a coalition. On May 12 he published a letter to the cen-

tral committee of the Socialist Revolutionary party. In it Kerensky
replied to the Soviet of Workers' and Soldiers' Deputies and to
the temporary committee of the State Duma, stating that henceforth "representatives of the workers' democracy can assume the
burden of power only through direct election and formal authorization by those organizations to which they belong," and that he
"will bear the full weight of actual discharge of obligations. . . ."

The more influential leaders of the Soviet, together with Tseretelli, were not at all inclined to bear responsibility for the use of
government authority at such an important and difficult moment.
They had counted their forces quite correctly and realized that
the process of organization they required had hardly started in
the country. They were well aware that in this process it was far
more advantageous to be on the side of the critics than on the side
of those criticized, and they also knew that if the more influential
of them were to leave the Soviet for the government this would
greatly weaken their influence in the Soviet and open the way to
the increased influence of their opponents on the left—the Bolsheviks. After long discussion at the May 12 session of the Executive Committee of the Soviet, the committee decided *against*
participating in the government by a majority of 1 vote: 23 to 22,
with 8 abstentions. . . .

On the evening of May 12, however, Guchkov had already told
the Provisional Government he was leaving it, and on May 13,
Prince G. E. Lvov received a letter from him stating that "in view
of the conditions in which governmental authority has been placed
in the country, especially the authority of the minister of war and
marine, he cannot in conscience act any longer as minister of war
and marine and share responsibility for the great crime which is
being committed against the homeland."

The news of Guchkov's resignation caused the Executive Committee, following explanations by Kerensky, to reconsider its
decision not to enter the government. At an evening meeting May
14 the Executive Committee of the Soviet decided by a majority
of 41 to 18, with three abstentions, to take part in a coalition
government.

At an evening meeting on May 15 Kerensky informed Miliukov
that the seven members of the Provisional Government had decided, in Miliukov's absence, to appoint him minister of public

education, rather than minister of foreign affairs, in the new assignment of ministries. Kerensky himself was to become minister of war and the navy. Miliukov categorically refused to accept the comrades' proposal and left the session. In view of the implicit victory of Zimmerwald [antiwar] tendencies . . . he did not consider it possible to bear his share of the future actions of the coalition cabinet.

Moribund Socialism under Attack from the Left—the July Revolt

Matters had become more complicated by the beginning of July. The soldiers of the Petrograd garrison were annoyed that there was reluctance to release the "forty-year-olders" from the front so that they could do field work, and they were also stirred up by rumors that certain regiments had been disbanded at the front and behind it for failure to obey orders. The center of agitation was the First Machine Gun Regiment, the same one that organized the military part of a demonstration in June. Emissaries were sent from the Machine Gun Regiment to other military units with the invitation to take part in the demonstration. . . . The emissaries of the Machine Gun Regiment even made these requests during the demonstration itself. This aspect of the preparations was undoubtedly Bolshevik in essence but evidently carried out outside of the close circle of Bolshevik leaders. Its results, expressed [in a demonstration] on the evening of July 16, were largely unexpected for them. But there is no longer any doubt that they kept close control over another aspect of the preparations—the creation of a central staff for the revolutionary demonstration. . . .

[On July 17] the Tauride Palace became the true center of the struggle. For a whole day it was approached by armed units which demanded in irritation that the Soviet finally seize power. A session of the soldiers' section began at two o'clock, but it developed that only 250 of 700 members had assembled. The session was not yet over when (at four o'clock) the hall was needed for a joint session of the Soviets. The forces from Kronstadt approached the Tauride Palace at that time and tried to break into the palace. They demanded that Minister of Justice Pereverzev explain why the Kronstadt sailor Zhelezniakov and the anarchists had been arrested at Durnovo's [a tsarist minister] summer house. Tseretelli came out and told the hostile crowd that Pereverzev was not there and that he had already resigned and was no longer minister. The first was true; the second was not. Deprived of a direct motivation, the crowd was somewhat confused, but then there were shouts that the ministers were all responsible for one another, and an attempt was made to arrest Tseretelli. He managed to hide in the doorways of the palace. Chernov came out of the palace to calm the crowd. The crowd immediately rushed toward him, demanding that he be searched for weapons. Chernov declared that if he were searched he would not speak, and the crowd quieted down. Chernov began to deliver a long speech on the work of the socialist ministers in general and on his own work as minister of agriculture in particular . . . . A tall worker shook his fist in the minister's face and shouted in a rage, "Take the power when it's offered, you s.o.b." Several persons seized Chernov in the commotion and tried to drag him toward an automobile. Others tried to drag him toward the palace. After the Kronstadters had torn the minister's coat they dragged him into an automobile and declared that they would not release him until the Soviet took all power. Excited workers broke into the meeting hall shouting, "They're beating up Comrade Chernov." Chkheidze declared amid the confusion that Comrades Kamenev, Steklov, and Martov were assigned to free Chernov. But he was freed by Trotsky when he drove up: the Kronstadters listened to him. Chernov returned to the hall accompanied by Trotsky. . . .

Finally, at about seven in the evening, the first consequences of government appeals to the troops which had remained loyal began to be felt. At that time the Ninth Cavalry regiment, the Vladimir Military Academy, and the First Cossack regiment came to Palace Square. The government took heart. The Lithuanian and 176th regiments came to the rescue of the Tauride Palace . . . .

One of the circumstances which shattered the mood of the "neutral" military units was the publication of certain intelligence documents. This was Minister Pereverzev's idea. . . . These documents included an affidavit by Lt. Ermolenko, who had been put through the German front "to agitate in favor of concluding a peace with Germany as soon as possible." Ermolenko pointed out Lenin's connections with the German General Staff and named the confidants in Stockholm through whom the Germans had monetary dealings with the Bolsheviks. . . . The impression produced by these documents can be judged by the fact that when they were read to delegates of the Preobrazhensky regiment these men declared that they would go out to suppress the revolt immediately. Indeed, they were the first of the guards units to go to Palace Square. They were followed by the Semenovsky and Izmailovsky regiments. . . .

In order to restore order completely, the Provisional Government, having cleared with the Executive Committee, decided on July 18 to set up a special commission in contact with the commander in chief of the troops of the districts. At the same time it was decided to set up an investigating commission to find those responsible. Vehicles with armed men in them still drove about the city during the day, but they were immediately seized by patrols of government troops. The mood and make-up of the populace on the streets had changed completely. Petrograd was completely calm by evening. . . .

The Bolsheviks acted without a program on July 16–18. If they had triumphed they would not have known what to do with their victory. But as a test the experiment was without doubt very valuable for them. It showed them what elements they had to deal with, how to organize these elements and, lastly, what resistance the government, the Soviet, and the military units could offer. The results of the experiment were extremely encouraging. The Bolsheviks saw how easily power could be seized, and it was obvious that when the time came to repeat the experiment they would conduct it more systematically and deliberately.

What did the other, the winning side, learn from this lesson? It can be said that the winners took their rapid victory too lightly and by no means appreciated the importance of those factors whose effect had caused them several unpleasant hours. The momentary fear passed, and everything seemed to have settled back into the old channels. Life with its problems of the moment, again hid from them those depths which for several moments had yawned before them. The main problems of the revolution remained unsolved, even though they had now been posed in full. The current was bearing the ship of state inexorably toward the abyss.

The Kornilov Insurrection

The two weeks before the Kornilov insurrection were passed in negotiations between the commander in chief, whose headquarters were in Mogilev, and Kerensky. Twice during August Kornilov went to Petrograd to confer with Kerensky. The two occupied themselves not only with the necessary military reforms, but also with the chances, in case of the resignation of Kornilov, of a military *coup d'état,* for which the Bolshevik military demonstration, expected in late September, would provide a pretext. Since the Petrograd regiments were manifestly disorganized by Bolshevik propaganda, the Third Division had arrived to protect the government against a larger repetition of the July uprising. The negotiations were guided by the intermediary Savinkov.· Both Kornilov and Savinkov wanted to destroy the Soviets and facilitate the realization of military reforms. But, under the influence of second-rate politicians, such as Zavoiko, Aladin, Dobrinsky, etc., Kornilov formed the plan of simultaneously modifying the ministry to reduce the influence of the Soviet in it. Since he could not ·dream of removing Kerensky, he planned to keep him, but as the minister of justice. Kornilov had many sympathizers, but his entourage and his methods alienated the best and most influential politicians. After having prepared a series of proclamations and having fixed the date of the *coup d'état* as September 9, Kornilov was naïve enough to tell Kerensky his plans the night before through the intermediary of V. L. Lvov, a former minister. Kerensky promised by telephone to come to headquarters, but this was only a maneuver to better unmask the conspiracy of the generals. Despite the opinion of a large party of the ministers, who resigned on the morning of September 9, leaving Kerensky and a "directory" of five, Kerensky hastened to declare Kornilov a traitor, and to order him to resign as commander in chief. Kornilov concluded from this that Kerensky was definitely bent to the power of the soviets, and decided to disobey, to arouse the army openly, and to oblige the ministry to reform itself and free itself from the tutelage of the Soviet. The troops that he was sending against the capital were to annihilate the Soviet, unhesitatingly killing its most influential members. Thus, Kornilov thought he would "assure the country of a firm and strong power."

But on this terrain the struggle was an unequal one for this general of no political experience. He further diminished his chances by remaining at Supreme Headquarters, instead of returning to his troops. When the latter approached Petrograd, Kerensky lost his head at first. He passed the day of September 10 and the following night in growing terror, shared by his followers. Several proposals were made for the reconciliation of the commander in chief and the premier. Only the Bolsheviks, for whom the success of Kornilov equaled a death sentence, retained their courage. They formed a "council of struggle" and a network of "committees of revolutionary war," which put an end to Kerensky's hesitation. The Bolsheviks returned to their old, proven methods: destruction of railroads, destruction of telegraph lines, the dispatch of propagandists ahead of Kornilov's troops, etc. The officers whom Kornilov had gathered in Petrograd in an attempt to raise the army there turned out to be unworthy. All of them took to flight at the decisive moment.

By September 11 the repulse of Kornilov was definite. The next day, General Krymov, commander of the expeditionary force to Petrograd, was forced to obey Kerensky and report to him. He was received by the premier with great brutality. He then returned to the ministry of war and committed suicide. On September 13 Kornilov and his accomplices were accused of mutiny and Kerensky proclaimed himself commander in chief, naming General Alexeev chief of staff. . . .

With the liquidation of the Kornilov insurrection the last hope of reinforcing the revolutionary government by an alliance with the military disappeared. It was no longer possible to count on the aid of the generals. At the same time, the period of reaction against the Bolsheviks, provoked by the July uprising, ended. Henceforth, the Bolsheviks held the trumps, and the political balance shifted as rapidly to the left as it formerly had to the right. Kerensky's impotence against the Communist fraction in the Soviet became evident when, by his decree of September 17, he tried to stop the direct action of the "committees of revolutionary war" by licensing them. Instead of submitting, they declared that they would continue their activity. . . .

The Final Struggle

At the first meeting of the Preparliament [a consultative body organized by Kerensky], the Bolsheviks ostentatiously left the room to go "to the barricades." They did not hide their intentions, and Trotsky openly declared that the new ministry was "a government of civil war." Taking advantage of the existence of the dual power, that of the government and Soviets, the Bolsheviks supported the rule of "revolutionary legality," publically violated the law, and almost openly prepared to overthrow the government. It only remained to set the date of the revolt. The fixing of the opening of the Second All-Russian Congress of Soviets for November 7 settled this matter. . . .

At dawn on November 7 Kerensky was able to ascertain that the revolt had broken out and that Supreme Headquarters had done nothing to defend Petrograd. He blamed the military for having been complacent. He then transferred to Kishkin, the minister of civil affairs, the command of the women's battalion, called the "Shock Battalion," and the detachments formed by the students of the military academy, who were assembled before the Winter Palace. Kerensky then hastened from the capital under the protection of an automobile of the American Embassy, to go out to meet the troops that had been recalled from the front. Toward the end of the afternoon the Winter Palace was surrounded and no longer could communicate with the city. The Provisional Government in vain awaited Kerensky's return with the troops. At night the cruiser Aurora, which had gone over to the Bolsheviks after its arrival from Kronstadt, bombarded the palace. Although one group of the defenders was convinced that the struggle was useless and left, the government refused to surrender, believing that until the convocation of the Constituent Assembly it was the repository of supreme authority and could be deposed only by force. . . .

Finally, the sailors, soldiers, and workers of the Red Guard penetrated the palace, and the commander surrendered on the condition that they spare the lives of the cadets. The members of the Provisional Government were led away, at the risk of their lives, to the other side of the Neva and were imprisoned in the fortress of St. Peter and St. Paul, where they again met the ministers of the tsarist regime, who had been imprisoned by the March Revolution.

It was similarly the irony of fate that Kerensky asked for help from the same troops that had marched on Petrograd in September to execute Kornilov's plan. What had happened under Kornilov was repeated exactly, but still more rapidly. The troops, composed largely of Cossaks, did not wish to fight for Kerensky, and dispersed. . . .

Russia had entered a new phase of her existence, a phase of disorganization and dispersal, in which a series of large and small "republics" was formed, arbitrarily assuming sovereign powers. General dissolution began under the Provisional Government. As early as the summer of 1917 the peasants had undertaken to redistribute the lands of the landed proprietors and to destroy the manors of the nobility. Earlier, disorganization had overtaken the army, exhausted by the war. Crowds of armed soldiers invaded the cities and towns and everywhere established an arbitrary reign. The deserters, whose numbers were unimaginable, started off for their home towns, pillaging whole districts and organizing pogroms. The disorganization of transportation set off a food-supply crisis. Famine appeared in many regions and the peasants refused to sell grain at the price that the government imposed, so that inflation brought about a rise in the cost of living which, under the Bolsheviks, soon attained terrifying proportions. The "control" of industry by the workers also bore fruit. Despite the powerful support that the state gave to all branches of war industry, the industries were unable to bear the continual wage increases and strikes. The workers left their plants, and the factories closed, one by one. All of this tended to accustom the populace to the disorganized way of life that was to characterize the Soviet regime. The disorganization resulting from the extraordinary military effort, the extreme lassitude of the army, the economic disarray, all this prepared Russia for Bolshevism. While the soldiers ended the war, the peasants made themselves masters of the land, and the workers took over the factories. Lenin had only to sanction an accomplished fact to assure the sympathy of the soldiers, peasants, and workers.

ZINAÏDA SHAKHOVSKOI

The Russian Revolution as Seen by a Child

Zinaïda Shakhovskoi (also Schakovskoy, 1906–   ) is a writer, literary critic, and journalist—editor-in-chief of the Russian daily in Paris, *Russkaya Mysl* (Russian Thought). A prolific writer in Russian and in French, she is the author of numerous novels and a series of personal memoirs, as well as historical studies including *Precursors of Peter the Great* (1964). The author belongs to a distinguished family of Russian nobility, the princes Shakhovskoi, who figured prominently in Russian history.

In the following memoir the author describes her childhood impressions of the February/March and the October/November Revolutions in Petrograd, Moscow, and the provinces.

I was ten years old and since September 1916 a pupil at the Empress Catherine Institute for Young Ladies of Nobility, in Petrograd, when the February revolution occured.

Sunday, the 26th of February 1917. In the large white-columned reception hall of the Institute, where once a week the pupils could see their parents (under the stares of two solemn looking Empresses, painted in majesty—Catherine the Great and the Dowager Empress Mariya Fedorovna) the usual crowd of visitors was on this particular day considerably thinner, but no rumors of disquietness had penetrated the walls of the Institute.

From *The Russian Review,* vol. 26, no. 1 (January 1967), pp. 68–73; vol. 26, no. 4 (October 1967), pp. 376–90. Slightly abridged.

As my sister and I took leave of my mother, who was accompanied by my brother Dimitry, in his uniform of the pupils of Alexandrovsky Lyceum, and by my two cousins, one of whom was finishing his studies in the Pavlovsky Military Officers School, I joined my classmates in a small neighboring hall where we were allowed to play on Sunday afternoons. There I heard a strange, soon to become familiar, sound: it resembled the dry and regular fall of hail and it was followed by shouting and screams and by the tramping of horseshoes on the pavement. We were even more startled by the hurry with which our mistress in charge, breaking with traditional composure, without even bothering to put us in pairs or order us to keep silent, led us to the corridor. At once the grave, somehow monastic atmosphere of the Institute which I found so boring, broke into pandemonium. There were our maids running up and down the stairs, some of them carrying mattresses (as I learned later, to be propped against the windows opening on the quays of Fontanka); our janitors, old bemedaled and bearded veterans of the previous war, were hurrying from the entrance hall to the upper floors, where they were never supposed to penetrate. We were shepherded into our classroom overlooking the relative safety of our garden and there our mistresses gave us a summary explanation of what was happening. The unfamiliar word entered my vocabulary: the Revolt, not yet "Revolution."

Of course, the event was beyond our comprehension. The world which I had entered without enthusiasm some months ago, was, in spite of its excellent educational program, remote from reality and nearer the eighteenth century than the twentieth. Over our tight corsets we wore long dresses—green, red or lilac depending on our respective grades—which would have suited the court ladies of Catherine the Great. Our bare arms and ample décolletage were modestly covered by white capes and detachable sleeves. It was a dress which hardly conveyed the idea of the struggle for life.

I must confess, this first day of the February Revolution seemed to us, the seventh-grade pupils, just an exceptionally exciting day which liberated us from the tedious obligation to behave ourselves in a lady-like manner—which meant walking demurely with hands gently crossed over our stomach and making deep reverences when we saw one of our teachers. Discipline was shattered, to our great delight.

While helping other maids to arrange our beds (we were to sleep that night on the floor of our classroom) our young maid Grousha, her arm in a sling, for she was slightly wounded while shutting windows in the great hall, chattered away: "Oh, my dear young ladies, it is terrible what is happening. You see, the crowd thought that they were fired upon from our attic, and they put us under fire. But the police are not here, they are on the roof of Sheremetiev's mansion next door! Oh dear me, what will happen to all of us?! They might well try and burn us during the night." The mysterious "they," who were they exactly? Would "they" roast us during the night? After much speculating on this question, the "young ladies" finally settled down to sleep despite their fears.

The excitement continued during the days that followed as rumors spread that the Pages of the Emperor and the Junkers (student officers) of Pavlovsky Military School would be sent to protect us. The young people of the opposite sex were never, never to be seen outside the great hall! But the awaited defenders didn't come and nobody took the Catherine Institute by assault or fire. . . .
But there came the day when even we, the youngest of the pupils, became aware that something tragic and final had befallen the Russian Empire and all of us. On March 3, all the pupils and teachers were assembled in the hall as usual for the morning prayers read by one of the highest-ranking pupils. For the first time in about two centuries the prayer for the Tsar and his family was to be omitted, the Emperor having abdicated on the previous day. The girl, who was about 18, stumbled over her words and was unable to pronounce, "Let us pray for the Provisional Government." She started to cry. The teachers and mistresses took to their handkerchiefs and soon the four or five hundred of us were sobbing over something that was lost forever.

The next day the mothers came to take their daughters away; Catherine's Institute was seeing its last days.

Following our mother, my sister Natasha and I stepped out, for good, from the Catherine Institute. I hardly recognized the capital which I had last seen two months ago returning from my winter vacation. All the glamor had left Petrograd; many shops were closed and in front of the others was an unfamiliar sight — long queues were waiting. There were few carriages and no policemen to be seen at the crossings; the streets were full of disorderly soldiers, with a few gloomy civilians hurrying along. Our driver kept saying: "Let's hurry, let's hurry, before the shooting, God forbid, starts again. . . ." And so we arrived at Furstadskaya Street.

My brother Dimitry was then only 14, but very much interested in the events. By chance I have in my possession the letters he sent to our uncle Peter Naryshkin who was living on his estate Kozlovka, in the Kashira district, in the province of Tula.

Sunday, February 27, 1917.

. . . "The tramways are not running. There are no more *izvosh-chiks*. We went with mother to see the girls at the Institute. The streets were calm but full of people. After our visit we joined Alexis and Yura and decided to cross the Nevsky, but after we had gone a hundred paces, gunfire broke out and we tried to get back into the Institute. Its doors, however, were already closed. So we hid in the entrance. The gunfire became more and more violent. The police were firing at the crowd from the roof-tops. In order to avoid being crushed by the mob we hurried to Semenovsky Street. Result from gunfire: 14 dead and many wounded."

From the apartment on Furstadskaya, Dimitry constantly kept in touch by telephone with his friends who lived in various parts of the capital, and continued his report to our uncle:

". . . Terrible things are happening in Petrograd. It has become a real battlefield. Five regiments have joined the revolt. Gunfire never ceases in our part of the city—Liteiny. The officers cannot go out into the streets, because the crowd disarms them, molests them, and even kills them. There is no police. Two prefects of the police were killed. Worst of all, the soldiers have got hold of the vodka and are drunk. There is bound to be terrible looting of shops, banks and private apartments. . . . Today, the Duma was closed and the State Council also. We, the students of the Lyceum, are on leave till the time when order can be restored; but when will this be?"

Confined to the apartment, we spent a lot of time looking through the windows. We saw Rodzianko, ex-president of the Duma, carried in triumph through the streets, and many other lively scenes. One evening, a cousin of my mother, Mara Bock, whose husband, a colonel, was arrested and whose apartment was ransacked by soldiers, arrived in distress and asked to sleep at our place. My mother could offer her only a couch in the drawing room. As she went to bed she spread over her blanket her uniform of a Red Cross nurse. "In case they should come here, it might protect me," she said. Many people these days preferred to sleep at some friend's house, as seizures of private property became more and more frequent. A family friend, General Grigoriev, having sent away his relatives, was awakened one night by a group of soldiers and escaped molestation only by dressing himself in his cook's apron and white cap and leading the soldiers through the house in search of himself.

The mail was functioning and my mother received letters both from my father, who was living on our family estate Matovo, district of Viniev, government of Tula, and from our estate-agent, who was in charge of another estate, Pronya, in the neighboring district of Epiphan. All seemed quiet at Matovo and my father insisted that my mother should come there with us as soon as possible. Quite another picture was conveyed by the estate-agent of Pronya, an estate not linked with our family by ancient ties, having been in our possession only since 1915. There the situation got out of hand: As soon as revolution was announced, the peasants came in force, broke the government seals on the reservoirs of spirits impounded in our distillery (during the war the production of alcohol was halted), and went for the liquor. Some of them drowned themselves in the huge containers, but others went on with their drinking spree, and upon leaving the place said that they would come back and burn down everything. The land-agent declared that, since he was unable to cope with the situation, he was leaving and returning to his native Baltic province.

My mother was undecided what to do. She could, of course, have gone with us to Finland while she still had some money, and there await the expected political appeasement. Incidentally, while passing one day before the Kshesinskaya mansion, she stopped to listen to a small, baldish man who was speaking to a large crowd. The man was Lenin and my mother didn't like very much what he was saying. Accompanied by my brother she went to see prince Lvov, then the head of the Provisional Government. She knew him through their common welfare work during the famine which struck the country before I was born. Lvov received her in one of the ministries not far from Nevsky. When she told him about what was happening in Pronya, Lvov raised both hands to his head and said that this was a small thing compared with all the difficulties that were confronting Russia. As to Lenin he said: "Do not worry about him. The man is not dangerous and the authorities can arrest him when they want to." Lvov also insisted that the land-owners must not leave the country, that their duty was to go back to their country places and help the peasants with their new tasks.

So, one day, we took the train to Moscow, where we children stayed for a few days with our relatives while mother went on alone to Pronya. Being a woman of great courage and determination, she decided to start where things were most dangerous.

Moscow was quieter than Petrograd. There was neither vivid apprehension nor vivid rejoicing in the streets. My governess took me to see some plays she wanted to see herself and I laughed a lot over a satire called "Liberation of Women," in which the actors were sitting at home in silk negligées, polishing their nails, while the actresses, in manish suits, talked about business and politics. And then we too left Moscow to join mother in Pronya.

At Epiphan station everything seemed exactly as it was before the revolution. We were warmly greeted by the stationmaster and the carriages sent from the estate awaited us and our luggage; they were driven by our friendly and faithful Austrian prisoners of war.

We were entering a picturesque, grotesque and tragic period of our lives. In the country, with the peasants, we were to live through the months preceding and following the October Revolution. . . .

The servants and workmen living on the Pronya estate remained faithful and stayed with us, as did about twenty Austrian prisoners of war; so at first glance danger seemed not immediate, and the situation was not too desperate. Still, to avoid being isolated in the master's house, which stood alone in the park, my mother decided to live in a two-story building in the court of the farm among a distillery and other buildings which were usually occupied by the manager, the servants and the dairy workers with their families. Our building was neither comfortable nor large enough for us, as we were joined by my aunt and her two sons, a friend of my brother who was cut off from his parents by recent events, our governess, and so on. Pronya already had a sinister record, for its original owner, my godfather, had been killed there in the master's house by revolutionary terrorists.

Still we were a rather jolly crowd and there was plenty to do to keep things going. News from the outside world was scarce and my mother decided to wait and see. . . . She did not have to wait long. One day the maid announced that a crowd from Dudkino, the nearest village, was approaching the estate. We looked down from the balcony: Here they were, and they seemed in a rather ugly mood. Mother wanted to go alone to meet them, but we all insisted on accompanying her, and finally the whole family went down to meet the intruders.

They were led by a deserter, a soldier named Chikin, who was still wearing parts of his rather frayed and floppy military uniform. Obviously, he and another man were the leaders and speakers. Chikin was full of new ideas and new words and used the latter in a manner which evoked hidden smiles from my elders. Constitution, retribution, revolution—all these "utions" not properly employed made his speech somewhat difficult to understand, but the core of it was that, although they did not know yet what they would do with us, they wanted to take over our forest located a few miles from the estate. The two or three nearest villages had decided among themselves that this "common property" had to be guarded in order to avoid uncontrolled looting. The woods now being theirs, they wanted us to stand guard over it. We were to see to it that only those who could show an order signed by the village authority were allowed to cut trees. . . .

I was happy to participate in guarding the woods. When my turn came I went with my sixteen-year-old cousin, feeling like a cowboy with a "Bulldog" (a small revolver with a mother-of-pearl handle) in my belt, my light shooting-gun over my shoulder, riding my little black horse and my dog following me. Alone in the wilderness, or what seemed to me a real jungle, I would push my horse in the direction of any sound of an axe, and so vigilant was I, that once I caught Chikin himself unlawfully cutting some trees near the road. He had an axe, I had a "Bulldog," and though I was scared to death I was determined to do my duty. "Hallo, Chikin, do you have a signed order from the village?" I asked. "I'll show you my order, you'll see it," he said menacingly and proceeded towards me without any slip of paper visible, but with his axe solidly gripped in his hand. I could not shoot him, but I didn't want to be killed either. "I see you haven't got a permit, so I will report you to the village," I said, trying to look unconcerned, but moving my horse away. Then I galloped out of the woods, stopping in a nearby village, where the atmosphere was very different, and the woman whom I asked for water, invited me to her *izba* and gave me a glass of *kvass* (a kind of cider) and a slice of rye bread.

Violence and friendliness were interlaced and very confusing for a child's mind. My brother and my cousin were for instance invited to be guests of honor at a village wedding and I went with them. We were treated with the utmost respect and courtesy, as if the revolution was only a word and nothing else. But the "armistice" did not last, and Chikin was again behind the next and final crisis. It must have been March or April when they came again, crowding the courtyard of Pronya, the peasants from Dudkino. This time they had come to take the horses and the cows, and to bid us, not too politely, to go away.

There were lengthy discussions between them and mother. The livestock was often transferred from Matovo to Pronya and from Pronya to Matovo and my mother flatly refused to leave all of it behind. The peasants tried to win over our workers and prisoners of war, but they did not succeed. Everybody stood behind us and the old Austrian sergeant Karatosh, who was chief stable-boy, said in his poor Russian that he preferred to be a valet to a gentleman than to be a valet to a valet. Other Austrians, in charge of the farm, protested against the seizure of their private pigs which my mother had given them and which they had lovingly bred and desired to keep. This Chikin refused to allow.

We started our first exodus. Our trunks were put on the carriages, the servants and we sat in different coaches, the Austrians shepherded some of the livestock, and off we went to Matovo, a little like Noah in his Ark, under the watchful eyes of Chikin. No tears were shed on either side.

Soon after we had settled in Matovo, one of the Austrians came to ask my mother's permission to make a personal raid on Pronya in order to retrieve two pigs confiscated by Chikin. Of course my mother said that since it was his property, unlawfully seized by Chikin, he could well try to get them back, but that for obvious reasons she could not grant "permission." However, she allowed the Austrians to take horses for their expedition. The "commando" force left Matovo by night and achieved complete victory. In the small hours of the morning they returned, killed the pigs, put them in jars with appropriate spices, and went to bed. Chikin with two of his men arrived the next day before noon, with an order to search for "stolen property of the people." My mother greeted them with a poker face and permitted them to go through the farm and look for the kidnapped animals. Of course no living pigs were found and Chikin returned empty-handed, probably planning revenge.

Matovo seemed a sure haven. Nothing had happened there and my father, a kind and simple man, considered a just man by the whole neighborhood—landowners and peasants—was not worried at all. He was determined to stay in Matovo whatever happened. And if some of the land should be taken from us, he did not care too much so long as he could remain there. What happened to us was a common phenomenon. On the estates recently acquired by "strangers," the peasants were much more intransigent and rude than in those that belonged to old families of landlords. The nearby village, two miles from our estate, was also called Matovo and its inhabitants were the descendants of our serfs. Shortly before the official abolishment of serfdom by Alexander II, my great-great uncle Dimitry had liberated his serfs, settled them on his land and helped the peasants to start a new life as free men. We knew all about the peasants and they knew all about us; we played with their children, whose fathers came to discuss their problems with my father, my mother organized schools, tended the sick and provided help in years of famine. Not that it was an absolutely idyllic relationship, but as far as human relations go, it was quite satisfactory in its patriarchal intimacy. Matovo had not changed a bit and for a while we could forget about the revolution. . . .

Soon our family circle was enlarged by newcomers: my elder cousin, an officer and his friend, also a captain returned from the Rumanian front. Weapons were now in profusion because the soldiers brought arms back with them. So our gun-stores, which consisted chiefly of hunting rifles, duelling pistols and a few small-caliber revolvers, were suddenly augmented by modern weapons and ammunition, including "Nagans" and even some hand-grenades. These would be useful if we should ever be compelled to face a siege.

There were many palavers between my family and the peasants who, though friendly to us, made frequent demands, being greedy as all men are more often than not. "Meetings" were held in our dining-room, our visitors explaining to our parents what they wanted and my parents trying to give them as little as possible. The greatest problem of our Matovo village-friends was, however, how to prevent other villages from getting hold of our commodities. They could bear the idea of leaving them to us, but would not tolerate seeing them pass on to "strangers." For this reason the Matovo peasants explained to us that rather than risk seizure of our tree nursery by peasants from nearby Savino and Gremyacheye, they had decided to cut the young trees that stood opposite our house and which my father treasured particularly, since he had planted them himself. My father tried to dissuade them. "Do not be fools," he said. "It is the only wood in the vicinity. You will have much more profit if you let the trees grow." But the future did not interest them. So they arrived one day, old and young, each family on its *telega,* and they were in such a hurry to cut down, load and carry away the trees, so as to bring home a bigger haul than their neighbors, that nobody paid attention to anyone else. One tree after another fell under their axes, in greatest disorder, and several of the peasants got hurt, a few even died. In our house the windows were shut so as not to hear the noise of the sacrilege, and my father closed the door of his study. He considered it less a personal offense than a stupid and senseless desecration. But so patriarchal was our relationship with the Matovo peasants that quite naturally they brought their wounded into our house and my mother tended them in the hall of the "Red Entrance."

The wood having been sacrificed, the cordiality of our relations was restored and sins forgiven. The summer field work went on as usual; the prisoners of war and the refugees from the Polish territories worked side by side with the young generation of our own family, myself included.

This peaceful coexistence of landlords and peasants was not appreciated by the new ruling circles of the nearest provincial town, Venev. One of the new masters there was a former clerk of my father's who had been dismissed for drunkenness and prevarication. He thought of course his time had come. One day the man sent to Venev for mail brought back the local newspaper. We read it aloud, roaring with laughter. The former clerk wrote about us with great gusto, saying that he would not rest until the "nest of vipers" in Matovo was destroyed, and he promised to "draw tears from the eyes of the former Satrap of His Majesty" — my father — "with his own rough fists." My father did not bother at all about these threats. My mother, younger and more energetic than he, went "canvassing" for public support. She was well liked and knew how to speak to an audience.

Periodically urban "propagandists" came to our vicinity, not only from Venev, but also from Tula and even from Moscow. They tried to arouse the peasants against the landlords, but they were townspeople and my mother was born a country-woman and knew everybody and everything that was going on. There was for instance an incident, not in Matovo, but in another village: One of our well-wishers had informed my mother that a meeting was to be held by two "foreigners" in that village. Jumping on her horse and accompanied by two or three of our boys, my mother went to the meeting, dismounted, and approached the crowd eagerly listening to the two townsmen, who were trying to persuade the peasants to burn the estates and to kill the landlords. My mother quietly took her place near the agitators and then, interrupting the speech, addressed the crowd: "Now, my friends," she said, "I have known you and you have known my family for many years; we shared the hard years of famine, and we helped you always when we could do so. What about those two, who come and try to make trouble between us? Who are they? Have you seen them before? What do they know about you and the peasants' life, about your needs and your expectations?" Crowds are changeable; the peasants around her, who had been listening to the propagandists with some interest, started suddenly to get excited. Some shouted: "To be sure, in fact, who are they?" and "What do they want, just to make trouble?" "Let us just drown them," cried somebody. . . . My mother, not asking so much, went away and the two agitators barely escaped the peasants' wrath.

This and other similar incidents were of course reported to the authorities, who considered the influence of my parents on the villagers as nothing less than a crime. Still the summer passed and nothing changed much. News was scarce and delayed, and word of the advent of the October Revolution did not reach the countryside immediately. There were more rumors than facts. Of course Lenin's wonderful promise "All land to the peasants" was accepted with joy, though it was not clear how this was to happen. In Matovo everything stayed quiet, a few more meetings were held in our house, and measures of redistribution of land were discussed. Some agreements were drawn up. With the titles abolished, my parents became "comrades of the estate," and the estate took the modern name "the Commune of Matovo." It took some calculation to know how much land the Commune of Matovo could keep, but so many of us were living on the estate (each member of the family had a right to a parcel of land) and in addition there were the old workmen, stable-boys, coach-drivers and maids who gladly became our partners, that finally not much land was to be relinquished to the peasants. We agreed of course to work on the land ourselves.

In Pronya—in contrast to Matovo—the new events provoked an upheaval. Chikin and his friends, furious because we were out of their reach, could think only of profaning the tombs of the dead. They dug up the remains of my godfather and my grand-mother who were buried near the church of Pronya. When the macabre news arrived in Matovo my mother reacted immediately. Taking with her some of our boys, well-armed, she went to Pronya, reburied the bones of her dead, and made the priest celebrate a requiem mass. Nobody dared to attack her, but Chikin did not forget this humiliation.

The snow fell and the country sank into its winter sleep. We spent the winter months undisturbed, playing the piano, sing-ing, reading, working, hunting and editing a humorous weekly in which old and young laughed about the menace hanging over our heads. At the news of a threatening famine, my mother took care to hoard provisions: casks of salted butter, sacks of flour, ham, and salted and dried meats were hidden in caves which could be reached by a secret trap in a corridor. . . .

Matovo soon became a self-sufficient unit. We could live on and on, without taking notice of the outside world. The farm provided food, the sheep provided warm coats for the boys. . . .

Since nothing could be bought any more, we discovered in our attics hidden treasures of our grandfathers' times: sumptuous overcoats for coach-drivers of best quality green cloth, lined (it seems funny to think of it now) with yellow-black fox, old cur-tains of gorgeous velvet, quite suitable for ladies' gowns—so many treasures forgotten and unused for so long.

We spent Christmas traditionally, riding sleighs to the church of Gremyacheye, a very friendly village, and on New Year's, following another tradition, the young folks and children, accompanied by servants, all dressed in fancy attire, went to Matovo village where everybody greeted the masqueraders with delight. It was the last *sviatki* in Matovo and I vividly remember the immensity of the snow fields sliding beneath the sleighs and stretching into the night silvered by the moon . . . wonderful moments of poignant intensity.

The spring as usual cut us off even more from the outside world. The roads were flooded and that gave us one more respite. But when the snow and the mud were gone, and the green winter corn had appeared in the black fields, we all felt the menace was near. Not from the peasants, who after having taken what they could, remained friendly and in a way even were reassured by our presence among them. . . .

However, the town and the communists had not forgotten us. The first sign that the incidents in Pronya, such as the pig-raid, my mother's impressive visit to the cemetery, or her speeches at peasant meetings, had been recorded, was the arrival from Tula of a young, rather handsome, black-eyed man in military uniform. He was sent to investigate the behavior of "the enemies of the regime." Victor Modlinsky was a young lawyer from Kharkov in the Ukraine. He belonged to a bourgeois but progressive-minded family and after the demobilization he became an investigating magistrate of the new regime. He was courteously met, invited to enter the house, and heard our side of the story concerning Chikin's complaint. Our jolly crowd, with three officers of his own age, aroused his sympathy and dispelled some of his suspicions. Maybe my mother's graciousness and courage impressed him, and certainly he succumbed to the charm of my older sister. We had won a friend, the new regime had lost a follower. Victor Modlinsky joined the "commune of Matovo" as a regular member and sent his resignation to his superiors. That of course was not welcome news to the authorities and made things look worse than ever to them.

There was another day when a three-man commission whose purpose was to arrest my parents arrived from Venev. But Vassily the stable-boy took it upon himself to gallop to the village of Matovo and soon a hefty crowd of peasants came to the rescue, armed with axes, pitchforks and anything that could persuade the intruders to flee. . . . Through the open windows the visitors heard the growing noise of the peasants.

"Would you like to speak to the peasants?" my mother asked the members of the commission. They were extremely reluctant to do so, and only after my mother assured them that she would try to arrange things peacefully, they finally went to the main entrance with my parents and faced the angry mob of our defenders. When they tried to appeal to their revolutionary feelings, the peasants answered sneeringly: "All right, so you tell us the land is ours and that we are free to do with it what we want. Then why shouldn't we keep the comrades of the estate with us?" —"You have nothing to say, it is up to us to decide whether we want them to stay or to leave," they shouted, and they were so vehement about it that our unwanted guests preferred to leave in a hurry.

We knew of course that we would not be left in peace much longer, and my mother, as commander-in-chief, held a war-council with us all, to decide what to do in case the enemy should return in strength.

Of course we should have given up all the arms and ammunition in our possession, and there were, as I mentioned earlier, many deadly weapons lying around, in addition to a fine collection of old arms lovingly assembled by my fifteen-year-old brother—including grandfather's spears and sabres. Everybody received instructions as to what he should do in case of emergency.

The Lenten season had begun, the trees were sprouting their first leaves, the singing birds had returned and we were in the midst of our short and vehement spring when we received the horrible news: On the estate of my grandparents, in the province of Riazan, my Uncle Sergei and my Aunt Natasha, a sweet old maid, had been arrested by a detachment of Red soldiers and taken away "to town." But they never arrived there, for they were horribly murdered on the way without any trial or court hearing. The peasants asked for their corpses to bury them, but were refused this favor, so my father's brother and sister were buried somewhere on the spot, nobody knew where. One of our cousins came from Moscow to take grandmother and her lady companion, both of them in their eighties, to the capital.

Grieving for their slain relatives and expecting that this kind of death might well be in store for them, my parents still were not contemplating flight. It was not the attachment to their earthly possessions that prevented them from taking this course, but rather their attachment to that particular piece of land which they loved so much.

In the early hours of an April day, it was Lida and not the maid, who woke me up. "Hurry up, hurry up," she said, "they have come to arrest the princess!"

The bed of my sister Natasha was empty. I was so well prepared for anything that might happen, that I was dressed in a few seconds. At the age of eleven I was very romantic, always dreaming of adventures, and seeing this as an occasion to face danger bravely, I chose to put on a "Russian costume" and go barefoot, so as to look like a peasant girl. I slipped out of the house with the purpose of sending Vassily again to fetch the villagers to our rescue. There was a soldier near the entrance, he let me pass, not suspecting me to be the daughter of the princess. I hurried to the farm, but there were soldiers there too and Vassily told me sadly: "It cannot be done, little princess. They have taken all the horses and there are machine-guns pointed on every road leading to the various villages."

I came back. The house was in an upheaval; Aniuta directed me to go to my mother's room. Victor Modlinsky was arrested, as well as my young cousin Yura, fourteen years old. They were kept under guard behind the closed doors of father's study. Strange people in various uniforms went from room to room, evidently searching for arms.

I followed two of them who seemed to be chiefs. They went with me to my room and one asked me: "Have you any arms?" I said yes and proudly produced my "Bulldog," which he took. "Any others?" I showed him my fists: "These, and you cannot take them away."—"So young and such a spiteful little aristocrat," said he, laughingly. I hated him. I went everywhere he went. He had found in a closet my brother's cap of the Imperial Lyceum and took it along, saying: "Well, it may be of some use to my son." I took him by the sleeve: "Take off your coat, and give it to me, it may be of some use to my brother." He laughed again.

Aniuta came to remind me that my mother was waiting for me. There she was. Her maid, crying, put some of her belongings in a suitcase, then went away to carry it downstairs. We were left alone—my mother, my brother, my aunt, my two sisters and I. Everyone of us thought about the death of our relatives but no one spoke about it, pretending to be confident. Now I learned what had happened. My brother Dimitry was the first to see the Red soldiers. Everybody in the family, including the children, had been in charge of some section of the country work. He took care of the dairy. On this fateful day, he went as usual, at dawn, to his work. Near the cowshed he spotted the arrival of a mounted detachment of heavily armed Reds. Some of them proceeded with machine-guns in the direction of nearby villages, to prevent a riot on our behalf.

My brother's friend, Pavlik, seeing the soldiers through the window, took his revolver and the two hand-grenades, as we had been instructed beforehand, and hurried to the cache. But when he emerged from the trap-door, two soldiers met him with pointed bayonets: "What were you doing?" they asked. "Hiding my revolver," he answered. "Well, bring it back!" He plunged down again, glad that the two soldiers were reluctant to follow him underground. He brought out his revolver, but not the grenades (retention of grenades was punishable by death). My cousin Yura, in a hurry, managed to hide his "Smith & Wesson" in a bucket of dirty water. But he forgot its sheath under the pillow, and a soldier told him: "You have two minutes to find the revolver that was in this, otherwise you'll be shot." So he had to bring it back.

Victor, seeing the soldiers surround the house, went up the stairs (all the women of the family lived on the second floor) to take the revolvers from my mother and elder sister and hide them. But there again everything went wrong. He had three revolvers on him when going downstairs; he was searched and arrested on the spot, just like Yura. Nobody knew why only the two of them were arrested and nobody else. The official order was strangely restricted: to arrest my mother only, not my father, and with her our coach-driver Andrey, the only pro-Communist of the commune of Matovo. This cured the latter of his sympathy for the new regime.

After a while, my mother said to us: "Remember, if you need some money, it is there, in that old suitcase, lying among the others. . . ." We prayed and got up. The carriages were at the Red Entrance, and the soldiers of the escort were ready. Some of them had already "requisitioned" our horses. . . . My father was not arrested but demanded permission to accompany my mother. The maid went to call him and I went with her. Father was drinking tea, alone in the dining-room.

"Your Excellency," said the maid, "the commissar is getting impatient."—"Let him be impatient, he will have to wait," my father answered. He kissed and blessed me, then we went together to the Red Entrance. I think it was my friend the stable-boy Vassily who was driving the carriage which my parents and Yura occupied. Victor Modlinsky and the coach-driver Andrey were in another carriage. Nobody spoke much. The carriages, surrounded by Red soldiers, moved on. The remaining family and the servants, in a tight group looked on, trying not to show their apprehension. This was the end of "the commune of Matovo," but not of its inhabitants. I was the last to leave Matovo, because for some time I was held as a hostage, alone in the house, with Red soldiers. . . . But this is another story.

SERGEI G. PUSHKAREV

1917—A Memoir

S. G. Pushkarev (1888–   ), historian and publicist, taught Russian history at Fordham University and Russian at Yale University. He is the author of *The Emergence of Modern Russia 1801–1917,* New York, Holt, Rinehart and Winston, 1963, and other works in the field of Russian history.

   In the reminiscences printed below, the author describes his activities as a student at Kharkov University, where he joined the Menshevik organization with primary sympathies with G. Plekhanov's *Edinstvo* (Unity) group, which favored Russia's continuance in the war to its successful conclusion. He also relates his subsequent activities in the Ukraine and in the Kursk province. Dates are according to the "new style."

I entered the historical-philosophical faculty of Kharkov University (which had the usual four-year curriculum) in the fall of 1907, but the end of my university studies were greatly delayed because of my political "deviation." My connections with the social-democratic Mensheviks led, in January 1910, to my arrest by the gendarmerie and, as a result, to my expulsion from the university. After two months of solitary confinement I was placed under so-called open police surveillance, and then asked for and was granted permission to go abroad.

   After several semesters at the Universities of Heidelberg and Leipzig, I returned to Russia in 1914 wishing to re-enter my *alma*

From *The Russian Review,* vol. 26, no. 1 (January 1967), pp. 54–67.

mater. To do that I had to obtain a "certificate of political reliability" from the Governor of my native Kursk province. The Governor, however, doubted that I was "reliable" enough. After a long
conference with my elder brother (whose political innocence and
reliability were above any suspicion), the Governor consented to
write a letter to "His Excellency, Rector of the Imperial University
at Kharkov" stating that, the Rector consenting, the Governor
would not object to my re-admission to Kharkov University.

In January of 1916, after an interruption of precisely six years,
I entered my familiar auditoriums. . . . My age, my "political past,"
and my Heidelberg studies put me a little above average in the eyes
of my professors and my fellow-students, and when the February
revolution came and all governors disappeared overnight, I together with millions of other Russians, was plunged into political
activities of various kinds. The revolution "conquered" Kharkov
without any resistance, and most people expected a bright future
for free, democratic Russia.

Two days after the Emperor's abdication manifesto was issued
in Pskov on March 2, the students of our department held a meeting to discuss the current political situation. It must be recalled
that the city of Pskov, annexed by Moscow in 1510, was the last
stronghold of the old Russian political freedom, and so I, being a
historian, began my speech with the statement: "The tsar signed
his abdication manifesto in *Pskov!* Historical fate willed that in the
same city where the old Russian political freedom perished four
hundred years ago, the Russian autocracy has now perished forever!" My prophecy proved to be quite erroneous, but I was eloquent
enough so that my speech, foreseeing a bright future for the young
Russian democracy, was a big success. As a result, I was chosen at
the same meeting to be one of the two students from our department to represent it in the Soviet of Students' Deputies, formed by
the students of higher educational institutions parallel to the Soviet
of Workers' and Soldiers' Deputies.

From now on the chief interest for me, as for the majority of the
active intelligentsia, was not in school affairs, but in political developments. My own primary sympathies lay with the group called
Edinstvo (Unity) founded and headed by G. V. Plekhanov. Members of the *Edinstvo* group were convinced "defensists" *(oborontsy),*
i.e., they insisted that Russia should repel the German aggression,
and by successfully ending the war, in unity with its Western allies,

make German imperialism unable to repeat the terrible bloodshed. In Kharkov, however, the *Edinstvo* group had so few members and so little influence that it was not noticeable in the boiling kettle of political life. Therefore, I decided to join the Menshevik organization (named *studencheskaya fraktsiya Rossiiskoi Sotsial-Demokraticheskoi Rabochei Partii*) as a more suitable organ of political influence. Endless meetings followed to discuss the current political situtation and the ways the young Russian republic was to go.

The most tragic and difficult question to decide was, of course, that of war and peace. The Mensheviks were sharply divided on this question. The "internationalists" forcefully condemned the war and wanted a peace without victors and vanquished, to be achieved as a result of the combined efforts of the European socialist parties. The "defensists" did not believe in socialist international solidarity and insisted on the necessity to defeat the German Empire.

So in the spring of 1917 I divided my time between the university exams and the meetings of the Menshevik organization. We talked, and talked, and talked, while the Russian front, under the corroding influence of Bolshevik and German defeatist propaganda became progressively demoralized and was losing what remained of its fighting spirit. In May this process of decline became evident enough, and our discussions more and more heated. Once when in an excited speech I insisted that the "revolutionary democracy" (*i.e.,* the Mensheviks and Socialist Revolutionaries) should help rebuild the fighting abilities of the army, and closed my speech with the words "if our army should perish, Russia will perish also," the internationalists shouted: *"Cadetskie rassuzhdeniya!"* (Cadet arguments!). In their opinion, to be in agreement with the Cadets and especially with their leader, P. N. Miliukov, on the question of the "imperialistic war" was the greatest shame for a good Marxist. One of them, comrade Leo, vehemently attacked my un-Marxist position and once more declared that it was not the business of the Social Democracy to support the imperialist war. I asked for the floor and said: "Comrades! Let us be consistent. If we are absolutely against this 'criminal war,' let us accept Lenin's program, bless 'fraternization' with the enemy and recall the army from the front. If not for fighting why do we need 15 million spongers under arms who are only becoming demoralized and are ruining the national economy? Therefore: either call upon the army to fight—or recall it from the front!" Comrade Leo answered angrily: "No, no, no! Comrade Pushkarev distorted my position! I do not accept the Bolshevik tactics. We, Social-Democrat Internationalists, neither call upon, nor recall! *(ne prizyvaem i ne otzyvaem)."*

Such were the results of our three months of debate. I came to realize that our heated discussions in Kharkov were entirely irrelevant and useless, because the question of defense could only be solved by the army in the field. My personal position with regard to the defense question was rather uneasy: I had never served in the army, and was exempt from military duty because of physical disabilities. But how could I preach the duty of defending the fatherland if I did not myself take part in the dangers and hardships of the Great War?

In the beginning of June I left Kharkov for the village Prokho-rovka in Kursk province, where my mother possessed a landed estate of some 620 acres and my elder brother was, until the revolution, the local justice of the peace. Meanwhile, the situation in the country and at the front went from bad to worse. Kerensky's June offensive ended in failure, and after the crushing and shameful defeat of the 11th Russian Army in Galicia in July, 1917, my patriotic sense was so depressed and shocked that I felt it my duty to join the army in order to defend the Russian republic against its external and internal enemies.

Because of the hopeless military situation at the front, all my relatives and friends regarded my decision as utterly foolish, but I was steadfast enough to insist on my purpose, and applied as a volunteer at the military recruitment office in Kharkov. The clerks at the office were rather amazed, and looked at me with a mixture of irony and pity: "You want to join the army now? What for?" Trying to be self-confident, I spoke about my duty to defend Russia in a dangerous situation. "Well, you can try," said the clerk and, without a medical examination, gave me in a few minutes an assignment to the 24th Infantry Regiment, stationed at that time in Mariupol on the Azov Sea.

At the regimental headquarters I was received with the same perplexed irony as in Kharkov. After brief questioning I was assigned to the 8th Company and went into the barracks for the first time in my life. The initial impression was discouraging and further impressions all the more so. The barracks were filled with a bored, grumbling, idle crowd. A Russian infantry regiment was composed of four battalions and each battalion of four companies; aside from these 16 regular companies there was a logistic company and a training company for future sergeants. Our company, a regular one, had about 300 men and was of a very mixed composition: there was a small group of battle-proven and well-trained sergeants and corporals, there were many young peasant boys who had not had time enough to be made into soldiers; the majority were middle-aged "uncles" who had left their families and their farms in the countryside and were longing to return home.

When I entered this peaceful army at the end of July 1917, military life in the rear-regiments was in full decline. There was no regular military training in our companies, there was no military order, there was no military spirit, there was only one overwhelming desire—to get over with the senseless life in the barracks and to return home. In proportion to the huge mass of soldiers there were very few officers in our regiment, and they rarely appeared in the barracks. Training was entrusted to the sergeants commanding platoons, but they fulfilled their duty with a great deal of liberalism. According to the schedule, training hours were from 8 till 12; from 12 to 2 o'clock there was lunch and rest, and from 2 o'clock on there was free time, with the right to go out; no passes or permission were needed. We were soldiers of the Russian democratic republic and therefore enjoyed all the rights of free Russian citizens. In the morning the platoon sergeants asked their subordinates: "Well, boys, who is going to drill?" From our whole platoon of about 70 men, about 15 to 20 would usually consent, the rest stayed quietly in the barracks. I was, of course, among the eager ones, but my eagerness did not help me very much, because more than half of our training was occupied with talking and smoking; after three or four weeks of such "training" I remained as miserable a soldier as I was in the beginning of my military career.

Initially I hoped that my political-educational work among my new comrades would bring more success than my military efforts, but these expectations were also betrayed. First of all, my personality and appearance (with eyeglasses, the mark of a *"burzhui"*) aroused perplexity, and perhaps suspicion, among the soldiers: "What the devil does this egghead want in these overcrowded, dirty, stinking barracks, which everybody is eager to leave as soon as possible?" I tried to arrange some discussions in our company concerning the current military and political situation, and to explain my views and ideas. From the very beginning, I found a strong opponent in the person of a middle-aged sergeant, wounded in the beginning of the war but now in excellent health, tall, robust, a convinced Bolshevik with a very loud voice, greatly exceeding my own. I had many heated debates with him, without much success. After listening to our vehement disputes, the soldiers would frequently say: "Devil only knows, which one of you is right." But the key argument of my opponent—"we don't need this war any more, we want peace"—was always nearer to their hearts than my patriotic appeals.

We spent our afternoons either at the seashore—lying on the sand or bathing in the warm, shallow water of the Azov Sea—or in the city square, where we attended noisy political meetings (composed mostly of soldiers) and listened to speeches by Bolsheviks, Mensheviks, and Socialist Revolutionaries. The main content of the Bolshevik speeches was simple: "Comrades! For 300 years the bourgeoisie and the landlords drank your blood! [Why exactly 300?] Now we have overthrown the tsarist regime, but are we free? Not at all! Instead of the tsarist government we have Kerensky. Who is Kerensky? He is a hireling of the Russian and foreign bourgeoisie! Kerensky forces you to continue this senseless, criminal war. Do you need this bloody, criminal war? (No, we don't . . .) Do you need Turkish or German territories? (No, we have enough of our own . . .) Do you want to shed your blood for the interests of English and American capitalists? (No, we don't want to . . .) Do you want peace? (Yes . . .) Listen, Kerensky, the Mensheviks and Socialist Revolutionaries are betraying the working people; they have sold themselves to the Russian, English and American bourgeoisie, that is why they want to send you into battle again and again. Only our party, the Bolshevik party, will give you peace!"

The other important issue was land. The Bolshevik speaker would ask the crowd: "Do you need more land? (Yes, of course we do . . .) Do you have as much land as the landlords do? (No, they have much more than we have . . .) You see! But will the Kerensky government give you land? No, never. It protects the interests of the landlords. Only our party, the Bolsheviks, will immediately give you land. . . . " And so on.

Several times I tried to take the floor and to explain that the

Bolsheviks make promises which they can never fulfill. I used figures from agrarian statistics to prove my points; but I saw that the crowded square was unsuitable for academic discussion, and especially for statistics. The crowd would be silent at first, but soon the "activists" became impatient and began to shout: "Leave! None of this rubbish! He is obviously for the *burzhui!* Down with him!"*

By the middle of August I realized my military and political failure in the 8th Company and, following my request, was transferred to the training company *(uchebnaya komanda)* where order and discipline were still in existence and where there was regular military training. Now I took part in the drill every day and was trying to do my best. I must confess, however, that my physical fitness left something to be desired. Among other military exercises we were taught to hit straw men with our bayonets; when I struck my straw man for the first time the lieutenant commanding our platoon smiled sourly and said: "Yes, Pushkarev, with such a stroke you could kill only a frog!"

I had more luck in the field of political activity. Each company at that time had a company committee, and I was soon elected a member of our company committee, and became its secretary. In general, the atmosphere in the training company was much healthier than in the regular companies. Our committee worked in full agreement with the commanding officer. My own relations with the soldiers were friendly and trusting, and the officers appreciated me if not as a future military hero, then as a reliable link between themselves and the privates.

* The promises to give land to the peasants were in fact a great hoax. By 1917 there were over 170 million *desiatinas* of arable lands in the possession of peasants and Cossacks, while the possessions of the nobility shrank to only 40 million (G. T. Robinson, *Rural Russia Under the Old Regime,* 1949, p. 270). The general redistribution of the *pomeshchiki* lands among peasants in 1918 increased the average peasant holding by only 16 per cent (A. Bolshakov, *Derevnya posle Oktyabrya,* Leningrad, 1925, p. 28). For the national economy as a whole, the dismemberment of the more productive private estates brought more harm than good. In the early twenties competent Soviet agrarian experts candidly recognized that "the slogan of the confiscation of land and its equal distribution was, so to say, a technical device for revolutionizing the peasantry and was devoid of serious economic significance." (I. A. Kirillov, *Ocherki zemleustroistva za tri goda revoliutsii,* Moscow, 1922, p. 112; also B. N. Knipovich, *Ocherk deiatelnosti Narodnogo Kommissariata Zemledeliya za tri goda,* Moscow, 1920, p. 9.)

Toward the end of September our training and our normal life in the barracks were suddenly interrupted and we were called to prove our military fitness and our loyalty to the government by deeds. Our training company was sent to quell a riot and to restore order in the city of Bakhmut (now Artemovsk) in the Donets Basin.

The cause for the riot was not so much political as alcoholic in nature. It should be remembered that from the end of the nineteenth century the Russian government operated a monopoly on the sale of vodka, from which the treasury derived huge revenues. Each locality had government-operated liquor retail stores, and major cities, such as Bakhmut, had large vodka warehouses. During the war sales of alcoholic beverages were suspended, the retail stores were closed, and the warehouses were guarded by watchmen. Such full prohibition was probably too drastic a measure. The soldiers in the trenches missed their favorite drink—so useful to heat the body and enhance the spirit—and the peasants helped themselves by producing *samogon* or moonshine, a detestable and often harmful substitute for the high-quality tsarist vodka.

The Provisional Government persisted in the policy of prohibition, but was not strong enough to enforce it. After months of walking around the locked vodka warehouses with longing and licking their lips, soldiers and workers in many cities lost their patience and began to break in and loot the warehouses. Drinking sprees were followed by brawls, plundering and general disorder. Such was the situation in September of 1917 in Bakhmut, where the 25th Infantry Reserve Regiment broke into the local vodka warehouse by force and started heavy drinking, inviting all those who wished to participate. Our training company from Mariupol and a company of military school cadets *(iunkerskoe uchilishche)* from Chuguev near Kharkov were sent to restore order in Bakhmut.

We entered the streets of Bakhmut in strict military formation, to the visible astonishment of the local population, both sober and drunk. In the city square we were ordered to stop and rest, until our commander received needed instructions. On a sidewalk nearby a drunk soldier of the 25th Regiment was standing; he was not able to move and could preserve an erect posture only by embracing a lamppost with both arms. He looked at our ranks and asked: "Comrades, comrades, what regiment are you from?" Our boys answered: "The 24th Infantry Reserve Regiment!"—"Very well, very well, comrades," he answered. "Now we will drink vodka together."

I became indignant and said in a sharp voice: "We did not come to drink vodka with you, we came to restore order in your city!" He was visibly surprised, became seemingly half-sober and answered with biting irony: "That's very strange! That means the 25th Regiment will drink vodka and the 24th will pray to God. . . . " Then he looked piously to heaven. Our boys answered with loud laughter and my eloquence was dissipated without result.

Finally we arrived at the source of the disturbances, the vodka warehouse. It was a large, three-story brick building with windows protected by iron bars, U-shaped in plan, with the open side protected by a massive iron railing. The fence and the gate were not damaged, only the lock and the bolts were broken. Two or three days passed before these were replaced. In the meantime the entrance had to be guarded by two armed sentries; one from our company and one from the military cadets.

During the night, one after another, soldiers of the 25th Regiment came to the gates and whispered: "Comrade, comrade, give me a little bottle! At least one little 'scoundrel'" (*merzavchik* — colloquial name for the smallest size vodka bottle). We tried to chase them away and when I became angry and threatened to fire, the soldiers outside also became furious: "You damned sons of bitches! Whom do you guard this vodka for! We will shoot you all. . . . " Nor were these threats only words. On the second night of our guard duty one of the cadets was shot in the head and died instantly. It was a most unpleasant feeling — to be in danger of being killed in the defense of vodka.

This vodka war lasted for about two weeks, and during this difficult time our officers and the members of the company committee were hard put to restrain our own soldiers from drinking more than one or two "little scoundrels." . . .

Soon after our return to Mariupol, in October 1917, our regiment received orders to send all soldiers who had higher education to the military cadet school in Poltava (the *Vilenskoe Voennoe Uchilishche* was evacuated from Vilna to Poltava in 1915). This changed once more the field of my military and political activity.

The bulk of the military cadets were loyal to the Provisional Government and ready to defend it, but many cadets and most of the officers resented the passive and lenient policy toward the Bolshevik menace, which the Kerensky regime adopted. The cadet schools had, like other military units, their meetings, their political discussions, and their elected committees. I took part in this political life and was elected to the school committee.

In the beginning of November the Bolsheviks seized power in Petrograd. The local Soviet of Workers' and Soldiers' Deputies in Poltava, after some time, recognized the Petrograd Sovnarkom (Council of People's Commissars) as the legal government of Russia. We, the two representatives of our school in the local Soviet, experienced many times very unpleasant feelings among hundreds of soldiers' deputies, with the active, loud and hostile Bolshevik faction; but we steadfastly attended the meetings of the local Soviet and pretended that we were not at all afraid. Also, most of the Poltava garrison was in such a state of disorder and dissolution that the Bolsheviks were not able to gather enough military force to "liquidate" our school, armed and excellently organized under the guidance of our distinguished and highly respected director, General Adamovich.

In the beginning of December, when it became obvious that the Bolshevik regime in Petrograd would last more than three or four weeks, as many of us had hoped, the commanding officers of our school and our school committee decided that, whereas Poltava is situated in the Ukraine and whereas our school is located in Poltava, we should recognize as our legal government not the Sovnarkom in Petrograd, but the Ukrainian government, the so-called Central Ukrainian Rada in Kiev. A delegation of six members (three officers and three cadets) was sent to Kiev. I was a member of this delegation.

In Kiev we were received by *pan* Simon Petliura, the War Minister of the Ukrainian government. I was silent during the audience because my spoken Ukrainian was rather poor, and merely looked at and listened to the new War Minister. He had sharp features and a proud Napoleonic posture, but we were sorry to discover that he possessed almost no real power and commanded no real army. . . .

Having returned to Poltava, we reported the meager results of our mission, and General Adamovich, in agreement with the school committee, made the decision to disband our school, because the general situation looked hopeless and there was no sense in sending 600 cadets into battle against the external and internal enemies of Russia. . . . We said good-bye to our honored General and to each other, took off our shoulder-straps and dispersed from Poltava in different directions.

I returned to our Prokhorovka several days before Christmas. My mother and brother lived in our house undisturbed by the local peasants. The peasants adopted a neutral wait-and-see attitude towards the "Soviet power" which had recently come to the countryside. They were, of course, glad to read Lenin's "land decree" which abolished the right of the *pomeshchiki* to own land, and waited (with exaggerated expectations) for the coming spring when the distribution of the newly acquired lands would be realized.

At that time, Soviet power in the countryside did not yet possess a system of local administrative organs; its commissars appeared only in cities and in the rural districts, while the slogan for the provincial administration was *vlast' na mestakh, i.e.,* power to the local population. In villages, therefore, the higher organ of power was the peasant *skhod,* the assembly of the peasant *mir.*

The commissar for our district was a tall and robust sailor, of bandit appearance and behavior, always with a revolver and a belt of cartridges. The day after Christmas he came to Prokhorovka and called the *skhod.* The meeting took place in the local school. The crowd of peasants in their sheep-skin coats was standing in the empty room (the benches were removed for the occasion), while the speaker mounted the desk. I was also in the room, in my soldier-gray overcoat.

The commissar conveyed to the *skhod* greetings from the newly established Soviet power, which had *"abolished the pomeshchiki";* but, he continued, "in your Prokhorovka live the Pushkari (*i.e.,* the Pushkarevs) who should now be expelled from here." My mother at that time was seriously and chronically ill, spending the daytime in a wheelchair, and for her the expulsion from our house during the severe winter cold could only mean an agonizing death. I decided to ask the *skhod* for justice and mercy. I read the land-decree of October 26 and pointed out that the decree only abolished the property right of the *pomeshchiki* to their land, but said nothing about expelling them from their homes. The peasant crowd hub-bubbed: "That's right, that's true. The land must go to the people, but they themselves can live in their house as before! Let them stay! They can remain there!" and so on.*

---

* Not just in Prokhorovka, but in all of Russia the local peasants usually permitted the landowners to remain in their houses, if they wished to. The general expulsion of the former *pomeshchiki* from their homes was ordered only by the repeated decrees of the central government issued on April 3, 1925 and March 5, 1926.

When all the attempts of the angry commissar to pass the vote on our expulsion remained futile, he resorted to the last argument. At that crazy time a hat on a lady's head or a pair of eyeglasses on the nose of a man were regarded as indications of belonging to the hated class of the *burzhui,* and our commissar shouted angrily: "Listen, comrades! Why argue? Just look around. All of us here, toiling proletarians, are without eye-glasses, there is only one who has them, and that is *gospodin Pushkar!*" A contemptuous gesture in my direction followed. I mounted the desk again and addressed the *skhod:* "Citizen peasants! I have weak eyesight and the doctor ordered me to wear glasses. I think this is not such a serious crime that it should be punished by the expulsion of my sick mother from her house!" The peasant crowd agreed again: "That's nothing, the eyeglasses. That's not bad. Let him wear eyeglasses, *eto mozhno, eto nichevo.*"

Thus, the people's assembly in our village unanimously and generously granted my mother the right to stay in her house, and to me even the right to wear eyeglasses. Later that night, the commissar appeared in our house to search for weapons and, having found none, departed angry and menacing. The night and the day of January 1, 1918 we spent in our house, but that was the last New Year at home. As it turned out, the events of the year that had passed were only the beginning of the upheavals and bloodshed to come.

N. N. SUKHANOV

Sketches of Revolutionary Leaders

N. N. Sukhanov (pseudonym of N. N. Himmer, 1873–?) was a re-
nowned chronicler of the Revolution of 1917 from February through
October. In his famous seven-volume *Zapiski o revolutsii (Notes on
the Revolution),* first published in the Soviet Union in 1922, he gives
a full eyewitness account of the entire revolutionary period.

Originally an SR, the author left the party in 1906, and in the middle
of 1917, he joined the SD party, inclining toward the Menshevik
faction. Between the two Revolutions he was an ardent advocate of
"peace now," the Zimmerwaldian position. A cantankerous and
politically rather unstable, but honest intellectual, he managed
throughout 1917 to be at the right place at the right time. He had
widespread connections in the socialist movement and was a lively
and colorful, though not always objective, witness for posterity. He
managed to survive until the purge trial of the Mensheviks in 1931,
when he was convicted and sent to a concentration camp in Siberia,
where he perished.

V. I. Lenin

. . . We waited for a long time. The train was very late.

But at long last it arrived. A thunderous *Marseillaise* boomed
forth on the platform, and shouts of welcome rang out. We stayed
in the imperial waiting-rooms while the Bolshevik generals ex-

The following excerpts are taken from the English translation of Sukhanov's
memoirs *The Russian Revolution 1917,* ed., abr., and trans. by Joel Car-
michael, New York, Oxford University Press, 1955, pp. 272–75, 290–92,
305–7, 352–56, 362–63. Reprinted by permission of Oxford University Press.

changed greetings. Then we heard them marching along the platform, under the triumphal arches, to the sound of the band, and
between the rows of welcoming troops and workers. The gloomy
Chkheidze, and the rest of us after him, got up, went to the middle
of the room, and prepared for the meeting. And what a meeting
it was, worthy of—more than my wretched pen!

Shlyapnikov, acting as master of ceremonies, appeared in the
doorway, portentously hurrying, with the air of a faithful old police
chief announcing the Governor's arrival. Without any apparent
necessity he kept crying out fussily: "Please, Comrades, please!
Make way there! Comrades, make way!"

Behind Shlyapnikov, at the head of a small cluster of people
behind whom the door slammed again at once, Lenin came, or
rather ran, into the room. He wore a round cap, his face looked
frozen, and there was a magnificent bouquet in his hands. Running to the middle of the room, he stopped in front of Chkheidze
as though colliding with a completely unexpected obstacle. And
Chkheidze, still glum, pronounced the following "speech of welcome" with not only the spirit and wording but also the tone of a
sermon:

"Comrade Lenin, in the name of the Petersburg Soviet and of
the whole revolution we welcome you to Russia. . . . But—we
think that the principal task of the revolutionary democracy is
now the defence of the revolution from any encroachments either
from within or from without. We consider that what this goal requires is not disunion, but the closing of the democratic ranks. We
hope you will pursue these goals together with us."

Chkheidze stopped speaking. I was dumbfounded with surprise:
really, what attitude could be taken to this "welcome" and to that
delicious "But——"?

But Lenin plainly knew exactly how to behave. He stood there
as though nothing taking place had the slightest connexion with
him—looking about him, examining the persons round him and
even the ceiling of the imperial waiting-room, adjusting his bouquet (rather out of tune with his whole appearance), and then,
turning away from the Ex. Com. delegation altogether, he made
this "reply":

"Dear Comrades, soldiers, sailors, and workers! I am happy to
greet in your persons the victorious Russian revolution, and greet
you as the vanguard of the worldwide proletarian army. . . . The

piratical imperialist war is the beginning of civil war throughout Europe. . . . The hour is not far distant when at the call of our comrade, Karl Liebknecht, the peoples will turn their arms against their own capitalist exploiters. . . . The worldwide Socialist revolution has already dawned. . . . Germany is seething. . . . Any day now the whole of European capitalism may crash. The Russian revolution accomplished by you has prepared the way and opened a new epoch. Long live the worldwide Socialist revolution!"

This was really no reply to Chkheidze's "welcome," and it entirely failed to echo the "context" of the Russian revolution as accepted by everyone, without distinction, of its witnesses and participants.

It was very interesting! Suddenly, before the eyes of all of us, completely swallowed up by the routine drudgery of the revolution, there was presented a bright, blinding, exotic beacon, obliterating everything we "lived by." Lenin's voice, heard straight from the train, was a "voice from outside." There had broken in upon us in the revolution a note that was not, to be sure, a contradiction, but that was novel, harsh, and somewhat deafening.

Let us admit that essentially Lenin was right a thousand times over. Personally I was convinced that he was quite right, not only in recognizing the beginning of the worldwide Socialist revolution and establishing an unbreakable connexion between the World War and the crash of the imperialist system, but in maintaining that we had to steer towards world revolution and evaluate all contemporary historical events in its light. All this was beyond question.

But it was far from enough. It was not enough to acclaim the worldwide Socialist revolution: we had to understand what practical use to make of this idea in our revolutionary policy. If we didn't then the proclamation of the worldwide proletarian revolution would not merely be completely abstract, empty, and futile, but would obscure all the real perspectives and be extremely harmful.

In any case it was all *very* interesting!

The official and public part of the welcome was over. The crowd, burning with impatience, envy, and indignation, was already trying to break through the glass doors from the square. It was noisily and insistently demanding that the newly arrived leader should come out to it in the street. Shlyapnikov again cleared a way for Lenin, shouting: "Comrades, please! Make way there!"

To another *Marseillaise,* and to the shouts of the throng of thou-

sands, among the red-and-gold banners illuminated by the searchlight, Lenin went out by the main entrance and was about to get
into a closed car, but the crowd absolutely refused to allow this.
Lenin clambered on to the bonnet of the car and had to make a
speech.

" . . . any part in shameful imperialist slaughter . . . lies and
frauds . . . capitalist pirates . . . " was what I could hear, squeezed
in the doorway and vainly trying to get out on to the square to hear
the first speech "to the people" of this new star of the first magnitude on our revolutionary horizon.

Then I think Lenin had to change to an armoured car and in it,
preceded by the searchlight and accompanied by the band, flags,
workers' detachments, army units, and an enormous crowd of
"private" people, proceed to the Sampson Bridge and over to the
Petersburg Side, to the Bolshevik headquarters—the palace of
Kshesinskaya, the ballerina. From the top of the armoured car
Lenin "conducted a service" at practically every street-crossing,
making new speeches to continually changing audiences. The procession made slow progress. The triumph had come off brilliantly,
and even quite symbolically.

. . . Lenin is an extraordinary phenomenon, a man of absolutely exceptional intellectual power; he is of first-class world magnitude in calibre. For he represents an unusually happy combination of theoretician and popular leader. If still other epithets were
needed I shouldn't hesitate to call Lenin a genius, keeping in mind
the content of this notion of genius.

A genius, as is well known, is an abnormal person. More con-
cretely, he is very often a man with an extremely limited area of
intellectual activity, in which area this activity is carried on with
unusual power and productivity. A genius can very often be extremely narrow-minded, with no understanding or grasp of the
simplest and most generally accessible things. Such was the generally accepted genius Leo Tolstoy, who (in the brilliant though
paradoxical expression of Merezhkovsky) was simply "not intelligent enough for his own genius."

Lenin was undoubtedly like this too: many elementary truths
were inaccessible to his mind—even in politics. This was the source
of an endless series of the most elementary errors—in the period
of his dictatorship as well as in the epoch of his agitation and
demagogy.

But on the other hand, within a certain realm of ideas—a few "fixed" ideas—Lenin displayed such amazing force, such super-human power of attack that his colossal influence over the social-ists and revolutionaries was secure.

In addition to these internal and, so to speak, theoretical qual-ities of Lenin's, as well as his genius, the following circumstance also played a primary role in his victory over the old Marxist Bol-sheviks. In practice Lenin had been historically the exclusive, sole, and unchallenged head of the party for many years, since the day of its emergence. The Bolshevik Party was the work of his hands, and his alone. The very thought of going against Lenin was frightening and odious, and required from the Bolshevik mass what it was incapable of giving.

Lenin the genius was an historic figure—this is one side of the matter. The other is that, except Lenin, there was nothing and no one in the party. The few massive generals without Lenin were *nothing,* like the few immense planets without the sun (for the moment I leave aside Trotsky, who at that time was still outside the ranks of the order, that is, in the camp of the "enemies of the proletariat, lackeys of the bourgeoisie," etc.).

In the First International, according to the well-known descrip-tion, there was Marx high up in the clouds; then for a long, long way there was nothing; then, also at a great height, there was Engels; then again for a long, long way there was nothing, and finally there was Liebknecht sitting there, etc.

But in the Bolshevik Party Lenin the Thunderer sat in the clouds and then—there was absolutely nothing right down to the ground. And on the ground, amongst the party rankers and officers a few generals could be distinguished—and even then I daresay not in-dividually but rather in couples or combinations. There could be no question of *replacing* Lenin by individuals, couples, or combina-tions. There could be neither independent thinking nor organi-zational base in the Bolshevik Party without Lenin.

That is how matters stood in the Bolshevik general staff. As for the mass of party officers, they were far from distinguished. Amongst the Bolshevik officers there were many first-rate tech-nicians in party and professional work, and not a few "romantics," but extremely few political thinkers and conscious socialists.

In consequence every form of radicalism and external *Leftism* had an invincible attraction for the Bolshevik mass, while the natural "line" of work consisted of demagogy. This was very often what all the political wisdom of the Bolshevik committee-men boiled down to.

Thus the "party public" of course quite lacked the strength or any internal resources to oppose anything whatever to Lenin's onslaught.

Lenin's radicalism, his heedless "Leftism," and primitive demagogy, unrestrained either by science or common sense, later secured his success among the broadest proletarian-muzhik masses, who had had no other teaching than that of the tsarist whip. But the same characteristics of this Leninist propaganda also seduced the more backward, less literate elements of the party itself. Very soon after Lenin's arrival they were faced by an alternative: either keep the old principles of Social Democracy and Marxist science, but without Lenin, without the masses, and without the party; or stay with Lenin and the party and conquer the masses together in an easy way, having thrown overboard the obscure, unfamiliar Marxist principles. It's understandable that the mass of party Bolsheviks, though after some vacillation, decided on the latter.

But the attitude of this mass could not help but have a decisive influence on the fully conscious Bolshevik elements too, on the Bolshevik generals, for after Lenin's conquest of the officers of the party, people like Kamenev, for instance, were completely isolated; they had fallen into the position of outlaws and internal traitors. And the implacable Thunderer soon subjected them, together with other infidels, to such abuse that not all of them could endure it. It goes without saying that even the generals, even those who had read Marx and Engels, were incapable of sustaining such an ordeal. And Lenin won one victory after another.

• • •

Victor Chernov

I had heard Chernov, as well as Lenin, Martov, and Trotsky, in 1902–3 abroad. Afterwards, in 1905–7, I became acquainted with him personally as well, in Russia and Finland, seeing him on political but more often on literary matters. Then we separated until this ceremonial meeting—keeping up (rather feebly) a "literary" correspondence between Moscow, Archangel, and Petersburg on one side and Italy on the other.

In spite of my extreme heresies Chernov was always glad of my contributions to the journals he edited. In general my writing owed a great deal to his encouragement.

In the creation of the SR Party Chernov had played an absolutely exceptional role. Chernov was the only substantial theoretician of any kind it had—and a universal one at that. If Chernov's writings were removed from the SR Party literature almost nothing would be left.

Without Chernov the SR Party would not have existed, any more than the Bolshevik Party without Lenin—inasmuch as no serious political organization can take shape round an intellectual vacuum. But the difference between Chernov and Lenin was that Lenin was not only an ideologist but also a political leader, whereas Chernov was *merely a littérateur.*

Scarcely anyone would deny Chernov's really immense literary talent. But the essential character and the basic aims of his literary creation must not be forgotten. He was always beset, after all, by the unattainable, false, and internally contradictory task of impregnating the black-earth, muzhik Russian soil with the most modern scientific international socialism; or else wresting equal rights in the European working-class International for our black-earth muzhik, for "independent" populism.

But Chernov—unlike Lenin—only performed half the work in the SR Party. During the period of pre-revolutionary conspiracy he was not the party organizing centre, and in the broad arena of the revolution, in spite of his vast authority amongst the SRs, *Chernov proved bankrupt as a political leader.* Here, where ideology should have yielded to politics, Chernov was fated not only to wear out his authority but also to break his neck.

Further on, in our frequent encounters with Chernov, we shall see how he lost not only his authority but also his adherents and his position as leader in the "biggest Russian party." We shall see how he writhed and wriggled, grew confused and lost his way among people, events, movements, and tendencies. We shall see how, under an unbearable burden, he arrived at his naïve and silly personal tactic of washing his hands of everything. We shall see the founder and leader of the SR Party in a tragi-comic position.

But one must not only be fair: the *reasons* for the tragedy (or if you like the tragi-comedy) of Chernov must be correctly understood.

Chernov never showed the slightest stability, striking power, or fighting ability—qualities vital for a political leader in a revolutionary situation. He proved inwardly feeble and outwardly unattractive, disagreeable and ridiculous. But that's only one side of the matter. I'm convinced that no less a role was played by the above-mentioned falsity and internal contradictoriness of his doctrine and world outlook.

While it was possible to write, and do nothing but write, things went splendidly. But in revolutionary practice how was it possible to wriggle out from under in the din of the hammer and anvil?

Chernov wanted to plant a proletarian, European, and also Zimmerwald socialism* in the Russian soil of petty-bourgeois darkness and philistinism. This was a hopeless business. But Chernov could not tear himself away either from his socialism or from his soil. This is by no means the least important aspect of the drama of Chernov.

From the very beginning of the war Chernov had taken a Zimmerwald position. And now, on my way to the Finland Station for the triumphal welcome to the SR leader, I was thinking: Where will he get to, in this moss-covered swamp, with his Zimmerwaldism? How is he going to manage with his internationalism against the background of the growing bloc between the imperialist bourgeoisie and his blood-brothers of the muzhik-soldier, radical-intellectual groups?

There had been bitter disillusionments already. I was far from optimistic.

•   •   •

Julius Martov

Martov—a vast theme. I won't attempt a thorough-going treatment of it, in view of my constant references to him: we worked side by side both before and after October. Nevertheless it's very tempting

---

* Zimmerwald socialism refers to the international socialist conference called in September 1915 in Zimmerwald, Switzerland. This conference adopted a resolution condemning the "imperialist" war and proposed a general peace treaty "without annexation or indemnities on the basis of self-determination of nations." Lenin proposed to change the imperialist war into a civil war, but the majority of the socialists at this conference agreed to limit their activities to pacifist propaganda [Ed.].

now to note his basic traits, to establish, so to speak, the general pattern of this distinguished figure, not only of our own but of the European working-class movement. All the more so since there was relatively little interest in him during the revolution. The fates decreed that he should not play a prominent part in the events of these last years, but nevertheless he was and remains a star of the first magnitude, one of the few whose names were characteristic of our epoch.

I had seen Martov for the first time in Paris in 1903. He was then 29 years old. At that time he, with Lenin and Plekhanov, made up the editorial board of *Iskra,* and he gave propaganda lectures to the Russian colonies abroad, waging a bitter struggle against the SRs, who were increasing in strength. He was already famous among the expatriates and lived somewhere on Olympus, amidst other such deities, and people in the Russian colony, meeting his spare, hobbling figure, would nudge one another.

Although I was not convinced by his arguments at that time, I remember very well the enormous impression made on me by his erudition and his intellectual and dialectical power. I was, to be sure, an absolute fledgeling, but I felt that Martov's speeches filled my head with new ideas; without sympathizing with him, I watched him emerge victorious in his bouts with the populist chiefs. Trotsky, in spite of his showiness, did not produce a tenth of his effect and seemed no more than his echo.

In those days Martov also revealed his qualities as an orator. These are rather singular. He has not a single external oratorical gift. A completely unimpressive, puny little body, standing if possible half-turned away from the audience, with stiff monotonous gestures; indistinct diction, a weak and muffled voice, hoarse in 1917 and still so now; his speech in general far from smooth, with clipped words and full of pauses; finally, an abstractness in exposition exhausting to a mass audience. Tens of thousands of people retain this impression of him. But all this doesn't prevent him from being a remarkable orator. For a man's qualities should be judged not by what he does but by what he may do, and Martov the orator is, of course, capable of making you forget all his oratorical faults. At some moments he rises to an extraordinary, breath-taking height. These are either *critical* moments, or occasions of special excitement, among a lively, heckling crowd actively "participating in the debate." Then Martov's speech turns into a dazzling firework

display of images, epithets, and similes; his blows acquire enormous power, his sarcasms extraordinary sharpness, his impro-
visations the quality of a magnificently staged artistic production.
In his memoirs Lunacharsky acknowledges this and says that
Martov was the incomparable master of the summing up. Anyone
who knew Martov the orator well can confirm this.

In our Paris days I didn't know him personally. Then, in 1904–5,
cooped up in the *Taganka** in Moscow, and carefully studying
Iskra,† I perceived other qualities of Martov's—as a remarkable
writer and journalist. Our foreign, illegal, Social Democratic press,
thought to be beyond the pale of Russian journalism, introduced
a whole group of first-rate writers—Plekhanov, Martov, Trotsky,
and perhaps Lenin. All these of course should stand in the front
rank of our journalistic history. But surely Martov must be given
the palm; no one had a pen like his; no one showed himself so completely its master in the full meaning of the word. He was capable,
when necessary, of giving his writing the brilliant wit of Plekhanov,
the striking power of Lenin, the elegant finish of Trotsky.

One of Martov's basic traits is effectively illustrated in his writing. Here, however, it may not appear uniquely exceptional; but in
any personal encounter with him, whether private or concerned
with public affairs, it leaps to the eye at once. This trait is a *mind*
of extraordinary power and development. In my time I've had the
fortune to meet not a few remarkable contemporaries—scientists,
artists, and statesmen with world names. But I have never doubted
for a moment that Martov is the most intelligent man I've ever
known.

It used to be said of our ancient magicians that they saw three
yards into the earth beneath you. Martov constantly reminds you
of this. An incomparable political analyst, he has the capacity of
grasping, anticipating, and evaluating the psychology, train of
ideas, and sources of his interlocutor's argumentation. Hence a
conversation with Martov always has a special character, as with
no one else in the world, and always provides a peculiar enjoy-

* A prison in Moscow, for both criminal and political offenders [Ed.].
† A Social Democratic paper founded in 1900 by Lenin, Martov, and Potresov
under the sponsorship of Plekhanov, Axelrod and Vera Zazulich; after the Social Democratic split into Bolsheviks and Mensheviks in 1903 it was in Menshevik hands until 1905 when it ceased publication. In 1917 Martov started
a bulletin also called *Iskra* [Ed.].

ment, however disagreeable the theme, however sharp at times the disagreement and virulent the recriminations. When you talk to him, it does not occur to you that you won't be *understood;* you can feel no doubts on this score. Here the slightest hint or gesture is enough to provoke a response that pierces to the very hub of the question and forestalls any further arguments around its periphery.

Martov is an incomparable political thinker and a remarkable analyst because of his exceptional intellect. But this intellect dominates his whole personality to such an extent than an unexpected conclusion begins to thrust itself on you: Martov owes not only his good side to this intellect, but also his bad side, not only his highly cultivated thinking apparatus but also his *weakness in action.*

Of course it's impossible to blame only his omnivorous intellect for his incapacity for practical combat. A lot must be ascribed to other general qualities. Nevertheless, in speaking of Martov, it would be perfectly just to develop the theme of [Griboedov's] *Woe from Wit.*

First of all, to understand everything is to forgive everything. And Martov, who always has an exhaustive understanding of his opponent, is to a substantial degree condemned by virtue of this very understanding to that mildness and submissiveness to his ideological adversaries that characterizes him. To a considerable extent it is precisely Martov's breadth of view that ties his hands in intellectual combat and condemns him to the role of critic, of perpetual "Opposition."

Secondly, it must be said that since the birth of the most famous of analysts, Prince Hamlet, analysis, as the supreme quality of a character, is never divorced from Hamletism. That is, an intellect that dominates everything is a source of softening of the will and of indecisiveness in action. With Martov, who is a thinking apparatus *par excellence,* the centres of restraint are too strong to allow him the free and reckless acts of combat, the revolutionary feats that no longer demand the reason, but only the will.

"I knew," Trotsky said to me much later, not long before these lines were written, "I knew Martov would be destroyed by the revolution!"

Trotsky expressed himself too one-sidedly. His words actually mean that in a revolution Martov could not occupy a place corresponding to his specific weight, for reasons inherent in himself. This is not so. Reasons outside himself had much greater significance. But it is true that Martov's sphere is theory, not practice. And when this epoch of fabulous exploits, of the greatest deeds in history began, then this star of the first magnitude of the underground period, the equal of Lenin and Trotsky, was eclipsed by the light even of comparatively minor luminaries like Dan and Tseretelli. There are a number of reasons for this—as we shall see later on. But again the same paradoxical reason stands out among them: Martov was *too* intelligent to be a first-class revolutionary.

His excessive, all-embracing analytical thinking apparatus was no help and was sometimes a hindrance in the fire of battle, amidst the unprecedented play of the elements. And later we shall see— even in my account, the account of a follower and apprentice—to what criminal inactivity Martov was condemned more than once by his Hamletism and his ultra-refined analytical web-spinning at moments demanding action and aggressiveness. These moments— critical moments!—will always remain my bitterest memories of the revolution. For the consequences of his errors in these critical moments were enormous, if not for the revolution as a whole, at least for his party and for himself.*

• • •

Alexander Kerensky

At this time [spring and early summer 1917] Kerensky displayed astonishing activity, supernatural energy, and the greatest enthusiasm. Of course he did everything within human power. And not for nothing does the chilly and malevolent historian Miliukov, in whose interests Kerensky was working at this time, recall, with a shade of tenderness and gratitude, the "comely figure of the young man with a bandaged arm" appearing first at one point then at another of our limitless front (apparently everywhere at once) and calling for great sacrifices, demanding that the wayward and indifferent rabble should pay tribute to the impulses of idealism.

Kerensky, who as Minister of Justice had put on a dark-brown jacket in place of his sports coat, now changed it for a light-coloured, elegant, officer's tunic. His hand had been bothering him nearly all that summer, and in a black sling gave him the appearance of a wounded hero. I have no idea what was wrong with Ke-

---

* After the October Revolution, to which Martov was hostile, he emigrated to Germany in 1920, where together with Dan he edited the influential Menshevik journal *Sotsialisticheskii Vestnik*. He died in 1923 [Ed.].

rensky's hand—it was a long time since I had talked to him. But it is just like this that he is remembered by tens and hundreds of thousands of soldiers and officers from Finland to the Black Sea, to whom he addressed his fiery speeches.

Everywhere, in the trenches, on ships, at parades, at meetings at the front, at social gatherings, in theaters, town-halls, Soviets —in Helsingfors, Riga, Dvinsk, Kamenets-Podolsk, Kiev, Odessa, Sebastopol—he kept speaking about the same thing and with the same enthusiasm, with sincere and unfeigned emotion. He spoke of freedom, of the land, or the brotherhood of nations, and of the imminent glowing future of the country. He called upon the soldiers and citizens to defend and conquer all this by force of arms, and show themselves worthy of the great revolution. And he pointed to himself as a guarantee that the sacrifices demanded would not be in vain, and that not one drop of free Russian blood would he shed for other, secondary goals.

Kerensky's agitation was (almost) a complete triumph for himself. Everywhere he was carried shoulder-high and pelted with flowers. Everywhere scenes of unprecedented enthusiasm took place, from the descriptions of which breathed the legendary air of heroic ages. Men flung their Crosses of St. George at the feet of Kerensky, who was calling on them to die; women stripped off their valuables and in Kerensky's name laid them on the alter of the (for some unknown reason) longed-for victory. . . .

Of course a sizeable portion of all this enthusiasm was generated by the middle classes, the officers and the philistines. But even amongst the front-line soldiers, in the very trenches, Kerensky had an enormous success. Tens and hundreds of thousands of fighting soldiers, at tremendous meetings, vowed to go into battle on the word of command and die for "Land and Freedom."

There is no doubt that the army had been roused by the agitation of this Minister, the "symbol of the revolution." The commanding officers cheered up and said good-bye to Kerensky with assurances that now the army would justify the hopes of the country. . . .

• • •

Leon Trotsky

. . . But the active and deciding role [in the October Revolution] belonged to Petersburg, and partly to its suburbs. Forces were mobilized here most of all, in the main arena of the drama.

Trotsky, tearing himself away from work on the revolutionary staff, personally rushed from the Obukhovsky plant to the Trubochny, from the Putilov to the Baltic works, from the riding-school to the barracks; he seemed to be speaking at all points simultaneously. His influence, both among the masses and on the staff, was overwhelming. He was the central figure of those days and the principal hero of this remarkable page of history. . . .

On October 21st the Petersburg garrison *conclusively acknowledged the Soviet as sole power, and the Military Revolutionary Committee as the immediate organ of authority.*

Two days earlier the District Commander had again reported to the Premier [Kerensky]: "There is no reason to think the garrison will refuse to obey the orders of the military authorities."

One could remain calm. The Winter Palace was calm. "Steps had been taken."

. . . I spent that night in the Karpovka because I had to speak the next day at noon at a mass-meeting in the People's House.

The decisive day came. The Cyclopean building of the People's House was packed to the doors with a countless throng. They filled the enormous theaters to overflowing in the expectation of mass-meetings. The foyer, buffet, and corridors were also full. Behind the scenes people kept asking me: Just what did I intend to talk about? I replied—about the "current moment," of course. Did that mean—*against the coup?* They began trying to persuade me to speak on foreign policy. After all, that was my specialty! The discussion with the organizers took on such a character I absolutely refused to speak at all. But that was no use either.

Irritated, I went out from backstage, to watch events from the hall. Trotsky was flying along the corridor towards me on to the stage. He glanced at me angrily and rushed by without any greeting. That was the first time. . . . Diplomatic relations were broken off for a long while.

The mood of the people, more than 3,000, who filled the hall was definitely tense: they were all silently waiting for something. The audience was of course primarily workers and soldiers, but more than a few typically lower-middle-class men and women were visible.

Trotsky's ovation seemed to be cut short prematurely, out of curiosity and impatience: what was he going to say? Trotsky at once began to heat up the atmosphere, with his skill and brilliance. I remember that at length and with extraordinary power he drew a picture (difficult through its simplicity) of the suffering of the trenches. Thoughts flashed through my mind of the inevitable incongruity of the parts in this oratorical whole. But Trotsky knew what he was doing. The whole point lay in the mood. The political conclusions had long been familiar. They could be condensed, as long as there were enough highlights.

Trotsky did this—with enough highlights. The Soviet regime was not only called upon to put an end to the suffering of the trenches. It would give land and heal the internal disorder. Once again the recipes against hunger were repeated: a soldier, a sailor, and a working girl, who would requisition bread from those who had it and distribute it gratis to the cities and front. But Trotsky went even further on this decisive "Day of the Petersburg Soviet."

"The Soviet government will give everything the country contains to the poor and the men in the trenches. You, bourgeois, have got two fur caps!—give one of them to the soldier, who's freezing in the trenches. Have you got warm boots? Stay at home. The worker needs your boots. . . ."

These were very good and just ideas. They could not but excite the enthusiasm of a crowd who had been reared on the tsarist whip. In any case, I certify as a direct witness that this was what was said on this last day.

All round me was a mood bordering on ecstasy. It seemed as though the crowd, spontaneously and of its own accord, would break into some religious hymn. Trotsky formulated a brief and general resolution, or pronounced some general formula like "we will defend the worker-peasant cause to the last drop of our blood."

Who was for it? The crowd of thousands, as one man, raised their hands. I saw the raised hands and burning eyes of men, women, youths, soldiers, peasants, and—typically lower-middle-class faces. Were they in spiritual transports? Did they see, through the raised curtain, a corner of the "righteous land" of their longing? Or were they penetrated by a consciousness of the *political occasion,* under the influence of the political agitation of a *Socialist?* Ask no questions! Accept it as it was. . . .

Trotsky went on speaking. The innumerable crowd went on holding their hands up. Trotsky rapped out the words: "Let this vote of yours be your vow—with all your strength and at any sacrifice to support the Soviet that has taken on itself the glorious burden of bringing to a conclusion the victory of the revolution and of giving land, bread, and peace!"

The vast crowd was holding up its hands. It agreed. It vowed. Once again, accept this as it was. With an unusual feeling of oppression I looked on at this really magnificent scene.

Trotsky finished. Someone else went out on to the stage. But there was no point in waiting and looking any more.

Throughout Petersburg more or less the same thing was going on. Everywhere there were final reviews and final vows. Thousands, tens of thousands and hundreds of thousands of people. . . . This, actually, was already an insurrection. Things had started. . . .

IRAKLI TSERETELLI

Reminiscences of the February
Revolution—The April Crisis

Irakli Tseretelli (1881–1959), a Georgian, was a central figure in the events of 1917. A Menshevik leader, he was a respected and influential member of the Executive Committee of the Petrograd Soviet and was Minister of Post and Telegraph and of the Interior (May–August 1917) in the Provisional Government.

Tseretelli's reminiscences of the February/March Revolution, carried only through the "July uprising," were published in Russian under the title *Vospominaniia o fevralskoi revolutsii*, 2 vols., The Hague, Mouton & Co., 1963.

The author was endowed with an exceptional memory. In the excerpts below, written in emigration, he gives a precise and minutely detailed account of the first crisis of the Revolution—the conflict between the Executive Committee of the Petrograd Soviet and the Provisional Government over the question of foreign policy. This conflict resulted in the resignation of two leaders, Octobrist A. I. Guchkov and Cadet P. N. Miliukov, and the formation, early in May, of a coalition government.

From *The Russian Review,* abridged from a four-part article. Vol. 14, no. 2 (April 1955), pp. 103–8; vol. 14, no. 4 (October 1955), pp. 301–21. Reprinted by courtesy of A. M. Bourguina.

On April 19 the long-awaited notification by Prince Lvov, addressed to me, at last reached the Tavrichesky Palace. I opened the envelope in the presence of Chkheidze,* Skobelev,† Dan,‡ and several other members of the Committee, and read out the text to them. We were stunned by what it contained.

The message apprised us that the Minister of Foreign Affairs [Miliukov] had directed our ambassadors accredited to allied powers to communicate the text of the address "to the citizens" [of Russia] of March 27 to the respective governments. The "address," however, was supplemented with a commentary to the effect that "the general principles stated by the Provisional Government (in its "address to the people of the world") were in full accord with the lofty ideas constantly voiced by many prominent statesmen of the allied powers," and that the Provisional Government "having abiding confidence in the victorious completion of the present war in full accord with the Allies, was firmly convinced that the problems raised by this war would be solved in such a spirit as to lay solid foundations for a lasting peace, and that the progressive democracies of the world, inspired by the same ideals, would find a way to establish the guarantees and the sanctions necessary to prevent new bloody conflicts in the future."

To understand the effect of this note upon us,** one has to conjure up the atmosphere of the revolutionary Russia of those days and the campaign then conducted by the Soviet democracy. In our appeals to the socialist parties of the world, in our press, in our resolutions and speeches addressed to the people and the army, we constantly emphasized that the declaration of the Provisional Government of March 27 was the first act, since the beginning of the war, by which one of the belligerent powers renounced all imperialistic war aims. We never tired of urging the public opinion of the democratic countries to support our initiative

* Menshevik; Chairman of the Petrograd Soviet [Ed.].
† Menshevik; member of the Executive Committee of the Petrograd Soviet [Ed.].
‡ Menshevik Soviet leader [Ed.].
** The reference to "guarantees" and "sanctions" contradicted the appeal of March 27 [Ed.].

and to compel their own governments to repudiate imperialistic aims and to work out a new platform for a general democratic peace. It was for these reasons that we had insisted on a formal note to communicate the declaration of March 27 to the Allies.

A fight against this policy of a democratic peace was being waged, both in Russia and abroad, under slogans "war to the victorious end" or "war till the establishment of sanctions and guarantees" imposed on the defeated enemy. And now, in a note ostensibly intended to elucidate the meaning of the act of March 27, Miliukov declared these very slogans, abhorrent to the revolutionary democracy,* to be those of the Provisional Government! And this note, which was nothing but a repudiation of the basic principles of the Soviets' foreign policy, was being presented to the revolutionary democracy as a compliance with its request.

The worst of it was that the note had already been dispatched, and the text had been given to the press.

If Miliukov had consciously striven to cause a rift between the Soviets and the government, he could not have used a better method than this document. This was the impression of all those present. Amazement and indignation were shared by all. Chkheidze said nothing for a long while, listening to the angry exclamations of the others. Then he turned to me and said in a low voice, with the accent of deep conviction: "Miliukov is the evil genius of the Revolution."

The news that the text of the note had been received, quickly spread through the Tavrichesky Palace, and members of the Executive Committee dropped in, one after another, to acquaint themselves with the message. Before the opening of the session a kind of improvised conference of those who were present took place.

---

* The terms "Soviet democracy" and "revolutionary democracy" frequently occurring in this article, were used in the Spring of 1917 to refer to the majority in the Soviets. The term "democracy" emphasized the fact that the majority in the Soviets at that time strove for a free, democratic state, as distinct from the Bolsheviks, who sought socialist dictatorship. At the same time, the terms "Soviet" and "revolutionary" served to emphasize that the Soviet majority wished to disassociate itself from the bourgeois democratic parties. One reason for that was that the latter had not taken part in the revolutionary struggle to overthrow the autocracy; nor had they advanced any program of radical democratic changes. It was the lack of such a program which had rallied the masses of workers, soldiers, and peasants around the Soviets from the outset of the Revolution.

In an animated exchange of opinions not only the members of the left-wing opposition but also some of the majority characterized the note as a provocation, an act of defiance. Feelings were running high. Skobelev, myself, and some others tried in vain to soothe the rising passions. Eager to hear some reassuring information, Bramson asked me whether in my opinion, based on my experience in negotiating with the government, the note had been phrased as it was on purpose, in order to disavow the policy of the Soviet democracy.

To this I replied that, in my judgment, the only member of the government actually intent on opposing a government foreign policy to that of the Soviets, was Miliukov. As for the majority of the ministers, they had, in all our negotiations, displayed the desire to establish a line of conduct in harmony with ours. This being the case, I said, I can explain the adoption of this text by the government only as an act of amazing thoughtlessness on the part of the majority of its members. Very likely Miliukov, with his usual insistence, had kept hammering on the theme that his consent to communicate to the Allies the declaration of March 27 in a formal note was already an enormous concession to Soviet democracy, in which he had acquiesced with great reluctance; and probably as a compensation for this concession he had obtained the assent of the others to the inclusion of his commentary. The other ministers may have assumed that the gratification of our desire to have the "Address" transmitted to the Allies would make us ready to accept the accompanying commentary, to which they apparently had failed to give their close attention.

"All these misunderstandings," said one of the left-wing members of the Executive Committee, "are only possible because we fail to use our full voice in talking to the government. Why has the contact commission failed up to now to urge the government to submit to the Allies the issue of a democratic peace as it was formulated by the Soviet manifesto of March 14?"

"I understand your displeasure with the note," replied Skobelev. "Still, we should not run to extremes. When the Soviet was drawing up its Manifesto, it had to consider only the Russian Revolution, the Russian wide-gauge track. The government, on the other hand, in addressing itself to foreign governments through diplomatic channels, has to keep in mind the conditions in foreign countries, the foreign narrow-gauge track. The cause of a general peace encounters obstacles in the public opinion of these countries, obstacles the Russian Revolution will have to overcome gradually, step by step, if it wants to avoid a collapse. What we find unacceptable in Miliukov's note is not the consideration of existing difficulties but the fact that these difficulties are used as a pretext to substitute the imperialistic slogans for those of the Russian Revolution."

By then most members of the Executive Committee had arrived, and Chkheidze opened the meeting in an atmosphere of extreme tension.

The excitement was due to the awareness that a crisis was imminent. There were no differences of opinion with regard to the note. All were agreed that it could not be accepted by the Executive Committee as satisfactory. The debate, therefore, centered on the question of ways and means to solve the conflict.

At that time the spokesmen for the left-wing opposition were still the Internationalists, to whom the Bolshevik fraction of the Executive Committee [readily] left the initiative of extremist proposals. The Internationalist Yurenev now took the floor to deliver a forceful speech. He insisted that the note had exposed the utter uselessness of negotiations with the government; now was the time for the masses to step in; an appeal to the masses should be our reply to the provocation of the government. Mass action alone would reveal to the government and to the whole world the true will of the Russian Revolution.

Shliapnikov, then a left-wing Bolshevik, also insisted on an appeal to the masses. His spiteful comments on Miliukov and the whole Provisional Government were marked by a deep-rooted class hatred of the bourgeoisie.

But even among the leading majority of the Executive Committee the resentment was so great that some of its members could see no other way out than to call on the masses to demonstrate against the government. Bogdanov,* normally even-tempered and unruffled, yet capable of impulsive speech and action under stress, was beside himself with rage. Miliukov's note, he said, strikes a blow first of all against us, the representatives of the majority of the Executive Committee. Direct negotiations between the Executive Committee and the Provisional Government have no longer any justification.

* B. O. Bogdanov was a Menshevik member of the Executive Committee of the Petrograd Soviet [Ed.].

The time has come for the masses to go into action. Their appearance on the scene is the only thing that would have any real influence on the government.

Members of the Labor Group (Trudoviki) Stankevich and Bramson tried to soothe the storm. There was no need, they said, to exaggerate the importance of the accompanying note. After all, the full text of the declaration of March 27, which contained the repudiation of imperialistic war aims, had been officially communicated to the allied governments. Those acquainted with the situation inside the government realize that Miliukov's commentary was but another of his misplaced stratagems and in no way reflected the views of the government as a whole. Bramson pointed out that even Miliukov's best friends regarded him as a "genius of tactlessness." Was it permissible, because of the tactlessness of a single minister, to gamble with the fate of the national Revolution?

Kamenev, who better than Shliapnikov represented the then dominant tactics of the Bolshevik organization, made a plain attempt to release the Bolsheviks from the responsibility for an eventual call to the masses. Miliukov's note, he said, only served to confirm what the Bolshevik party had maintained all along: that not a democratic peace but "war to the victorious end" was the true slogan of the bourgeoisie. Miliukov and his colleagues were representatives of that class and unable to carry out a different policy. An anti-imperialist policy could be put into effect only after the removal of the present government and its replacement by a government of the revolutionary democrary. The Executive Committee was opposed to this. If some of its members were now supporting an appeal to the masses, they were doing this with the purpose to compel a bourgeois government to carry out policies alien to it. The Bolsheviks had no such illusions. However, should a majority of the Executive Committee decide in favor of such an appeal, the Bolsheviks would support it in a body, since street demonstrations are the best school for the political education of the masses and the best method to pave the way for the replacement of the bourgeois government by one of the revolutionary democracy.

Of the members of the contact commission, Chernov* and Sukhanov† were absent. On behalf of the three members present,

* SR leader in the Soviet [Ed.].

†Journalist, at one time an SR, later a United Internationalist, author of *Zapiski o revolutsii* [Ed.].

Chkheidze, Skobelev, and myself, I declared that, in principle, there could be no disagreement about the evaluation of the note; it was a clear violation of the agreement which had made possible our co-operation in foreign policy with the government. The government ought to give us some tangible satisfaction, to show to the nation and to the world that its foreign policy still followed the line laid down by the declaration of March 27 and not that of Miliukov's accompanying note.

Yet as regards the appeal to the masses, I went on, we disagree not only with the Bolsheviks, who plan to use street demonstrations for their propaganda ends, but also with those among our comrades who have no intention to overthrow the government yet are willing to urge the masses to fight against it. In the present tense and emotional atmosphere it is not difficult to arouse the masses against the government; yet it is very doubtful whether these energies once released could be kept under control and from developing into a civil war. Soviet democracy is certainly strong enough to overthrow the government; yet it possesses neither enough solid influence with all circles of the population nor enough trained democratic cadres to organize on its own a government that would be indisputably recognized by the majority of the nation and would be able to ensure the fulfilment of the pressing economic and political needs of the country.

This is the situation, I continued, and it compels us to act with caution. Even more so it compels the Provisional Government to proceed cautiously, since it knows that without the support of the Soviets it cannot exist. This being so, we have every reason to presume that even without calling the masses into action we shall be able to make the government comply with the demands we are going to submit to it.

For all these reasons I proposed that, before issuing an appeal to the masses, we attempt to settle the conflict through new negotiations with the government. This proposition, supported by Dan* and Gots,† was adopted by the majority.

Nevertheless, the conflict with the government had come to a head, and the consequences of this fact soon became manifest. . . .

---

*Menshevik Soviet leader [Ed.].
† Member of Central Committee and the Combat Organization of the SR party [Ed.].

During the April demonstrations the chief task of the authorities, the restoration of order, had been performed not by the government but by the Soviet. And to achieve this end, the Soviet had had to resort to extraordinary measures which involved the assumption of certain functions of the executive power.

So long as the crisis lasted and only the energetic action by the Executive Committee appeared able to check the street fighting that might have developed into a civil war, the intrusion of the Soviet into the functions of the government, far from being denounced, was generally welcomed by public opinion and by the Provisional Government itself. As soon as the conflict was settled, however, the problem of strengthening the government was more urgent than ever before.

Even before the April events public opinion had been watching with growing anxiety the increasingly frequent outbreaks of violence and lawlessness in many parts of the vast country already deeply disturbed by the Revolution. In all such cases, whether it was a matter of Anarchists seizing a printing shop, of a military unit refusing to obey orders, or of some provincial committee deciding to declare itself an independent revolutionary authority, the government usually had recourse to the Soviet as an intermediary, relying on this authoritative democratic organization to restore order through moral pressure. Yet, while public opinion prior to the April crisis, had more or less acquiesced in such a situation, accounting for it by the reluctance of the government to use coercion without extreme necessity, now, after the events had exposed the government's impotence, every new manifestation of lawlessness caused a deep sense of alarm. The creation of a strong central power was now demanded by people of every political persuasion.

The democratic section of public opinion regarded a closer bond between the government and the democratic organizations, together with a better coordination between its policies and the aspirations of the revolutionary democracy, as the best way to strengthen the government. Accordingly, a considerable part of this democratic public opinion now demanded, with growing insistency, that the Executive Committee participate in the government.

This trend was strongest in the army organizations. On April 23, at the Tavrichesky Palace, a meeting was organized, composed of delegates from regimental and battalion committees of the Petrograd garrison, to discuss the issue of the attitude to be taken towards the Provisional Government, Bogdanov, addressing the assembly on behalf of the Executive Committee, informed the audience of the settlement of the conflict and of the decision of the Executive Committee to resume its former relationship with the Provisional Government. Yet despite the high prestige of the Executive Committee among the delegates, the majority of the speakers recommended that the former policy be replaced by one of direct participation in the government. A resolution was adopted, expressing the wish "that the Executive Committee submit the problem of the relations between the democrary and the Provisional Government to the assemblies of workers and soldiers for discussion, and that the Executive Committee formulate its opinion regarding the formation of a coalition Cabinet."

This resolution reflected the frame of mind of a large element of the democrary. From every part of the country and of the front, from army organizations and peasants' soviets, a flood of letters and telegrams poured into the Executive Committee, all voicing the desire for a coalition government. Some of the frontline and peasants' organizations went so far as to send special delegations to present this demand to the Executive Committee. This campaign found a favorable response inside the Executive Committee, not only among the Laborites (Trudoviki) and the People's Socialists, who all along had advocated coalition, but also among the Socialist Revolutionaries.

The Provisional Government, on the other hand, was showered with similar demands for the formation of a coalition government, coming from left-wing bourgeois groups, local self-government agencies, the liberal intelligentsia, the civil service, and the officer body.

Once, during those days, I was stopped in the lobby of the Tavrichesky Palace by V. N. Lvov, Procurator of the Holy Synod. He was smiling benignly and seemed greatly pleased by the change in the public mood. Ever since the beginning of the Revolution, he told me, he had advocated the inclusion of Soviet representatives in the government. "Up to now," he said, "you have opposed it. However, the matter can no longer be postponed. It is impossible to govern Russia without the Soviet democracy. Today this is generally understood. Yesterday some young officers from the staff of the Petrograd military district called on us at the Mariinsky Palace and urged us to accept any compromise, provided the Soviets help us to maintain discipline in the army and in the rear. They don't want Guchkov,* they don't want Miliukov, all they want is a government enjoying the confidence of the nation. We in the government," continued Lvov, "feel the same way. Come to us with your program, it makes sense, we accept it. But you must join us in the government."

V. N. Lvov went on in that vein for a long time, and from his words it became apparent that Guchkov and Miliukov, who both were opposed to a closer tie with the Soviet, were completely isolated in the government. Listening to him, I recalled a remark once made about him by Prince Lvov in conversation with Skobelev and myself: "V. N. Lvov does not rack his brains about program issues," Prince Lvov had said with a twinkle in his eye, "but he is very useful to the government. He is the most sociable of men, with an extraordinary range of connections. He has an infallible flair for the trends of public opinion."

V. N. Lvov, indeed, reflected the sentiments of the man in the street like a barometer.

However, the temper of the right section of public opinion was vastly different.

The right-wing bourgeoisie used the anxiety caused by the April events as a starting point for a political attack on the Soviet. For the first time since the beginning of the Revolution, these circles thought the moment opportune for an open, large-scale, organized campaign to provoke a rift between the government and the Soviet. Dismayed not only by the weakness of the government but also by the general direction of its domestic and foreign policies pursued in agreement with the Soviet, these elements, under the guise of opposition to a "diarchy," demanded the elimination of any kind of political control over the Provisional Government. The disorganization of the national life, resulting from a devastating war and the collapse of the old order, they attributed solely to the influence of the Soviet democracy, which they also held accountable for the general yearning for peace, both at the front and in the rear. To counteract the policy of cooperation with the Soviet, these groups, led by the Committee of the Imperial Duma, advocated, as a means of strengthening the government, the adoption by the latter of the

---

* Octobrist; War Minister in the First Provisional Government [Ed.].

program of the rightist bourgeoisie with its militant slogan of "war to the victorious end."

In conformity with this point of view, a prominent member of the Cadet Party, Professor Kokoshkin, submitted to the government the draft of an "Address to the Country," in which the government was to ascribe to the Soviet responsibility for the crisis and was to solicit support, in the administration of the country, from the social elements not connected with the Soviet democracy.

This proposition was vigorously opposed by the majority of the ministers. Not only Kerensky, Nekrasov, and Tereshchenko, who represented the left wing of the Provisional Government, but also Prince Lvov, supported by Konovalov, V. N. Lvov, and Godnev, refused to break with the Soviet democracy. Nekrasov, who kept me informed about the situation inside the government, told me that even the Cadet ministers closest to Miliukov, Manuilov, and Shingaryov, objected to this version of an address to the nation which meant a rupture with the democratic organizations born of the Revolution.

The coming governmental crisis came into the open with the publication, on April 26, of the official version of the "Address of the Provisional Government to the Country." It declared that the Provisional Government had decided to seek a solution of the crisis, as desired by democratic public opinion, by inviting representatives of the Soviet to join the government.

I shall quote here a few passages of this "Address," vividly reflecting the moral atmosphere of that first period of the Revolution. The "Address" began with the enumeration of all the acts of the government in the domestic and foreign fields undertaken in agreement with the Soviet democracy. Next came the following description of the administrative methods applied by the first government of revolutionary Russia:

> Called into life by a great national movement, the Provisional Government regards itself as the executor and guardian of the people's will. It bases the administration of the state not on force and coercion but on the voluntary obedience of free citizens to the authority created by them. It relies not on physical but on moral force. Ever since the Provisional Government has been established in power, it has not once deviated from these principles. Not a single drop of the people's blood has been shed through its fault, nor has it set up forcible obstacles to any trend of public thought.

This benign, idealistic faith in the possibility of replacing the coercive functions of power by moral persuasion was characteristic of the initial period of the Revolution, and even the right-wing elements did not reject it at the time. The February upheaval had been christened "the bloodless revolution," and all new Russia took pride in the fact that the downfall of the centuries-old tsarist order had been so painless, without the streams of blood that had accompanied all former revolutions. Not only the socialists but also the bourgeois democracy cherished the hope that a democracy would be able to govern the nation without recourse to the repressive measures identified in the public mind with the tyrannical methods of the past, now loathed by all. For the time being even the rightists had reconciled themselves to this attitude, all the more so because this position of the new authorities had saved the representatives of the old regime, now in the hands of the government, from stern retaliation.

In discussing the text of the "Address," the government had regarded as debatable, not the statement about the new administrative methods quoted above, but that part of the text which dealt with the difficulties faced by the government in the task of maintaining law and order: the anarchic activities of certain groups and the violations of democratic discipline. The initial draft, as drawn up by Professor Kokoshkin, ascribed the responsibility for such acts to the Soviets, accusing them of trying to undermine the authority of the government. However, the majority of the ministers, overruling the objections of Guchkov and Miliukov, eliminated these attacks on the Soviets from the government's final version and replaced them with the following objective description of the difficulties and dangers confronting the Revolution:

> Unfortunately, the cause of freedom is greatly endangered by the fact that the formation of new social ties that would hold the nation together lags behind the process of disintegration caused by the collapse of the old political system. Under these conditions, and after the repudiation of the old coercive methods of government as well as of the external artificial devices formerly employed to raise the prestige of the authorities, the difficulties of the task that has fallen to the Provisional Government threaten to become insuperable.
>
> The elemental striving of various social groups to realize their desires and their claims, as it is now increasingly displayed by ever less conscious and less organized layers of the population, threatens to destroy the civic cohesion and discipline. It creates a favorable soil, on the one

hand, for acts of violence sowing the seeds of bitterness and enmity to the new order among those injured by them, and, on the other, for the growth of special interests and aspirations to the prejudice of the general interest, as well as for the evasion of the duties of citizenship.

The Provisional Government considers it its duty to declare plainly and unequivocally that such a situation makes it extremely difficult to govern the country and threatens, as it further develops, to lead the nation to internal disorganization and to defeat at the front.

Russia is faced with the frightful specter of internecine war and anarchy, threatening freedom with destruction. There is a somber and grievous road well known to the history of nations—the road leading from freedom, through civil war and anarchy, to reaction and the return of despotism. This road should not be that of the Russian people.

The "Address" concluded with a call to the citizens to support the authority of the government through example and persuasion and with the announcement, in the following terms, of the government's decision to invite representatives of the Soviet to join it:

The government, on its part, will resume, with greater determination, its efforts to enlarge its membership, by including those active creative forces of the nation which up to now have taken no direct and immediate part in the administration of the country, to join in the responsible governmental work.

The "Address" was received with notable approval by the greater part of the public. Within the majority of the Executive Committee opinions varied regarding the expediency of joining the government: the Socialist Revolutionaries were in favor of it, the Social Democrats were against. There was agreement, however, about the necessity to respond to the government's step with an expression of confidence and with actions intended to strengthen its authority.

Within the Cadet Party the differences of opinion were more substantial. While the Moscow City Council, on the motion of its Cadet members led by Astrov, went on record in favor of a coalition government, the newspaper *Rech,* inspired by Miliukov, warned against illusions about a coalition: "It is quite possible," wrote the Cadet organ, "that the disease requires a more radical treatment," implying with these words a break with the Soviets and the formation of a strong dictatorial power based on the propertied classes.

This rightist trend found its most effective expression the day after the publication of the "Address," at the anniversary meeting of the Imperial Duma.

The 27th of April was the eleventh anniversary of the convocation of the First Duma. The Committee of the Imperial Duma, headed by the president of the Fourth Duma, Rodzianko, decided to celebrate the day by a solemn meeting of members of the four Dumas at the Tavrichesky Palace, in the "White Hall," former assembly room of the Duma. The declared purpose of the meeting was the discussion of the national issues brought to the fore by the crisis. At the same time the organizers of the anniversary meeting wished to remind the country of the Duma and of the part it had played in the overthrow of tsarism. The public reaction to this would enable them to estimate whether there was a chance that a resurrected Duma— with a bourgeois majority—might become an authoritative permanent organ, to exercise political control over the government in place of the Soviet.

The meeting, coinciding with a moment of general anxiety, aroused keen interest both in the country and beyond its borders. The Provisional Government, led by Prince Lvov, as well as representatives of allied and neutral powers were present. The Executive Committee attended in a body, occupying the box of the Imperial Council. The visitors' gallery was crowded to overflowing, mostly with members of the Petrograd Soviet.

Rodzianko was in the chair. He opened the session with a program speech in which he described the role of the Duma in the overthrow of the old regime and the establishment of the new democratic system. Underscoring in this way the solidarity of the Duma with the Revolution and avoiding any direct criticism of the Soviet, he yet emphasized two basic points on which there was a divergence of opinion between the rightist groups and the Soviets. In foreign policy, he repudiated the campaign for a democratic peace in favor of the old slogan of war to the end, "until full victory over German militarism." In the domestic field, Rodzianko demanded that the Provisional Government be freed from any political control over it: "The country must give its full confidence and voluntary obedience to the single power it has created and which for that reason it has to trust. Active interference in the decisions of the government is inadmissible. The Provisional Government will be unable to fulfill its functions unless it has at its disposal all the might and strength of the supreme power in the state."

These two salient points: the endowment of the Provisional Government with the fullness of power and the restoration of the old war aims, were the recurring theme of all the right-wing speakers at the meeting. They avoided outright polemics against the Soviet democracy; yet the gist of all their speeches was the contention that the salvation of the country was dependent on the elimination of the influence of the Soviet democracy on policy-making, especially in the field of foreign affairs.

The address of Prince Lvov, who spoke on behalf of the Provisional Government, revealed a very different frame of mind. With great political tact he abstained from putting before the assembly the issue of the governmental crisis, which had been so forcefully and candidly expounded in the Government's "Address to the Country" the day before. Prince Lvov spoke of the spiritual essence of the Russian Revolution and made it unequivocally clear that the government of revolutionary Russia would not seek the salvation of the country in the methods recommended by the rightist speakers. With particular force he defended, in the terms of the Slavophile philosophy close to his heart, the orientation of the foreign policy towards a general democratic peace. . . .

The speech of Prince Lvov, obviously intended to stress the inner accord between the policies of the government and the aspirations of the Soviet democracy, had no effect whatever on the right-wing speakers who followed him. Only when speaking of the past, of the Duma's opposition to the old regime, of its part in the February events, and of the first days of the Revolution, did they sound conciliatory notes towards the Revolution. But as soon as the acknowledged leaders of the Duma, Rodichev, Shulgin, Guchkov, and others, touched upon current policies, all the fire of their eloquence was directed against the revolutionary democracy. The culminating point of their attack on the Soviet's policies was the speech by Shulgin.

Shulgin was one of the most eminent and original orators of the Duma. Speaking, now with wistful lyricism, now with irony and restrained passion, he recounted how, under the effect of the defeat of 1915 and the manifest inability of the old system to cope with the situation, he and some other rightist Duma members had sought a rapprochement with the opposition and, together with the whole body of the Duma, had taken part in the overthrow of the old order. "We cannot disavow the Revolution," he said, "we are linked with it, we are welded to it, and for this we bear the moral responsibility." Yet these admissions were made only to give stronger empha-

sis to the "grievous doubts" with which Shulgin and his friends
regarded the system that had emerged from the Revolution. "Despite all the achievements of Russia in these two months," he
continued, "the question arises whether Germany may not have
made the greater gains. Why is this so? What are the reasons for
it? For one thing, the honest and talented government, which we
should like to see invested with the plenitude of power, is in reality
powerless because it is treated with suspicion. A sentry stationed
to watch it was instructed: 'Look out, these are bourgeois, keep a
sharp eye on them, and if anything happens, you know your regulations.' Gentlemen, on the 20th of April you had occasion to see
for yourselves that the sentry knows his regulations and performs
his duty faithfully. Yet it is questionable whether those who have
assigned the sentry to his post have done right."

In the same sarcastic, impersonal way, without naming the
Soviets directly, Shulgin subjected to ruthless criticism the whole
system of the mutual relationship between the government and the
Soviet and intimated that the Soviet influence was a source of anarchy and would finally wreck the state. He listed various features
of the Soviet foreign and domestic policy, presenting them in an
utterly distorted form. Parodying Miliukov's famous speech against
Stürmer and the Tsarina, he asked after each of his charges against
the Soviets, "what is it, stupidity or treason?" He gave the answer
himself: "Each of these actions taken separately is an act of stupidity, but taken all together they add up to treason."

Shulgin formulated his accusations without asperity, always in
the same ironic manner, and without ever mentioning the Soviets
directly. "Demonstrations are being organized against imperialist
war aims," he went on, "peace at any price is being preached,
soldiers are being incited against their officers. Isn't this the best
way to set us at odds with our Allies and to disorganize the army?
Agitators are being sent to the villages, where they create anarchy
and confusion. Is it not plain that the only result will be to leave
Petrograd, Moscow, the army, and the northern provinces without
bread?"

The remarkable thing about this speech was the fact that Shulgin, in voicing these charges, chose to completely ignore the conditions created by the war and the break-up of the old order. He
forgot that the revolutionary intelligentsia at the head of the Soviet
organizations enjoyed the confidence of the army only because of its

peace program, which reflected the yearnings of the masses at the front and in the rear; and that these leaders had used this confidence not only to promote the political peace campaign but also to restore discipline in the army and to prevent the front from disintegrating. He forgot that if the struggle against agrarian violence was having any success, this was due entirely to the revolutionary democracy, which, in defending organized land reform, set the full weight of its authority against the spontaneous, lawless acts of the peasantry.

When I interrupted Shulgin from the floor to ask to whom he was directing his accusations, he still did not name the Soviets but referred to "people from the Petrogradskaya Side"* acting "under the label of Lenin."

At that moment, however, his assertions were wrong even with respect to Lenin, since the latter, aware of the general hostility to him in the ranks of the revolutionary democracy, had been compelled to disclaim the idea of a separate peace and was still hesitating to incite the masses to violence, waiting for the time when the majority of the democracy would be won over to the principle of dictatorship.

Yet these circumstances had no significance for Shulgin. Actually he aimed his arrows above Lenin's head at the foe he considered most dangerous, the democracy. After all, Lenin was only preaching dictatorship, while the Soviet democracy, as Shulgin and his set saw it, was already practicing dictatorship in what seemed to them the worst possible form.

Shulgin's vivid and forceful speech, interpreted by the audience precisely in this sense, made a strong impression. The majority of the deputies and a part of the public in the gallery gave him a prolonged, tumultuous ovation.

I took the floor immediately after Shulgin, and my appearance on the rostrum was used by the leftist sector of the Duma and the democratically minded public in the boxes and the gallery to give an even more enthusiastic ovation for the Soviet democracy.

To show how we put our case against the right-wing bourgeoisie

---

* One of the main sections of Petrograd in which was located the villa of the well-known ballerina Kshesinskaya. This spacious villa was seized by the Bolsheviks at the beginning of the Revolution and became the headquarters of the Bolshevik Party [Ed.].

before the nation, I shall quote here the essential passages from the stenographic record of my speech:

I shall begin with replying to all the questions put here by Deputy Shulgin. (Applause.) This was his first question: "Does our Provisional Government, whose integrity is doubted by none, possess the fullness of power? Are we not witnessing the spectacle of the sapping of its power, with sentries posted at the door of the Provisional Government and told: 'These are bourgeois, be on the lookout!'" Gentlemen, to this I can reply with the words of a member of the Provisional Government, N. V. Nekrasov who asks the meaning of "fullness of power." This is what Nekrasov said: "The Russian people have not overthrown one autocrat in order to install twelve autocrats in power." And before making charges against all those who refuse to regard the Provisional Government as a group of twelve irresponsible autocrats, Deputy Shulgin should have asked the Provisional Government itself how it views its situation. I know, gentlemen, that in the circles to which Shulgin belongs recriminations are heard not only against the "Petrogradskaya Side" but also against the organ that embodies the Russian Revolution, the Soviet of Workers' and Soldiers' Deputies. The Soviet stands for control over the Provisional Government because, as a powerful democratic organization, it expresses the yearnings of the broad masses of the population: the working class, the revolutionary army, and the peasantry. The position of the Provisional Government would have been immensely difficult, and at the moment of the Revolution it would have been unable to cope with its task, were it not for this control, were it not for this contact with the democratic elements. (Applause.) The member of the Duma, Shulgin, has said: "You are telling the people — these are bourgeois, keep them under suspicion." There is some truth in this sentence. We do tell the people: "these are bourgeois, this is the responsible organ of the bourgeoisie, the Provisional Government; but to this we add: this is that organ of the bourgeoisie, these are those representatives of the bourgeoisie who have accepted a general democratic platform, who have agreed to defend Russian freedom together with the entire democracy and have decided to make common cause with the democracy." (Stormy applause.)

Gentlemen, when we survey the work of the four Imperial Dumas, we note one common feature, their impotence, their utter helplessness in the field of constructive statesmanship, a helplessness to which Deputy Shulgin has called attention. Many have tried to lay a finger on the cause of that impotence. There were frictions, they have said, differences of opinion. Of course, there were differences in the Duma; they reflected the differences in the nation, and these differences have been a cause of the failure of all previous revolutionary attempts. But, gentlemen, I wish to call your attention to the following: the left-wing section representing the democracy, the proletariat, and the revolutionary peasantry, that section knew how to combine its class interests with a general democratic platform acceptable to the whole nation, and it has called the bourgeoisie to take its stand on the common democratic platform. And if the bourgeoisie at first failed to respond to this call, it was not because this step would have required it to renounce its class interests, no, it only required it to realize these interests by revolutionary means. Today, in the brilliant light of the Russian Revolution, it has become manifest that this platform is the only one capable of rallying all the live forces of the nation. And so, gentlemen, all the aims of the Russian Revolution, and even its very fate, are dependent on whether the propertied classes will understand that this is a national platform and not one of the proletariat alone. The proletariat, to be sure, has its own ultimate class aims, yet for the sake of the common democractic platform, for which the conditions are already ripe, it abstains for the present from the realization of its own ultimate class aims. Will the propertied classes be able to rise to this level? Will they be able to renounce their narrow group interests and take their stand on the common national democratic platform? (Applause.)

From this general standpoint I dealt with all the questions raised by Shulgin.

Concerning the agrarian violence and the land seizures by the peasants, which Shulgin, without naming the Soviets, had nevertheless attributed to the influence of Soviet agitators, I reminded the audience that the demand for the transfer of the land to the peasantry was by no means a partisan-socialist demand of the Soviets but a national claim of long standing, raised by the Russian democracy whenever it had had the opportunity to speak out freely. While pressing this demand, I said, the Soviets were using their immense authority to impress on the peasants the necessity to carry out this radical land reform in an organized way, through a decision of the Constituent Assembly and not through illegal seizures. Only in the cases of landowners refusing to sow their fields, did the Soviets call for extraordinary measures accomplished not in an arbitrary way, but in full accord with the agencies of the government and the organs of the democracy.

As for the peace campaign which, according to Shulgin, was the primary cause of the disintegration of the army, I reminded the assembly that this campaign was being conducted in agreement with the army organizations which were the sole factor holding the army together since the collapse of the old order. I pointed out that given the general longing for peace, the fighting capacity and discipline of the army that we were striving to strengthen could be maintained only if the troops could be convinced that the government was doing everything in its power to bring closer the conclusion of a general democratic peace.

I quoted the words spoken a moment before by Prince Lvov who stressed the aspirations of the liberated Russian people towards the achievement of democratic aims in domestic as well as foreign policies. I welcomed this declaration of the head of the Provisional Government and I said:

> I am deeply convinced that so long as the government persists in this course, so long as it states the aims of the war in accordance with the expectations of the Russian people, the position of the Provisional Government will be stable and "the people from the Petrogradskaya-Side" mentioned by Shulgin will not be able to shake it, nor will the irresponsible elements of the bourgeoisie, which do not recoil from a civil war, succeed in undermining it. (Applause.) Deputy Shulgin has spoken of the anxious days we have just lived through. He has tried to lay the responsibility for those anxious days at the door of "the people from the Petrogradskaya-Side." I shall have something to say about those people later, but now to you I say this: It was the slogans put forward here by Deputy Shulgin, it was precisely these slogans that nearly touched off a civil war; and the Provisional Government displayed extraordinary, statesmanlike wisdom, an extraordinary understanding of the historical moment, when it issued the clarification of its note so as to preclude any possible misinterpretation.

I told Shulgin that his own position on the main issues of foreign and domestic policy was evidence neither of stupidity nor of treason, but of narrow vision, limited by class prejudice, which prevented him from realizing that propaganda against the democracy was the surest way to strengthen Lenin and his party.

I went on to say, alluding to Lenin's behavior during the April events, that Shulgin's allegation that Lenin had been inciting violence was false. I said:

> Lenin conducts a campaign based on ideas and principles, and his propaganda feeds on the irresponsible public utterances of Deputy Shulgin and many others from among the so-called moderate propertied elements. This, of course, makes a certain section of the democracy

despair of the possibility of an understanding with the bourgeoisie. Lenin's platform is this: Since there exists such a trend in the ranks of the bourgeoisie, since the bourgeoisie is unable to understand the general national exigencies of the moment, it should be eliminated, and the Soviet of Workers' and Soldiers' Deputies should assume the full power. You may dispute Lenin, you may disagree with him. I myself disagree with him since I am deeply convinced that the ideas of Deputy Shulgin cannot be those of the Russian bourgeoisie. But if I did believe for a moment that these ideas are shared by the entire propertied class, I should have said that there is no other way in Russia to save the conquests of the national revolution than the desperate attempt to proclaim at once the dictatorship of the proletariat and the peasantry. For it is these ideas that involve the only real threat of a civil war. If they should triumph within the Provisional Government, this would be the signal for a civil war.

I concluded with the expression of my faith that the victory and the consolidation of the all-national revolution in Russia would awaken the forces of a democratic revolution in the whole world:

> In my opinion, citizens, members of the Imperial Duma, the present meeting should not create the impression that there is confusion in the ranks of the bourgeoisie, that there is vacillation, that there is a conspiracy in the ranks of the bourgeoisie with the purpose of driving the Provisional Government to irresponsible acts, for I maintain that this would be the first step toward wrecking the Russian Revolution, and wrecking the country itself. Let the Provisional Government continue on the road of understanding it has chosen; let it pursue the ideals of democracy with increased determination, both in its internal and in its foreign policy. If it does this, the democracy will support this revolutionary Provisional Government with the whole strength and weight of its authority, and in a concerted effort of all the live forces of the nation we shall carry our revolution to completion and maybe spread it to the whole world. (Stormy applause at the left and in the center.)

I have never cherished any illusions regarding my oratorical gifts. In the Duma the flower of the Russian intelligentsia was represented, and many of its members in the audience, had, of course, a greater mastery of the spoken word than I. Nonetheless a truthful account of what the revolutionary democracy was striving for and was doing in order to save the country made a stronger impression on the audience than the well-polished oratory of the speakers who opposed our point of view. It is for this reason that my speech called forth quite an unusual ovation, from not only the

left-wing section of the Duma, the members of the Executive Committee, and the Soviet, but also from many of that part of the
audience which had cheered Shulgin. Rightist Duma members
whom I did not know were coming up to me to shake hands. The
next day, a bourgeois newspaper with a wide circulation, the
Russkaya Volya, devoted an editorial to my speech, expressing
the view that the salvation of Russia should be sought not in the
course of action advocated by the rightist speakers but in that pursued by the leading majority of the Executive Committee.

Let me note, however, two harshly critical comments on my
speech. One came from the American Consul, Winship. In a report
to the Secretary of State on the anniversary meeting of the Duma,
he denounced my views on foreign policy and voiced the opinion
that the "sectarian spirit and fanaticism" of the socialists, which
he saw reflected in my "fervent defense of Lenin," represented
"the greatest danger to Russia at the present moment." "Tseretelli," wrote the American Consul, "had often delivered fiery
speeches against Lenin and his ideas in the Soviet of Workers'
and Soldiers' Deputies, yet he proved ready to defend Lenin's cause
against the spokesman of the bourgeoisie."*

The other sharp criticism, for opposite motives, came from
Lenin himself. In an article entitled "I. G. Tseretelli and the Class
Struggle," Lenin argued that in assenting to an agreement with a
part of the bourgeoisie I had abandoned the principle of class
struggle, and in characterizing the dictatorship of the proletariat
and the peasantry as a "desperate attempt" I had betrayed the
principles of democracy.†

At the close of the session Guchkov put in an appearance and
unexpectedly took the floor for a speech that proved his farewell
address, for two days later he left the government. Guchkov delivered, or, rather, read his address with intense emotion. With
his usual forceful eloquence he expressed his yearning for a strong
executive power, his dissatisfaction with everything that had been
erected on the ruins of the old order, and his unwillingness to understand the new aspirations and needs of the country. He failed,
however, to indicate a way out of the existing situation; he could
not have done it, since it was clear that any real basis for the establishment of a bourgeois dictatorship did not exist.

*Papers Relating to the Foreign Relations of the United States. *Russia,* vol. I,
pp. 59–60.
† *Pravda,* April 29, 1917.

This first open attack on the Soviets by the right-wing bourgeoisie did not find the sympathetic public response expected by those who initiated it. Of the two political flanks, the wealthy bourgeoisie on the one side and the Soviet democracy on the other, the middle classes still overwhelmingly preferred the Soviets.

The general interest of the nation continued to be centered on the problem of a reorganization of the government that would ensure for it the greatest possible support by the Soviet democracy.

The position of Kerensky within the government had become very difficult. During the April events he had remained in the background, being unable either to prevent or to mitigate the conflict between the government and the Soviet democracy.

Now, with the other left-wing members of the government, he favored the formation of a coalition and he informed the leaders of the Socialist Revolutionary Party, Chernov and Gots, that he was determined to resign unless the coalition were put into effect.

On the day the government's "Address to the Country" was published, Kerensky issued a letter, composed for him by Chernov, in which he declared that, having joined the government on his own responsibility, in order to serve as a connecting link between the government and the democracy of the laboring classes, he no longer could remain in the government without a formal mandate. The national situation, he wrote, had become so complicated, and the forces of the organized labor democracy had grown to such an extent, that this democracy might no longer be able to avoid responsible participation in the government of the country.

During the first months of the February Revolution, Kerensky had enjoyed an immense, giddy popularity. In the Fourth Duma, he had been the leader of the small group of Laborites (Trudoviki) but after the Revolution he declared that he always considered himself a member of the Socialist Revolutionary Party. At the decisive moment of the Revolution, when the rebellious regiments were marching to the Duma, Kerensky, with characteristic impulsiveness, was instantly fired with such a faith in the victory of the Revolution that he went out to meet the soldiers and declared his solidarity with them in the name of the Duma. He was elected vice-chairman of the Petrograd Soviet and was regarded by the rank and file of the soldiers as closely connected with the Soviet and with a socialist party. Actually, though nominally a member of the Socialist Revolutionary Party, he was by nature a non-partisan individualist. In his views he was less close to the social-

ists than to the democratic intelligentsia on the borderline between
the socialist and the bourgeois democracy. In the excited atmosphere of the Revolution, his speeches, rather vague, yet echoing
the thoughts and feelings of both these groups, aroused a strong
enthusiasm at the mass meetings of the soldiers as well as among
the plain people outside the Soviets.

Kerensky had the ambition of being a national figure above the
parties. It is a curious fact that this man, whose name became
the synonym of a weak, spineless government, had a pronounced
personal predilection for the exercise of strong, commanding power.
Had this tendency been combined with strength of character and
organizing ability, he might have played a much more substantial
and constructive part in the Revolution than the one he actually
performed.

The members of the Executive Committee did not regard him as
quite one of themselves. He liked gestures calculated for effect
and intended to show his independence of the organization to which
he nominally belonged. In his capacity as Minister of Justice, for
instance, he released General Ivanov from prison, who in the first
days of the Revolution had attempted to lead the troops under his
command against Petrograd. When he was denounced for this in
the Executive Committee, Kerensky, instead of taking the matter
up with this leading organ of the Soviet and explaining his motives,
suddenly put in an appearance at a plenary session of the Soldiers'
section of the Soviet and delivered a hysterical speech before this
mass audience. He spoke of his devotion to the Revolution, of how
he had "led the revolutionary regiments to the Duma," of the unjustified criticism directed at him, which he was not going to tolerate, and so on. The audience, uninformed about the whole matter,
listened to him sympathetically and, of course, rewarded him with
tumultuous applause, which he took as a sign of confidence on the
part of the Soviet.

Such incidents caused considerable annoyance to the Executive
Committee, and its left-wing members repeatedly proposed that
Kerensky be disavowed, a step that certainly would have shaken
his political position. However, the majority of the Executive Committee preferred to smooth over such incidents behind the scenes,
since, by and large, Kerensky's presence in the government and
his popularity were considered valuable assets.

On basic issues, domestic and foreign, Kerensky conformed his
attitude to the general line of the Soviet. Miliukov, in his *History,*

goes so far as to call him a "Zimmerwaldist." Actually, Kerensky's outstanding characteristic was a kind of high-strung nationalism. The ideology of Russian imperialism and expansion had a stronger appeal to him than, for instance, to Prince Lvov or Nekrasov. Nevertheless, Kerensky, bearing in mind the prestige of the Soviet and the temper of the masses, supported the demand of the Soviet for the revision of the war aims, and defended it in the government against Miliukov, with whom his personal relationship had never been of the best. It hurt his feelings deeply that the Soviet considered his oppositional activities insufficient and used the contact commission to exert a direct influence on the government.

Shortly after my arrival in Petrograd, N. D. Sokolov* invited me to his home to meet Kerensky at the latter's request. At Sokolov's house I found Kerensky, Bramson, and some other guests. Kerensky, holding forth in his usual emotional way, was saying that in the Executive Committee Steklov and other leftists were systematically trying to discredit him and to obstruct his efforts in behalf of a rapprochement between the government and the Soviet democracy; that the contact commission was ignoring him in its negotiations with the government; that the Soviet was exerting pressure on the government in a humiliating form, and so on. When I pointed out to him that if he wished to straighten out his relations with the Executive Committee and to prevent further misunderstandings, all he had to do was to establish a permanent liaison with that leading organ of the Soviets, keep it informed of his actions and remain in constant touch with it, Kerensky became even more excited and insisted on his inability to do this, burdened as he was with government work, receptions and public speeches. I remarked that both for his own sake and for that of the common cause the coordination between his activities and the policies of the Executive Committee was more important than any receptions.

Then, he suddenly proposed that we immediately go together to the Executive Committee to clear up any misunderstandings and to arrange for a permanent contact. We drove to the Tavrichesky Palace, and there, at a session of the Executive Committee, Kerensky again complained of being misunderstood by members of the Executive Committee and of the difficulties due to the excessive pressure of the Soviet on the government. Yet, when asked by various members what changes he considered necessary, he evaded

---

* Radical lawyer; member of the Executive Committee [Ed.].

any definite statement. He talked at length about his desire to up-hold his connection with the Executive Committee, about his exces-sive burden of work, and left without having satisfied anyone and without having reached an agreement regarding a permanent con-tact.

Those few members of the Executive Committee who were close to Kerensky, such as Filippovsky and Bramson, tried to explain his inability to establish a close connection with the Executive Committee by his being generally unaccustomed to organizational ties. I had the impression, however, that this was not the main reason for Kerensky's conduct. While he certainly appreciated a nominal connection with the Soviet in view of its enormous prestige with the masses of soldiers and workers, he yet consciously avoided a closer link with the Executive Committee in the belief that so long as he stayed on the boundary between the bourgeois and the Soviet democracy, he would appear to the country as the exponent of the all-national character of the revolution.

In those April days, when it became known that Kerensky, with the other ministers, had approved Miliukov's note which had pro-voked the first flare-up of civil war in the streets of Petrograd, his popularity was strongly shaken. The Bolsheviks and some other leftist members of the Executive Committee proposed that Keren-sky be deprived of his vice-chairmanship of the Soviet. The majority of the Executive Committee, however, still thought that, despite his weaknesses and shortcomings, he might yet play a positive part for the benefit of democracy. For this reason we protected him against attacks from the left.

In this connection, I remember a characteristic incident in which I happened to have had a part.

On April 29, when the decision of the Executive Committee not to join the government was still unchanged, I was asked by the organizers of the Conference of Front Delegates then in session at the Tavrichesky Palace to act as chairman of the Conference for the day. War Minister Guchkov and Kerensky were to address the assembly. Guchkov, who was to resign on that very day, spoke in a pessimistic vein. After him Kerensky took the floor and de-picted the national situation in the darkest colors. Irresponsible people and organizations, he said, were doing everything to sow distrust of the democratic government. "Can it be," he asked, "that the free Russian state is a country of slaves in revolt? I wish I had died two months ago. I should have died then with a great dream: that the new life kindled in Russia would last forever, that we did not need a whip and a club to make us respect one another, and that we could govern our country differently from the old despots."

These words were reproduced with sympathetic comment by many newspapers and found an unusual response among the readers: the papers of the Right referred the remark about "slaves in revolt" to the Soviet democracy, and the democratic press, to the extremists fighting against organized democracy. Yet at the Conference itself, contrary to the newspaper reports that Kerensky's speech had been enthusiastically cheered, it was received coldly by the majority of the delegates, for the over-emotional speaker had talked in nebulous terms and had failed to indicate clearly whom he had in mind.

Kerensky himself must have sensed the bewilderment of a large part of his audience, for, after having left the rostrum, he at once returned to it to ask whether the listeners had any questions.

I put the following question to him: "You have said that there were organizations and individuals putting obstacles in front of the constructive work of the government. Certain groups direct this charge against the Soviet of Workers' and Soldiers' Deputies. Are your accusations also aimed at this organization, which is the center of the revolutionary democracy and directs its activities?"

Kerensky replied that his words could not have been directed at the Soviet, since he was a vice-chairman of that organization himself and would have left it if he disagreed with its policies. Not only did he have no intention of denouncing the Soviet, but he regarded it as the most reliable bulwark of the democratic system.

After answering a few more questions, Kerensky left the meeting. The assembly, however, still did not feel satisfied. One of the delegates, a member of the presidium of the Conference, took the floor and said in effect:

We have just listened to A. F. Kerensky, and his words have made a painful impression on us. He has accused the democracy of sowing unrest and has urged us to accept the uncontrolled authority of a bourgeois government. Plainly we can no longer trust him. Of all the speakers who have addressed our Conference, Tseretelli alone has our full confidence. We must follow him and the Executive Committee.

This statement, warmly applauded by the majority of the delegates, showed that some members of the Conference, displeased with Kerensky's speech, had interpreted my question to him as an attempt to show the Soviet as opposed to Kerensky and the Provisional Government. This was confirmed by several notes I received from the ranks of the delegates. I was asked why Kerensky was allowed to remain vice-chairman of the Soviet, and whether the question I had put to him was an expression of non-confidence on the part of the Executive Committee. I took the floor again and replied that I had put my question to Kerensky not because I suspected him of enmity to the Soviet but because I anticipated the answer he gave me. My purpose, I said, had been to clarify the situation by obtaining from Kerensky a definite statement of his position which we could use to counteract the slanderous campaign against the Soviet conducted by those who strive to provoke a rupture between the Soviet and the Provisional Government.

After this I made a report to the Conference on behalf of the Executive Committee, in which I described the nature of the mutual relationship between the Soviet and the Provisional Government and stressed their agreement on all basic issues, notably, the problem of war and peace.

My speech cleared the rather gloomy atmosphere that had settled on the assembly. Before the close of the session, one of the delegates took the floor to declare that the attack on Kerensky by the member of the presidium who had addressed the Conference had been ill-considered; and the latter in his turn made a statement in which he, in effect, took back all he had said against Kerensky.*

This incident illustrates the peculiar relationship between Kerensky and the Soviet democracy which I have mentioned above.

* After this had been written, I chanced upon the issue of the newspaper, *Rech,* containing an account of this session. The incident described by me, as well as the explanations that followed it, are reported correctly but have been considerably toned down. The chief difference between the *Rech* report and my own exposition consists in the rendering of the speech of the presidium member who spoke immediately after Kerensky and expressed his lack of confidence in the latter.

Rech quotes the speaker as follows: "The delegates from the front have had to listen to a great many speeches during this session. These speeches may have been honest and disinterested, but we are prepared to follow only one of the speakers, who, better than all the others, understands the needs and the sufferings of our brothers in the trenches. This man is Tseretelli. We shall not trust any speeches but his. (Loud applause directed at Tseretelli.)" *Rech,* April 30, 1917.

VICTOR B. SHKLOVSKY

At the Front—Summer 1917

V. B. Shklovsky (1893–   ), poet and critic, was one of the founders of the Formalist school of criticism. After the February Revolution, he was attracted by the right-wing SRs, was made commissar of the army by the Provisional Government, and left in June for the front to prepare the army for the ill-fated Kerensky offensive against the Central Powers.

The excerpts below are from his brilliant account of life in Russia during the Revolution and Civil War, *Sentimentalnoe puteshestvie*, Moscow and Berlin, 1923, which was recently made available to the English-speaking public (*A Sentimental Journey*, trans. and ed. by Richard Sheldon, Ithaca, Cornell University Press, 1970). This selection provides a vivid description of the army's demoralization in Galicia in the summer of 1917. The footnotes are by the translator, Richard Sheldon.

The council tried to talk us out of a rally, but we decided to call one anyway. There was a rostrum in the middle of the meadow. The soldiers assembled; an orchestra showed up. When the orchestra played the "Marseillaise," they all saluted. We got the impression that these men still had something; the regiment hadn't completely turned into mush. Life in the trenches over such a long period had worn the men down; many used sticks and walked with the practiced steps of blind men: they were suffering from ophthalmia. Worn out, cut off from Russia, they had formed their own republic. The machine-gun detachment was once again the excep-

From *The Russian Review*, vol. 26, no. 3 (July 1967), pp. 219–30.

tion. We conducted the rally. They listened restlessly, interrupting with shouts:

"Beat him up; he's a bourgeois dog; he's got pockets in his field shirt," or "How much are you getting from the bourgeois dogs?" I succeeded in finishing my speech, but while Filonenko* was talking, a crowd under the leadership of a certain Lomakin ran up to the rostrum and grabbed us. They didn't beat us up, but shoved against us with shouts of "Come to stir us up, huh!" One soldier took off his boot and kept spinning around, showing his foot and shouting: "Our feet! The trenches have rotted our feet!" They had already decided to hang us—as simple as that—to hang us by the neck, but at this point Anardovich† rescued us all. He began with a terrible string of curses, mentioning the soldiers' mothers more than once. They were so taken aback that they calmed down. To him, a revolutionary for fifteen years, this mob seemed like a herd of swine gone berserk. He wasn't sorry for them or afraid. It's hard for me to reproduce his speech; I only know that, among other things, he said: "And even with the noose around my neck, I'll tell you you're scum." It worked. They put us on their shoulders and carried us to the car. But as we drove off, they threw several rocks at us.

Ultimately Anardovich got the regiment under control. He went by himself, ordered them to hand over their rifles, divided them into companies, separated out 70 men and sent them under guard (one Cossack) to Kornilov's battalion,‡ where they said they were "reinforcements" and where they fought no worse than anyone else. The rest went with him.

They too turned out no worse than the other regiments. All this, of course, came to no avail: we were trying to keep the individual regiments from disintegrating, but this disintegration was a rational process, like all that exists, and was taking place all over Russia. . . .

---

* An ambitious captain, serving at this time as a commissar to the Russian army. When General Kornilov was made Supreme Commander-in-Chief of the Russian army, Filonenko served as the chief liaison between Kornilov and Kerensky.

† A commissar to the army.

‡ General Kornilov was at this time commander of the Eighth Army on the Southwestern Front. After the July Offensive, he became Commander-in-Chief of the Southwestern Front and then Supreme Commander-in-Chief. In late August, Kornilov made an unsuccessful attempt to overthrow the Provisional Government.

We drove back. Past ravaged, burned-out villages, past forests no longer whispering, past chapels burning with the yellow flame of candles someone had lit, I drove into Stanislau.

Here I was told to go to the 16th Corps, in the vicinity of Nadworna. There were hardly any enemy troops there—perhaps a few outposts left in the trenches or perhaps only watch dogs. The enemy was withdrawing, but still our reserve divisions couldn't make up their minds to advance, even though this Torricellian vacuum was sucking them in. I was sent to get the units moving. I set off again, saw General Stogov,* who tried to hide the disgraceful condition of his units, but, of course, couldn't. Kornilov had written him: "Occupy the village of Rosulna."

He answered: "The enemy is in the village of Rosulna."

Kornilov very pointedly telegraphed: "If the enemy is there, dislodge him."

But the troops weren't fighting and weren't dislodging anybody.

I got there. To intimidate our men, the Austrians had put one single cannon on the Kosmachka, that same round, wooded mountain I had seen from the Alexandropol Regiment. It was shooting to the right, to the left, along the roads—wherever it supposed our headquarters to be and where, of course, it was. Our artillery was silent and for good reason. The men knew there was no enemy line in front of them. You shoot at the village—hard on people; you shoot at the forest—hard on shells; so, for the sake of conscience, they shot only at the Kosmachka. In the field, you could see a flame—a local, latter-day burning bush; oil ignited two years before in a bore-hole was still burning.

We drove along the front. The Austrians had already pulled back and cleared out of their old trenches.

Good trenches, and dry, even though it was a swampy spot with a few groves of spruce—a regular Petersburg swamp. Little houses everywhere, everywhere the same little shelters made of birch with the bark intact.

I reached our front. While going through the forest, I kept running into stray soldiers with rifles, mostly young men. I asked: "Where are you off to?"

"I'm sick."

In other words, deserting from the front. What could you do with them? Even though you know it's useless, you say, "Go on

* Commander of the 16th Corps.

back. This is disgraceful." They keep going. I finally got to the edge of the forest. Snatches of conversation. Here and there, small groups of men. The regimental commander was giving a report:

"Yesterday this company deserted; yesterday that one panicked and opened fire on its own men."

I called the council together. The whole council was on the front line, being used to plug up the holes. I went up to one company, making myself understood almost entirely by interjections: "Comrades, what's going on?"

"Nothing. We're staying put."

"Go to Rosulna!"

They began to explain that to get to Rosulna, you had to cross a field, and while you were crossing, they would cut you down from the Kosmachka. Frustration.

I took a rifle and a grenade. "Who's going with me to Rosulna?" One scout volunteered. We went through the fields, sometimes in the grass, sometimes in sparse patches of grain—rye, maybe. We got to the village; the road was deserted.

We walked into the first hut. Some terrified peasant women asked us in a whisper, "What's going on? Will you come soon?" We didn't say anything. A quiet blond boy about seven or eight invited us in his hard-to-understand Galician jargon to come and look at the Austrians. We went on our bellies.

Standing in the river by a bridge, a small band of Austrians was throwing up an entanglement of barbed-wire, a single-strand necklace on thin steel rods.

It was out of the question for one or two men to run them off. Frustration. I picked up various bits of paper left in the abandoned battery and set out straight across the field toward our men. When I got there, I left the scout and departed. I thought, let him tell it.

I advised them to bombard the "front" with artillery fire, send armored cars into Rosulna and maybe then our infantry would tag along behind them.

These things were done and, with practically a knee in their backs, the troops plodded into Rosulna. In Rosulna, they perked up a bit: they had bypassed the terrible Kosmachka, whose taking they thought would have caused such fantastic bloodshed (another famous mountain, Kirlya-Baba, had been actually paved with bones); but because of our delay, the Austrians had saved all their artillery.

It was in Rosulna that we found a German staff guide to fraternization. . . .

Was it worth bothering with such troops? Why didn't we understand that you can't fight with such a concoction at the front?
Partly because we had no other way out of the war except a major
victory over Germany, which was the only way, in our opinion, to
stir up a revolution there. And, in fact, tanks did eventually crush
Wilhelm's throne. We didn't dare see how impossible it was, so we
proceeded to do the impossible.

Furthermore we knew that what lay in front of us was not an
army, but a hash—distinctly worse than our 16th Corps and a
good deal more cowardly; but unfortunately the Germans did,
however approximately, follow orders.

And so we entered Rosulna. . . .

The troops' morale left something to be desired. During a relatively easy march, they had thrown away their overcoats. They
were freezing, wrapping themselves up in blankets. I was told that
the shock troops of the 74th Division were refusing to move up to
the front line.

This just seemed too cowardly for shock troops, even though I
was used to such things. I went to see what was going on and immediately found myself in a crowd of exhausted and overwrought
men. Then came their grievances. It turned out that the battalion
consisted of regular soldiers and non-commissioned officers who
had run away from the disintegration of their previous units. But
even in their new unit, they found the same disintegration—not
from the reluctance of the soldiers to fight, but from their inability
to organize. The battalion had no vehicles, no cartridges for its
Japanese rifles—in short, was unarmed, unless you consider the
grenades picked up in the Austrian trenches. And it was being
ordered to move up to the front line.

Through Vonsky, who had just arrived, I somehow got rifles
and cartridges, and sent the men into battle. Nearly the whole
battalion was wiped out in one desperate charge.

I understand them. It was suicide.

I went to bed. That night the Ruthenian innkeeper got me up
with a desperate wail: the soldiers were cutting down his unripened
grain. I got up and spent the night running around in the dew. In
the morning Kornilov arrived and ordered us to bring all the shells
captured from the Austrians as soon as possible.

The front now ran along the edge of the village [Lodzjana]; the people were uneasy. During the day, the soldiers had killed two Jews; they said the Jews had been signaling. I'm convinced that wasn't the case. This combination of cowardice and spy-mania was unbearable. And all the same, this blood somehow was on my hands. The front had to be pushed forward. Our artillery was shooting more and more often, pushing back the Austrians, who did not hold their ground very well. To our right in the area of the 42nd Division, where Anardovich was then, they would run even from shrapnel fire. . . .

On the next day, a real battle broke out. It started either by the Lomnitsa, or by the Povelcha River. We kept receiving the most vague and contradictory information, all kinds of military gibberish. I set out for the front. The forest was full of stray men. I found a regimental headquarters; there too they knew almost nothing. There were no communications along the front. I went forward and crossed the river; the warm water immediately got into my boots and began to squeak and gurgle. After crossing a series of small glades, I came to a spruce forest, where bullets were whistling and ricocheting off the trees with a staccato whine.

While walking through the forest, I stumbled upon our line. Individual holes had been dug in the ground, still wet from the rain during the night, and the stumps torn roughly out of the ground showed their broken roots. There was water in the holes and tired, wet men were lying in the water. Two or three officers were hiding behind trees, but they were standing up. They obviously didn't know what they were supposed to do. The machine guns were firing without interruption and apparently to no avail. You could hear the ragged, nervous sound of rifle bullets. Various soldiers were grumbling about the officers.

"Why should they stay in the rear? Where they should be is about 200 yards up ahead." Someone explained that the troops hadn't made up their minds whether to move forward. Some Hungarians were in front of them. The regiments to the right and left were already almost half a mile ahead. I turned to the soldiers:

"Move forward." They were still silent. . . . It was so depressing in that forest, in the dense forest of the revolutionary front. I picked up two Russian tin bombs lying by the head of some soldier and put them in my pocket; I picked up a rifle, stepped over our line and moved forward. The shots ahead of us had died down. I went about sixty steps, I guess—a ditch, a road, another ditch and just beyond it were the Austrians. I almost stepped on them. I threw the bomb to the side; if I'd thrown it straight ahead, it would have gone over their heads. A yellow flame flared up with a muffled roar; I felt the concussion. . . . Time seemed to stand still. Sometimes during a storm, when lightning illuminates the clouds, they seem that still. . . .

And at that moment I heard a shout and our regiment ran forward, ran past me in a complete frenzy.

They didn't hold back; they ran forward.

I remember the charge. Everything around me seemed remote, sparse, strange and still.

I remember the yellow straps on the gray uniform of a German lieutenant. The lieutenant was the first to jump up in front of me; after a second of stupefaction, he rushed forward, turned and fell, tucking his knees under his chest as if he were looking for a place to lie down. The yellow strap crisscrossed his back. It wasn't I who killed him.

I ran past the enemy trenches and looked around: one of our soldiers, hastily removing the pack off a dead officer, suddenly fell beside him.

We were going into battle on a gray day, among the wet trees. Some German shouting "I give up" fell on his knees and put his hands up. One of our soldiers ran past, half-turned and, aiming on the run, shot at him.

The troops ran faster than I did; I fell behind. I knew that you never attack standing at your full height, but we had lost our senses. Fatigue, hatred for the war and for ourselves kept us from thinking about self-preservation.

Somewhere off to the left in some elder bushes, a German machine gun opened up with a sporadic rattle.

Behind us appeared a group of Austrians, hurrying to surrender.

We made a running jump into a swiftly flowing stream that almost bowled us over and took care of some enemy troops trying to dig in on the opposite bank.

Then a deserted little village with chickens running around in the streets. One of the men tried to catch one. There were just a few of us left; most had been wiped out.

On the other side of the village, there was another barbed-wire entanglement; we reached it.

At that moment, we realized we had no more cartridges left. The regiment had shot them up while lying in the forest. I yelled, "Get down and dig in." We were already deep in enemy territory.

At that moment, I felt something warm in my side and I found myself being knocked to the ground. More accurately, I found myself lying on the ground. I jumped up and again yelled, "Dig in. The cartridges will be here soon."

I was wounded right in the stomach. . . .

About a week later, Filonenko and Kornilov came to see me. Kornilov brought a Cross of St. George, for which I was grateful, but somehow I couldn't bring myself to go through the whole elaborate ritual of acceptance. Kornilov was somewhat disappointed. Filonenko was cheerful. He was on his way up. Now he was already a commissar of the Rumanian front. I found out from him about the debacle at Tarnopol, about what our troops did at Kalusz, about how the Bolsheviks had made their bid for power on the 3rd and 5th of July and been squelched.* I didn't guess the seriousness of these events right away.

But a few days later, the senior doctor came to see me; this lame, gray-bearded, slightly balmy native of Kronstadt announced that we were being evacuated right away.

The packing up began, got faster and faster until the evacuation gradually turned into a rout.

The enemy wasn't pressing us hard, but about two weeks before, in the region of Tarnopol, two regiments had simply left their positions, then a third; then still another didn't go where it was supposed to and the undermined front collapsed. The Germans had sent their cavalry into the breach; all it had to do was stand aside so as not to be trampled by fleeing Russians.

There's a certain children's game: you stand wooden blocks on end, one after another in a spiral, in such a way that when they fall, they hit each other; then you push one and havoc quickly runs

---

* After Lenin's return to Petrograd on April 16, 1917, the Bolsheviks directed a steady stream of propaganda against the Provincial Government. The growing tension among the workers and soldiers led to demonstrations in early July. When the moderate elements of the Soviet refused to accede to the demands of the demonstrators, the Bolshevik leaders decided to postpone their coup. The Provisional Government then succeeded in suppressing the uprising. Zinoviev went into hiding, Trotsky and Kamenev were arrested and Lenin fled to Finland.

through the whole spiral. The 7th Army had pushed us. Our right flank was exposed. . . .

The supply depots were burning. Almost by force of arms, the wounded were fighting for places in the very last train, which was slowly pulling out . . . men on top of the cars, between the cars, men tying themselves under cars . . . a tiny locomotive, straining every fiber, moving backwards and forward, pulled at the long line of cars, about to burst asunder at any moment.

The infantry was on the move. The artillery too. First-aid stations were replacing the hospitals. Artillery fire was again heard, the shells apparently landing not far away.

I tried to straighten out the columns of vehicles and to assign cargos to the empty ones, but couldn't; I didn't feel well.

I was put in an overcrowded makeshift ambulance and carted to Kolomea.

Kolomea was packed. I went to headquarters and found Cheremisov,* who was then already an army commander. He was composed, but agitated. He didn't recognize me, didn't even see me. He had other things on his mind.

I found somebody I knew, got in the commander's train and set off for Czernowitz. The headquarters telegraph operators were traveling in the same car, calmly playing guitars and carrying on their telegraphic conversations.

I didn't get to Czernowitz; the train stopped. Up ahead they were letting freight go through. I got off the train, hopped in a freight wagon and reached Czernowitz. There I went to the Kauffman Infirmary. Clean, quiet, organized—definitely a city place. They told me I had an infiltrate. This apparently means an internal hemorrhage. They said it was a serious case. I was lying down. It was quiet in the ward. A very young officer with a broken back was lying there embroidering; he would never be able to stand up or even sit up.

The other wounded officers were reproaching me for what we had done to Russia. . . .

I will try to relate how I understand everything that happened.

The Russian army was ruptured even before the Revolution. Revolution, the Russian Revolution, with the "maximalism of

---

* Previously commander of the 12th Corps, General Cheremisov was promoted to Commander of the Northern Front (Ninth Army).

democratism" by the Provisional Government, freed the army from all constraints. There were no laws left in the army—not even rules. But there was a complement of trained men, capable of sacrifice, capable of holding the trenches. Even without constraints, a short war was possible—a blitzkrieg. It so happens that at the front the enemy is a reality: it's clear that if you go home, he'll come right behind you. In any army, three-fourths of the men don't fight; if there had been troops in this war that fought as well as men work for themselves, they could have not only attacked Germany, but gone across Germany into France. When the Rogatin Regiment, about 400 strong, saw the Germans bayonet their commander right before their eyes, they went wild with rage and slaughtered the entire German regiment to the last man. The potential for this kind of fighting did exist, but two things killed it. The first was the criminal triple-damned, foul, ruthless politics of the Allies. They wouldn't go along with our peace conditions. They, no one but they, blew up Russia. Their refusal allowed the so-called Internationalists* to come to the fore. For an explanation of their role, I'll cite a parallel. I'm not a Socialist: I'm a Freudian.

A man is sleeping and he hears the doorbell ring. He knows that he has to get up, but he doesn't want to. And so he makes up a dream and puts into it that sound, justifying it in another way— for example, he may dream of church bells.

Russia made up the Bolsheviks as a justification for desertion and plunder; the Bolsheviks are not guilty of having been dreamed.

But who was ringing?

Perhaps World Revolution.

But not all had fallen asleep or not all could have the same dream. To my description of the army, the following amendment must be added. Mine was a killing occupation: I had to be in the worst units during their worst moments. We did have entire infantry divisions that were in good shape. I'll name the first that comes to mind—well, for example, the 19th. For that reason, the Bolsheviks had to hamstring the army, which Krylenko† succeeded in doing when he destroyed the apparatus of command and its surrogate—the councils.

---

* Those left-wing Socialists, including the Bolsheviks, who opposed continuation of the war.
† Commissar of Military and Naval Affairs after the October Revolution.

Why did the army take the offensive? Because it was an army. For an army, it's no harder to take the offensive, no harder psychologically, than to stand still. And an offensive is a less bloody business than a retreat. The army, feeling its disintegration, couldn't avoid using its strength in an all-out effort to end the war. It was, after all, an army and therefore it took the offensive rather than die and did not die because it took the offensive. The offensive could have succeeded, but it didn't succeed because of political circumstances; the units were already "falling asleep." They escaped into Bolshevism the way a man hides from life in a psychosis.

I will write more; I'll describe the Kornilov affair, as I know it, and my session in Persia, but what I wrote just now I consider important; I wrote it remembering the corpses I saw.

One word more. When you judge the Russian Revolution, don't forget to weigh in the balance of sacrifice—a balance too light—the blood of those who accepted death among the cornfields of Galicia, the blood of my poor comrades.

VICTOR MANAKIN

The Shock-Battalions of 1917,
Reminiscences

Victor Manakin (1887–1964), a colonel of the Russian army attached
to the general staff headquarters of the southwest army, was made
commander of the first storm troop regiment in the summer of 1917.
He subsequently fought in the White Armies of Generals Denikin and
Wrangel. After the collapse of the White Movement, he lived in Yugo-
slavia until 1949 and subsequently in the United States.

The following text is from the author's reminiscences of the formation of the shock battalions during the fateful months preceding
and immediately following the Bolshevik seizure of power.

In April 1917, in my capacity as Chief of the Political Staff Section
of the front at Kamenets-Podolsk, and with the approval of General
Dukhonin, Chief of Staff of the front, I gave a report at the conference of the southwestern front, which had been convoked by
order of the Provisional Government, "On the strategic situation
in the theaters of the World War." In this report, I showed that the
efforts of the Bolsheviks to demoralize the Russian army were
directly benefiting the Germans, who were waging war on two
fronts. After I had secured the backing of the presidium of the conference, we took up next the question of voting for continuation of

From *The Russian Review,* vol. 14, no. 3 (July 1955), pp. 226–32; vol. 14,
no. 4 (October 1955), pp. 332–44.

the war. This was a vote, unprecedented in history, taken by soldiers' deputies at the front, in time of war. The motion of the presidium was accepted by the conference. Ensign Krylenko, deputy from the Petrograd Soviet and subsequently Commander-in-Chief of the Soviet armies, was defeated.

After that, I introduced a motion for the formation of social shock-battalions to be made up of civilian volunteers, so that by the example of their personal bravery we might raise the fallen morale of the armies and endeavor to lead them along with us, in order to save the honor of Russia and fulfill her obligations to her Allies. The conference accepted my motion unanimously. This was the last attempt to arrest the disintegration of the front. General Brusilov, who was appointed Commander-in-Chief at that time, confirmed the decision of the conference on the very same day and issued an order to have it circulated on all the fronts.

In fulfillment of this order of the Commander-in-Chief, the formation of shock-battalions and death units was begun on all the fronts, at the rate of one battalion to a division. They were made up of volunteer soldiers and of civilian volunteers.

The front-line shock battalions remained in their divisions in order to maintain order and discipline in the individual units. The collapse of the front was temporarily checked, but the battalions, which were scattered among the divisions, were powerless to undertake any action on a larger scale. The higher command could not make up its mind to concentrate these battalions for a larger-scale undertaking of a political nature, namely, the dispersal of the Soviet of Workers' and Soldiers' Deputies in Petrograd, because the Kerensky government was, to its own ruin, supporting the latter.

The formation of shock battalions of civilian volunteers was more complicated and required time. I took this task upon myself. On the very next day after the Commander-in-Chief had issued his order, I set up a central committee for the formation of shock battalions composed of civilian volunteers, and was elected its chairman.

On the same day we invited the delegation of sailors of the Black Sea Fleet, which had come to the front with the same goal, upon the initiative of Admiral Kolchak, and which had supported my motion at the conference.

I proposed to the delegation that they join us and send delegates around to all the fronts and throughout all Russia in order to propagandize our patriotic idea and to recruit volunteers. My proposal was accepted and psychological warfare was begun in the fire of the Revolution.

Within three weeks, the first civilian volunteers, with no military obligations, began to arrive at headquarters of the southwestern front. These were primarily young people, members of the intelligentsia, and peasants, under the command of war veterans who had been wounded many times. At first, they came singly, then in groups, and finally in whole detachments.

In two months time, entire battalions started to arrive, some from such nests of Bolshevism as Oranienbaum, near Petrograd, and Tsaritsyn, later Stalingrad. There were battalions from Orenburg, Omsk, Kiev, Kharkov, and even Moscow. Most of them fought their way through to the front by force of arms.

The committee took care of receiving the arriving volunteers, of making arrangements for them, and of organizing them into units. The volunteers were arriving in excellent psychological condition and, even though they were untrained, they were inspired with the idea of performing a heroic exploit in the interests of their fatherland.

Junior command personnel was arriving with them, but we had to look for battalion commanders ourselves, since we were not authorized to accept officers from the front, lest their units become weakened. The task was more than difficult in time of war, but we nevertheless found ways of solving it, by taking disabled men and those whose own soldiers had wanted to kill them.

We set about the work of organizing and of military training. When enough of the first arrivals among the volunteers had assembled for one company to be formed, the question came up of who would be the commanding officer of this company. The question was one of unusual importance for the consolidation of discipline among the volunteers.

At this time, cavalry Captain Lomakin of the Cuirassier Guard Regiment turned up at my office, having barely escaped lynching by his soldiers. He offered me his services as a volunteer. I said, "Go to the first company as an ordinary volunteer, leaving your officer's Cross of St. George on your chest, and go to sleep on a plank-bed like all the other volunteers. Tomorrow you'll be the company commander." That is just what he did, and the next day the company unanimously declared that it wanted Lomakin as commanding officer and that it would follow him wherever he ordered it to go. The committee approved the company's choice, and the company kept its word. It was the best company of the first shock-battalion and it carried out the most responsible assignments. The secret lay in the fact that he was the first combat officer to have turned up among the volunteers. And they responded to him with enthusiasm and confidence. One had to take into account the fact that this was a time of complete breakdown of discipline and confidence in officers.

A few days later, I was informed that in the Front Revolutionary Committee, which was led by Communists, a question had been raised about our battalions being possibly counter-revolutionary and about me as the chief instigator. I immediately sent over two members of our committee, both of them workers, to have a talk with the Front Committee. Both of my delegates were former "political prisoners" who had been amnestied after the Revolution.

In the evening they returned and gave me an account: "We came to the Committee, laid our revolvers down on the table of the presidium and said, 'We did fifteen years at forced labor. Which one of you did more than that? Nobody. Well, listen then. We ourselves know what kind of battalions we have and what kind of man our colonel is. If any one of you dares to say even one more word, he'll be dealing with us! Understand? And that's that!'" And they left. The Committee was at a loss for an answer. The primitive psychology of the masses had to be dealt with in an even more primitive fashion. We were left in peace.

In June, our committee already had four activated battalions armed with Japanese rifles that Admiral Kolchak had sent us. In addition there were several thousand volunteers who had not yet been organized into units.

At this time, General Kornilov, who had escaped from German captivity and had been named Commander-in-Chief of the front, came to Kamenets-Podolsk, where the headquarters of the southwestern front was located. He summoned me and asked: "I have been told that you have some battalions. Where are they? And do they obey orders?" The latter question is unusually significant for understanding the circumstances of that period. I explained and said that the battalions were completely reliable. "Who can give them orders?" asked Kornilov. I replied, "You, your Excellency, as Commander-in-Chief." Kornilov at once summoned General Dukhonin, the Chief of Staff, and ordered me to send our four shock-battalions to the front immediately with the mission of checking the armies of the southwestern front which were fleeing before the Germans.

When I reported that the battalions had no field-kitchens as yet, the General said that that made no difference for the moment, the main thing being that they had rifles. When I asked what to do with the remaining volunteers, who were not yet organized, General Kornilov appointed me commanding officer of the first shock regiment formed out of three as yet unactivated battalions.

A day later, the General summoned me again and said, "I have decided to demand that the Provisional Government take decisive measures for the restoration of discipline in the army, up to and including application of the death penalty. Can your battalions carry out this order?"

"Exactly the same as any other order," I replied.

"Then transmit this order of mine to your battalions, and I'll send a telegram to the government."

There was no other way. The only question was: who could carry out this order? In view of the tremendous upheaval in the demoralized army, infantry units of supreme reliability were necessary for such a purpose. There were no longer any such units at the front. Indeed, it was only by our shock-battalions that this assignment could be carried out, and at that only by those battalions that were composed of civilian volunteers, since these were not connected with their divisions. The shock-battalions of the southwestern front were the ones who carried out this assignment.

The first shock-battalion under Captain Talalaev was sent to Tarnopol, the contact point of the retreating armies which had lost the capacity to resist the advancing German armies. The battalion consisted of one company of civilian volunteers under the command of cavalry Captain Lomakin, two companies of non-commissioned officers who had deserted their disorganized division, and one company of cadets who had come to the front in response to our call.

As Talalaev reported to me later, he found complete chaos upon his arrival at Tarnopol. There was neither military nor civilian authority there. The city was clogged with transports, artillery, and ammunition belonging to the retreating armies. In the city itself, widespread looting of the stores was going on, and, from the west, the Germans were advancing.

Talalaev dispatched the two companies of non-commissioned officers to cover the city, kept Lomakin's company at his own disposal, and sent the company of cadets to the east of the city to stem the wave of fleeing deserters. The two companies of shock-troopers dispersed in skirmish formation in the western outskirts of Tarnopol, along a front of about four kilometers, without machine-guns, without entrenching tools, and without reserves.

A German regiment was approaching the city, with the commanding officer and a band playing music at the head of the column. This was the customary triumphal march of the Germans against the armies of the revolution, which were absolutely without any discipline whatsoever.

The shock-companies opened fire. The band stopped playing. The commander of the German regiment, caught by surprise, ordered his men to disperse in skirmish formation, and sent for artillery in order to prepare an attack. He could not suppose it likely that there were only two companies at the front of the division.

An unevenly matched battle began, with two companies of shock-troopers against a foe many times stronger and equipped with machine-guns and artillery. The battle lasted for an entire day. The Germans were cautious and prepared the attack under cover of artillery fire. Our companies bore heavy losses for they had no entrenching tools, but they did not waver in spirit. They were made up of seasoned Russian soldiers, for whom nothing is impossible.

Towards evening, Talalaev ordered them to fall back. Ninety men did so, but 310 remained on the field of battle, killed or wounded. There was no one to remove them. But time had been gained. This was the first battle of the shock-troopers with the Germans and they had withstood their baptism under fire.

At this point, the volunteer company captured the city and then and there arrested thirteen looters. In accordance with General Kornilov's order, they shot the looters on the spot, after a brief trial. The effect was astounding. The looting stopped immediately. The soldiers, who had been wandering about the city, took their places on their vehicles, the transports started moving, and by evening the city was cleared out. The artillery and ammunition of the army had been saved.

The company of cadets seized the bridges to the east of the city, and began to hold back the fleeing soldiers to organize them into companies with cadets in command, and to occupy trenches along the front towards the west. Four battalions were formed in all, and a position was occupied along a front six kilometers long. The breakthrough of the front in this sector was deflected and the front was re-established. This sector was taken over on the following day by the Petrovsky Brigade and by the Preobrazhensky and Semyonovsky Regiments of the Russian Guard, all of which had continued to maintain order.

The second Orenburg shock-battalion came to Kamenets-Podolsk directly from Orenburg, commanded by a second lieutenant. I did not even have time to see the battalion before it was sent off to Trembovlya, another critical sector of the front. Colonel Bleysh, a fellow-student of mine at the military academy, arrived at Kamenets-Podolsk the next day. As a disabled officer with only one arm, he had the right to enlist in our battalions. I explained the state of affairs to him and suggested that he take over the command of the second Orenburg battalion. He readily agreed. I wrote out an order to the second lieutenant to turn over the command of the battalion to him, Bleysh rode off in an automobile to overtake the battalion en route, and after he had overtaken it, he assumed command without even having seen his men.

Before reaching Trembovlya, Bleysh received an order from the commanding officer of the 22nd Corps to dismount at once and occupy a position on a mountain located at the corps' limiting point, at the break in the front, towards which the Germans were rushing. Bleysh led his men to the position. It was the eleventh hour. One German battalion advanced onto the same mountain from the west. The shock-troopers came out onto the ridge first, and since they had only a small amount of cartridges, Bleysh gave the order "Follow me!" and without firing a shot led the battalion in a bayonet counterattack. As one man the battalion rushed after him and with their bayonets they hurled the Germans back.

The Germans sent a second battalion. A second bayonet attack followed, with the same result. The Germans could not make up their minds to attack again, called out their artillery, and began to bombard the battalion. Uninterrupted artillery fire went on for forty-eight hours. The battalion sustained heavy losses, for it had no entrenching tools, but it held out until the end, when the order came to fall back.

"I can understand everything," Bleysh told me later. "I can understand that the shock-troopers, once they had made up their minds to accomplish something heroic, were able to withstand such heavy losses and thus hold their position. I can understand the fact that not even one of them asked me why I wasn't retreating, but I can't understand why not a single shock-trooper asked me why I wasn't feeding them for two whole days."

We did not have any field-kitchens or bread supply or even water.

On the third day, the battalion withdrew, according to orders. Four hundred men had remained out of twelve hundred. The casualties amounted to sixty-six percent. But the break-through by the Germans had been closed. Upon the recommendation of the corps commander, General Kornilov issued a telegraphic order that all of the survivors were to be awarded the Cross of St. George. This was the only occurrence of its kind in the history of that period.

I reviewed the battalion a few days later. It was a battalion of heroes. They looked with pride at Colonel Bleysh, their commanding officer. In the Volunteer Army, Bleysh later became the commander of one of the best officer regiments, the Markovsky Regiment, subsequently the Markovsky Division, and he died of wounds received in Novorossiisk in 1920.

The third shock-battalion, led by Captain Ott, was sent to Volochisk. This was a road junction in the rear of the army. Three days later, Captain Ott reported "I have organized six battalions of former deserters. More deserters are coming in by very roundabout routes." In the end no battles were fought there.

The fourth battalion was composed of cadets under the command of Lieutenant Popov, who was also disabled, having only one arm. By the time the battalion had arrived at Proskurov, an important road junction on the left flank of the front, there were no longer any civil authorities there. The city itself was crammed full of soldiers fleeing from their units.

After he had established order, Lieutenant Popov proceeded to round up deserters. On the very first day, four battalions were formed, which I reviewed a day later. The soldiers stood at attention, said they were satisfied, and asked to be accepted as shock-troopers. This was an extremely significant incident. People had grown weary of disorder and confusion and wanted a firm guiding hand. But we had neither the means nor the time to retrain such an enormous number of men with whom we were totally unfamiliar.

A few days later, Lieutenant Popov was summoned by the commanding officer of the combat engineers, who asked him to restore

order among 20,000 civilian workers, who had refused to dig
trenches for the second line of the front and were threatening the
engineers with lynching. Popov took a platoon of cadets and two
machine-guns and rode out to the work site on a truck. There stood
a huge crowd of striking workers. Driving directly into the midst
of the crowd. Popov unloaded the machine-guns, lined up the
platoon with their rifles ready, and, turning to the crowd, demanded
that the instigators be handed over to him. He set a time limit of
three minutes for the surrender and then, taking out his watch,
started to study the minute hand.

During the course of the first minute, he ordered the cadets to
bring feed-belts up to the machine-guns and to check the breech-
blocks. During the course of the second minute, he ordered them
to aim at the crowd, and he started to count out loud "Fifty seconds
left, forty . . . , thirty . . . , twenty . . . , ten. . . . "

The crowd stirred, and, before the end of the third minute, thirteen men were pushed out from its ranks. We were lucky with number thirteen. It was the same number as that of the looters executed
at Tarnopol. Popov greeted these thirteen men by saying: "Aha! My
dear comrades! Very happy to see you! You're just the ones I
needed! So you think that our army is defeated and that it doesn't
need any trenches at all? There's nothing else I can do. I have to
hand you over to be court-martialled!"

Paper and a table covered with green felt had been brought along
from Proskurov. The court, composed of three cadets, proceeded to
examine the case on the spot, before the very eyes of the crowd. In a
few moments the presiding judge announced "The case is clear. All
thirteen men are guilty. All thirteen are sentenced to be shot!"

Popov ordered the condemned men to be given shovels and then
commanded them to dig graves for themselves with their own
hands. The crowd watched in silence. No one stirred. The effect
was overwhelming. Eleven of the condemned men fell on their knees
and begged for mercy, pointing out that they were not guilty and
that they had been talked into it. They said that they had not known
what they were doing and that the whole affair had been started
by two ringleaders. They then pointed out which of the group had
been the ringleaders. These latter proved to be the chairman and
vice-chairman of the Bolshevik Party's Military Revolutionary
Committee of the Front. Popov pardoned the eleven men and
ordered the other two to be shot. The crowd made room for the

shooting. When the cadets passed by the newly dug graves at parade march, the crowd as one man kneeled and promised to be obedient and not to act contrary to the orders of the military authorities.

Thus General Kornilov's command to restore order and discipline on the front lines of the demoralized armies was carried out. The effect of these initial actions by the shock-battalions was overwhelming. The news of the executions spread over the front like wildfire, and, along the entire front, soldiers who only yesterday had been killing their officers, started to salute all officers. This was a phenomenon totally unheard of since the issuance of Order No. I. The psychological moment for restoring the front was at hand. Unfortunately, there was no longer any civil authority to clinch the matter.

By order of General Kornilov, I assumed command of a regiment composed of about three thousand volunteers, unorganized, untrained, and unclothed, together with a very small number of officers who had just completed their training at a school for second lieutenants. . . .

In October, my regiment was located in a position facing the Austrian city of Gorodok, on the left flank of the Seventh Army. I had been ordered to attack Gorodok and had already carried out reconnaissance and issued all the orders necessary for an attack at dawn. Deserters from the Austrian side informed me that a Czech regiment was waiting for the attack in order to come over to our side.

At eleven o'clock in the evening, I received a telegram in which General Dukhonin, acting Commander-in-Chief of the Russian armies, summoned me to take my regiment to Mogilev, in order to guard *stavka*. At dawn, after calling off the attack, I set out with my regiment to entrain for *stavka*. In breaking through the demoralized armies of the southwestern front by force of arms, our regiment lost two battalions, which were cut off by a railroad strike, and it arrived in Mogilev at the beginning of November, after the Bolsheviks had already seized power in Petrograd.

We found *stavka* in its death throes. There were generals and other officers there, but there was not even a single military unit which could be relied upon or which was carrying out the orders of the Commander-in-Chief. Colonel Intskirveli, the Commandant of *stavka,* and General Bonch-Bruevich, the garrison commander, had gone over to the side of the Bolsheviks.

We were in an enemy camp. In order to raise morale and to put on a demonstration, I ordered that patrols be sent around through the city and that the shock-troopers salute their officers by standing at attention. Such a scene had been unknown since the beginning of the revolution. The officers of *stavka* took heart at the sight of the shock-troopers. No one knew how many of us there were. The Bolsheviks became frightened, and all the time there were only three hundred of us.

At this time, my committee reported to me that it had received an invitation to a meeting at the garrison Commander's. I said "Go ahead." I did not issue any instructions, for the shock-troopers themselves knew what to do. Our regiment, although reduced to the strength of only one battalion, was one closely knit family, surrounded by enemies, and in imminent danger. But not one of us had any doubts or hesitations.

That night, my delegates returned from the meeting and reported that General Bonch-Bruevich had proposed that the units of the garrison form a military-revolutionary committee of *stavka,* a procedure usually followed by the Bolsheviks for the purpose of seizing power. Whereupon our delegates asked him if he knew that this was a Bolshevik term. The General, who had not expected such a question, began to justify himself, saying that we were all military people and that this was a post-revolutionary period, and that the term was completely innocuous.

To this the shock-troopers replied, "General, don't try to wiggle out of it. We understood you perfectly. Now we want you to know that in the event that a committee is formed, we'll destroy both you and the committee." The General became disconcerted, for he had not supposed that soldiers could teach a general his duty of honor to his country. The delegates of the other units had become silent. The attempt to form a military-revolutionary committee of *stavka* was broken off.

That same night, the shock-troopers requested my permission to liquidate the General, who had forgotten his honor. I turned down this proposal, for we had more important tasks to carry out.

The next day, I received an invitation from General Wrangel, who was in *stavka,* to visit him in his railroad car with a delegation of shock-troopers. This meeting was attended by our central committee and also by delegates of the shock-battalions and death-units of the western and northern fronts, who happened to be in *stavka.*

General Wrangel said to us: "I have invited you here, gentlemen, in order to inform you that I have submitted a report to the Commander-in-Chief containing a project for re-organizing the Russian Army on a volunteer basis, like your battalions, for the purpose of restoring the Russian front, even if it is on the Volga. I request your support for this project."

I answered in the name of those present: "That fits in perfectly with the ideas of our battalions and we can only welcome your initiative. Go to it, General, our hearts are with you."

The General thanked us and we left. That same day, he went to Petrograd, but . . . the opportunity had already been missed.

A few days later, I was informed that General Dukhonin was calling a meeting of the ranking personnel of *stavka.* This meeting was attended by the commanding officers of the battalions and by the delegates of other shock-units. A crowd of Bolshevik supporters had gathered in a large room at headquarters. A second lieutenant was chairman. We waited. General Dukhonin came in and excitedly informed us that he had received a telegram to the effect that the Allies were permitting him to conclude a separate peace with the Germans, in order to save the Russian Army. His question was, could he count on the support of the ranking personnel of *stavka.*

I then spoke out in the name of the shock-troopers and said that two thousand shock-troopers were awaiting the orders of their Commander-in-Chief. "No one and nothing can stop us," I said, "and if anyone has any doubts on that score, let him try. We'll show him what it means to try to stop us. We request orders!"

After me, the representatives of the battalions repeated the same threat. The crowd remained silent. The Bolsheviks are brave only when they can kill with impunity, when they outnumber their opponents by at least ten to one. But it was dangerous to try anything with the shock-battalions. This was the first open manifestation against the Communists.

General Dukhonin showed indecision. He said to us: "Thank you. Your proposal is honorable and noble. But I don't want blood to be shed on my account. Our country will still have need of you alive." And he went out. We left after him.

Under the pressure of an almost hopeless situation, Dukhonin lost his will and backed out of the fight. The shock-troopers were no longer needed by their Commander-in-Chief. But it was impossible for us to reconcile ourselves to this.

We were notified that the Finnish division, located to the north of Mogilev, had set up batteries in order to shell the city. That night, however, I rode out with some shock-troopers on two trucks and removed the breech-blocks from their heavy weapons, which were actually standing in position. The crew manning the weapons did not put up any resistance.

The next day, I was informed that Ensign Krylenko, who had been named the new Commander-in-Chief by the Soviets, was advancing upon Mogilev with groups of sailors of the Baltic Fleet, and that he was already in Orsha, six hours away. I took a detail of scouts and rode out towards him on two locomotives in order to blow up the bridges. At the first station, however, I received a telephone call from *stavka*. It was Colonel Kusonsky talking: "What are you doing, Colonel? The Commander-in-Chief has ordered you to return at once and has forbidden you to blow up the bridges!" I submitted, for I could not refuse to obey the Commander-in-Chief.

When I returned to headquarters, I was told that General Dukhonin had decided to turn over his command to Krylenko. Naturally, he could not destroy the bridges in front of him. The situation was becoming absurd. We had come to defend *stavka,* but *stavka* itself did not want to be defended. We had nothing further to do in Mogilev. . . .

I left a scout in the corridor and entered the room. General Dukhonin was alone. I said, "General, you have nothing further to do here. My automobile is standing at the entrance, and at the railroad station my squad is waiting for me. No one will dare to stop us. We'll take you wherever you can commence the formation of a new Russian army free of Communists. Let's go!"

General Dukhonin looked at me in hopeless dejection and said, "I can't answer you." He then covered his face with his hands and said, "It's so horrible to be a lump of flesh," and he went out. He had a foreboding of his own death, but he thought his duty was to stay at his post.

General Dietrichs, Chief of Staff to the Commander-in-Chief, came out of a neighboring room. The talk I had with him was so interesting that I remember it in full. He asked whether the nature of my proposal was that General Dukhonin should go along with us as the Commander-in-Chief or as an ordinary general. I replied that as an officer of the Russian army I had only to carry out the orders of the Commander-in-Chief, but since there were no longer any units here to which he could issue orders, there was no sense at all in staying behind, to meet certain death. I was therefore inviting General Dukhonin to leave with the shock-troopers.

General Dietrichs answered: "General Dukhonin as a general can go with you, but as Commander-in-Chief of the Russian Armies, he cannot leave his post. Do you really think that we didn't consider this matter? Only yesterday the General and I were in a private apartment, in civilian clothes. We looked at each other, became ashamed, and returned to headquarters."

I realized that General Dietrichs was the one that was standing over Dukhonin like Fate, prompting him with the idea of sacrificing himself. The question was, why? It was a beautiful idea but a useless death. And I said, "And how do you picture the future, General?"

"Your venture is hopeless," he replied. "You will perish. Communism is an elemental force against which it is impossible to fight right now. It has to rush throughout all of Russia, sweeping away everything in its path. It is hopeless to oppose it."

"In other words, you're folding your arms and doing nothing?"

"No, when the first wave has passed by, we shall rise up and renew the battle!"

"I wish you success in your plan," I said, "but it doesn't suit us shock-troopers. We'll fight here and now!"

At one o'clock in the morning of November 18 (new style), the last group of shock-troopers left *stavka.* Krylenko was waiting to be notified of this, but not, of course, out of considerations of honor. He arrived in Mogilev, as we found out later, at six o'clock in the morning, with six squads of sailors form the Baltic fleet. General Dukhonin was summoned to the railroad station "in order to hand over his command" and was bayoneted by the "guard" of the new Commander-in-Chief.

At four o'clock in the morning, our troop-trains arrived before Zhlobin. The railroad-yard was jammed full of trains carrying deserters to their homes. This was a peculiar method for demobilizing the Russian army at that time. I went to the railroad station with two scouts in order to find out when we would be able to move on. The station was crammed full of deserters. In unbuttoned over-coats, with a dirty, dishevelled appearance, they presented a fright-ful spectacle of the seamy side of the Revolution.

Bleysh's shock-troopers were not there, for the battalion had left for the branch line to Minsk, where it was fighting two armored trains which had been sent to cut us off. I went through the crowd to the Commandant's quarters. My officer's epaulettes and shock-trooper insignia produced their effect. The crowd made way for me.

The Commandant was in the throes of confusion. We went out into another room. In a trembling voice he told me that the bridge across the Dnieper had been prepared for demolition, and that a Bolshevik division with artillery was waiting for us on the other bank. What alertness after the coincident confusion of their Com-mander-in-Chief!

The Commandant advised me to take a detour by way of the still open branch line to Kalinkovichi. While we were talking, the room was filling up with deserters. All of them were looking at me with interest. The crowd was unarmed. Two men came in with rifles. One asked me, "And who might you be?"

"The commanding officer of the shock-regiment," I replied. The soldier stepped back. I went out onto the platform.

At the exit stood a dense mob of soldiers, who were waiting for me to come out. I took two steps and was hemmed in. They grabbed me and tore away my revolver. I broke loose and took a few more steps. Near me stood Zorkin, my scout, secretary of the regimental committee. He addressed the mob. Someone struck him on the head from behind. He fell.

I tried to walk on, but the mob became thicker and would not give way. In front of me stood men with dull eyes, such as one finds in murderers and Bolsheviks. I started to talk to the crowd. Sud-denly it was as though I had become the chairman of a meeting. The question under discussion was whether to kill me on the spot or to wait. Those standing in front of me kept their eyes lowered, as though they wanted to say, "We have nothing to do with this!"

From the back, men were shouting, "kill him!"

I said, "It won't do you any good to kill me. My shock-troopers will come and kill all of you. You'll be better off if you keep me as a hostage. Then my shock-troopers will do anything you want."

At this point my glance met the eyes of my second scout. He was asking me what to do. I motioned to him with my head to go get help. He understood and disappeared. I remained alone in the midst of the maddened mob. Undoubtedly there were many among them who had taken part in murdering officers. But no one could make up his mind to take the first step. My rank as commanding officer of the shock-troopers impressed them. From the rear, the yells kept getting stronger and stronger, "kill him!"

I had to stall for time. I started to speak of our striving to save the honor of our Fatherland, of our country. It was impossible to kill me at this moment. Those standing close by began to back away, and from behind, the yells were growing louder and louder. A circle was cleared around me. I realized that the most important thing was for me to remain on my feet. At this point I was struck on the head by something thrown from the rear ranks. I turned around. The men were still standing with their eyes lowered. No one could bring himself to strike me in the face. They began to push me around in the circle from one edge to the other. I was clearly aware of the fact that if I should fall, they would trample me to death. A fallen enemy is no longer frightening.

Psychologically, I still had the upper hand over the mob, but I realized clearly that the situation could not continue this way for long. My strength was giving out. A little longer, and I would fall and then the affair would be finished.

With this feeling, I closed my eyes. I had no desire to see the act of murder itself. I was ready for death. I no longer saw or heard anything. In my brain was a sensation of blankness. In my eyes appeared two fiery wheels which rotated rapidly as they came near. Fire filled everything. I was sure that this was death itself, the moment of transition into a better world.

I suddenly wanted to verify this, and with a final exertion of will, I opened my eyes. I was alive . . . and I was alone. The mob had disappeared. I was standing on the platform, and men were crawling under the cars of a train which was standing there. They were lying on top of one another. I saw only feet, many feet, in military boots. . . .

I heard a few shots, and I understood. My shock-troopers had come to the rescue of their commanding officer! I walked in the direction of the shots. At the end of the station I saw my scouts running up with carbines in their hands. They were breathless from running. It was almost a mile from the troop-train to the station. Second Lieutenant Marinkovič, a Serb, and my detail commander, came running up to me. "You're alive, Colonel. Well, thank God! Get away. We'll take care of things here ourselves."

He ran on. Two scouts took me by the arm and led me away. In the train, I was able only to tell Yankevsky to go to Kalinkovichi and then I lost consciousness. My skull had been severely wounded, and I had lost a great deal of blood.

I did not regain consciousness until thirty-six hours later. . . .

At one of the following stations, an armored train came out towards our leading train and, drawing right up to it, fired a gun at our locomotive, exploding the boiler. The armored train then moved back two miles. I suggested to Bleysh that he go around the armored train and tear up the tracks, and I myself went along the roadbed of the railroad with only half a company. When we had come up to within a quarter of a mile of the armored train, it began to fire its guns at us. We continued to approach without shooting. When we were only one hundred paces away, several sailors jumped out ("the ornament and pride of the Revolution," as they were then called). They had come out in order to give battle on even terms. This was a peculiar kind of chivalry characteristic of sailors. We opened fire, and several men fell. The rest took cover in the train and defended themselves by firing their machine-guns. . . .

At the Oboyan station our detachment left the trains and proceeded to march. We were beginning the Civil War. Before starting out, I assembled the battalion. Inasmuch as the volunteers had entered the battalion for the sake of defending our homeland from a foreign enemy and not for the purpose of fighting a Civil War, and since, in leaving the trains, we were directly confronted by a Civil War in fact, I did not feel that I had the right to lead the men into battle without warning them and without having their consent to do so. . . .

We moved off in marching order. My battalion was in the advance guard. In the very first village, an interesting psychological incident occurred. When the peasant women saw the shock-troopers, they said, "Why, darlings, you're just like our children, like our own little sonny boys. And the Bolsheviks were telling us that you're 'Cadets' [Members of the Constitutional Democratic Party] and that you have one eye in your foreheads and that you eat peasant children alive. It's too horrible to talk about!"

Only then did we understand why the peasants had been looking at us in such a hostile manner and why they had been shooting at us occasionally from around corners. The only way it had been possible for us to enter a village was with our rifles in our hands. The Bolsheviks were making use of the ignorance of the village masses and were inciting the peasants against us by tales which were extremely stupid but had an effect on the imagination.

After marching for two more days, we stopped in a large village. There were three hundred of us, and the main forces were five miles behind us. All around, everything was peaceful, and I started to believe that our march would end happily. We did not even set up any forward outpost.

Suddenly, at eleven o'clock in the morning, Lieutenant Nacewicz, a former officer in the Polish Legion, came running up to me and reported that sailors were advancing upon the village. This was so unlikely in the backwoods of Kursk Province that I said, "Sailors? It can't be! Check up on it!" and I continued to give orders with regard to our messing and billeting facilities.

A few minutes later, Nacewicz returned and reported that sailors really were surrounding the village and had already entered it in part. I ran out into the street. There was no longer any time to give orders. I shouted down the length of the village, "Everybody out to the borders of the village with your rifles in your hands! Pass the word along!"

The shock-troopers rushed to the edge of the village right through the kitchen-gardens. I took my carbine and went there too. Suddenly someone pulled me back and I saw that it was my orderly, Andreev, who had tended my horse throughout the whole war. When I took over the regiment, he had gone along with me, since he did not want to leave me after the Revolution. At first I did not understand what it was all about, but when I heard the whistle of bullets, it became clear to me that Andreev had gone ahead of me in order to shield me from the bullets with his own body.

We went out to a small hill, where my scouts had already gone. Along the entire horizon, as far as the eye could see, over the snow-covered fields, sailors, wearing black overcoats, were advancing in three lines. There were several battalions of them. The first line was firing. It was our hill in particular that the fire was concentrated upon. The flanks were already entering the village. . . .

The battle kept growing hotter along the entire front. The lines of sailors came up to within two hundred paces of our lines. Matters were coming to a head. At this point, Lieutenant Nacewicz came running up to me again and reported, "A delegation of sailors is coming!" I saw that a group of sailors with rifles in their hands really was moving along our front line, from the left. Of course this was not a delegation at all. Nevertheless, I called them over to me. They came near. They were fifteen Goliaths, sailors of the Black Sea Fleet.

They were looking for the commanding officer. They could easily have killed me and thus produced chaos in our ranks. But they came up with a seemingly pacific manner. I asked, "Who are you?" They said that they had been sent up from the Black Sea specifically to fight against the shock-troopers. That meant that this was a large-scale operation, on orders from Leningrad. They asked, "And what are you fighting for?"

"For our people and for the future of our country," I said.

"We are too," they replied. (This was an extremely characteristic type of incident at the beginning of the Civil War.)

I asked, "Then why are you advancing against us?"

"Well, the commissars told us that you are 'Cadets' and that we could take you with our bare hands. But what a fight you're putting up! Look how many of our men have been killed!"

"There'll be more if you don't stop," I replied.

"Well why should we keep on fighting? Cease fire!"

"You stop first," I said.

They started to signal, sailor-fashion, "Cease fire!" In a few minutes, the firing actually stopped. . . .

At this point, I saw that one sailor with a rifle was running over to us from the sailors' rear lines. I said, "Let him through." He ran up panting, with his collar unbuttoned. His first words were, "Where's the commanding officer?"

I raised my hand. "I'm the commanding officer. What's the matter?"

"Well, I've been the orderly of our commanding officer, a mid-shipman, and, well, he was killed the very first thing, by one shot from a machine-gun. Our men are waiting for orders. What shall I tell them?"

The matter became clear to me. For him, the important thing was the job for which he was responsible, namely to transmit or-

ders. What kind of orders did not matter. His commanding officer
had been killed. He was looking for another commanding officer. I
gave the following order: "All of the lines of sailors are to start
immediate withdrawal back to where they came from. They are to
fall back in order, without bunching up. I'm giving them thirty
minutes. Whoever does not fall back will be killed! Understand?"

"Aye aye, sir," answered the sailor and ran off to transmit the
order along the lines. A few minutes later, the nearest lines began
to withdraw.

The "delegation" of sailors was stunned by all that they had seen.
They at once suggested sending some delegates from our side to
their commissars in order to put a stop to military operations as
being totally unnecessary. I said, "And who guarantees that your
commissars won't kill our delegates?"

"We guarantee it," they replied, and then they proposed that
half of their own men be kept as hostages, so that the other half
could be a guard for our delegates. "If," they added, "your delegates don't return by five o'clock in the morning, you can shoot our
men whom you'll be holding as hostages."

I asked the shock-troopers, "Who wants to go along as a delegate
on these terms?" Captain Blinov and Cadet Tikhonov volunteered.
They went off with eight sailors, and seven remained as hostages.

We returned to the village. There we found about thirty more
sailors. They were trembling with cold and asked to be allowed to
warm up and they also requested something to eat. We arrested
them and sent them back to the rear. I sent a report to Yankevsky
and asked for reinforcements. We went to sleep. Thus ended our
first battle with the sailors of the Black Sea Fleet—three hundred
against five thousand. . . .

The battle, which took place near Krapivna, was our swan song.
Instead of pushing through to the east, to the Don, through the
demoralized ranks of the adversary, General Yankevsky and Bakhtin had decided to retreat. Where could we retreat to? All of Russia
was already a seething cauldron in the hands of the Bolsheviks.
But Bleysh and I carried out our orders once more and went off to
join the rest of the battalions. When we arrived at the designated
point, there was no one there. At the same time, we were informed
that instead of the demoralized battalions of sailors from the Black
Sea Fleet, newly arrived units of sailors from the Baltic Fleet, with
cavalry and artillery, had been sent out against us. At the very first

clash, the Finnish battalion had been defeated, and the survivors, together with Colonel Bakhtin and General Yankevsky, had fled without waiting for us. We turned out to be in the rear-guard.

The agonized retreat of our detachment began. The men walked through the snow, frequently without any boots. We moved at night, and in the daytime we fought. The sailors even had tanks. The battle was becoming an uneven match. Day and night we were under artillery fire and we sustained heavy losses. Many men could not walk any more. The sailors were finishing off the survivors. There were no vehicles with which to remove our wounded. It was clear that we no longer had any strength to continue the battle. We had to reach a decision.

I assembled all the officers and members of our battalion committees, who were still alive, and opened the last meeting of the shock-troopers. I said, "Dear friends! We engaged in this struggle in the name of a feeling of duty to our Fatherland in the hour of its ruin. We fought as well as we could, so as not to lose our own self-respect. No one laid down his arms. Most of our friends have perished in an unevenly matched battle. Our ranks have grown thin. Our survivors and wounded are being killed off. I feel that we have fulfilled our duty to our own conscience. Further opposition will lead only to the destruction of each and every one of us. I propose that we stop fighting and disperse."

Thereupon, Cadet Tikhonov, the vice-chairman of the regimental committee, stood up and said, "Colonel, sir, we've been thinking about that for a long time, but we didn't want to say anything to you, because we didn't want to distress you. We've been waiting for you to bring the matter up yourself. Now you've spoken up. It's all clear. We agree. There's nothing else for us to do."

I removed the regimental banner from its staff and gave it to a sergeant-major from Siberia. He kneeled. I made the sign of the cross over him and said, "I am giving you this banner of our shock-regiment. Shock-troopers have died under it, sons of the Russian people, for the honor of their country. Hide it in your bosom, and if the Lord destines you to live to brighter days, when the shame of our native land will be wiped out, give this banner to the new national government of Russia and tell them about us, about our struggle, the struggle of our nation's sons, and about our destruction for the sake of its honor." He kissed the banner. This was a moment of the highest spiritual intensity and fervor. . . .

. . . On the Don at this time, the formation of a Volunteer Army was begun, under the command of General Alekseev, former Chief of Staff to the Commander-in-Chief, and of General Kornilov, who had fled at that time from Bykhov. The shock-troopers who had succeeded in making their way through together with me entered this army.

NICHOLAS N. GOLOVIN

Disintegration of the Army in 1917

General N. N. Golovin (1875–1944) was professor in the Russian Imperial General Staff College in St. Petersburg and was chief of staff of the Russian armies on the Rumanian front. He is a major authority on the Russian army in World War I.

Anti-War Propaganda

The army's attitude may be judged from the thousands of proclamations put in circulation. We may quote here a typical example.

Brothers, we beg you not to obey an order that is meant to destroy us. An offensive is planned. Take no part in it. Our old leaders have no authority now. The papers have said there should nowhere be an offensive. Our officers want to make an end of us. They are the traitors. They are the internal enemy. They would like everything to be as before. You know well that all our generals have been put on reduced pay, and they want this revenge. We shall be thrown back when we reach the enemy's wire. We can not break through. I have reconnoitred in the enemy lines, and I know well that there are ten rows of it, with machine guns every fifteen yards. It is useless to advance. If we do, we shall be

This excerpt is from General Golovin's authoritative account of the effect of the war upon the Russian army. His book was first published in 1931 under the title *The Russian Army in the World War* by Yale University Press, New Haven, Conn. (Reprint edition entitled *The Russian Army in World War I,* Hamden, Conn., Archon Books, 1969, pp. 267–82.) Reprinted by courtesy of Carnegie Endowment for International Peace.

dead men, with nobody left to hold our front. Pass this on, brothers, and promptly write other letters of the same sort.*

Views of the Commanding Officers

On May 2 the Commander-in-Chief, with the commanders of the various fronts, went to Petrograd to give frank notice, at a conference of the Provisional Government and the Executive Committee of the Soviet of Workers' and Soldiers' Deputies, that the army was collapsing. The minutes of that conference are of great historical interest because they present a record of the opinions of the responsible commanding officers. We quote them at length.†

> Faith in our Allies [said General Alexeev] is disappearing. You take this into consideration in your diplomacy, and I must do the same thing in handling the army. Though it might seem that the Revolution would mean better morale, greater energy, and therefore victory, unfortunately, we have so far been mistaken. Not only is there no new energy in evidence, but the lowest instincts, such as love of live, and self-preservation have come to the surface. The interests of the country and its future are forgotten, probably because of the spreading abroad of theories quite misunderstood by the masses. The slogan "peace without annexations and contributions" has been interpreted as meaning that no longer is there any reason why a man should sacrifice his life. The army is on the very brink of ruin. One step more, and it will go into the abyss dragging with it Russia and her liberties, and nothing can save us. . . .
>
> A thirst for peace [asserted General Dragomirov] is all-dominant in the army. Anyone preaching peace without annexations, peace with the right of self-determination becomes a popular man. The ignorant, giving their own meaning to "without annexations" and unable to conceive of conditions in other countries, ask, why do not the common people among our Allies join us in such declarations? The desire to make peace is so strong that reinforcements, on arriving at the front, refuse to take their rifles. "What for?" they say, "We are not going to fight!"

---

* *Razlozhenie armii v 1917 godu (The Break-up of the Army in 1917),* Moscow-Leningrad, 1925, pp. 35–36.

† The full text of these minutes is printed in A. I. Denikin, *Ocherki russkoi smuty (The Russian Turmoil).* Paris, 1921–1926. 5 vols., vol. 1, Part 2, pp. 48–78.

No work is being done. It is even necessary to take special measures to prevent the tearing down of trench timbering, and to repair the roads. On a section of the front held by one of the best of our regiments, a red flag was found carrying the motto: "Peace at any price." An officer who tore it to pieces, had to flee for his life. He was hidden by Headquarters — it was in Dvinsk — and, all through the night groups of soldiers were looking for him. The dreadful words "supporters of the old *regime*" has meant the dismissal of our best officers. We all looked for the Revolution; yet many officers — the pride of the army — have been put on the reserve list because they have tried to keep their troops from going to pieces, or because they have not known how to adapt themselves. . . .

It is difficult to persuade the troops to do anything for the country. Under various pretexts, such as the bad weather or the fact that some of them haven't yet had their baths, they refuse to relieve the front-line units. There has even been a case of a regiment refusing to relieve another because two years before, just before Easter, it had occupied the same position. Therefore it would not do so again. It has become necessary to make bargains with the committees of the regiments concerned. All pride in belonging to a great nation has been lost. This is especially true of the people of the Volga provinces. "We don't want German land," they say, "The Germans won't come here, nor will the Japanese." And while one can profitably argue with individuals, it is very hard to alter the general attitude. . . .

Nowhere has it been possible fully to put in practice the election of officers. In some instances those the soldiers did not like, have simply been driven out as supporters of the old *regime;* or men who have shown themselves absolutely unfit, and have been slated for dismissal, have been asked to remain. There has been no way of persuading the soldiers to cease demanding the retention of such undesirables. As for excesses, men have made attempts to shoot their officers. . . . In the instinct for self-preservation even elementary shame has been forgotten, and panic has been made easy. The Germans well understand this, and they have taken full advantage of this desire for peace. They began the fraternizing, and began it on our time of disorder and collapse, to give all encouragement to our yearning for peace. Later, they began sending us peace envoys, which was frankly provocative.

The army [said General Gurko] is on the eve of collapse. The country is in danger and nearing destruction. You must help us. To destroy is easier than to build. You knew how to destroy. You should know how to restore.

In the cavalry, artillery and engineers [General Brusilov estimated] 50 per cent of their *cadres* still remain. The situation in the infantry, which forms the bulk of the army, is very different. Heavy losses in killed, wounded and prisoners, and many desertions have meant that the effectives of some regiments have been renewed as many as nine or ten times, while there are companies with not more than three of their original men. As to new reinforcements, their training is inadequate, and their discipline is worse than anything before. There remain only from two to four of the original officers per regiment, and many such officers have been wounded. Those we have now are young men who have been promoted after short periods of training, who lack experience, and who have no authority. Now, such *cadres* have been given the task of restoring the army, and on a new basis. This has so far been beyond their powers. Although the need of a revolution has been felt, and it even broke out too late, the soil for it had not been prepared. It was regarded by our backward soldiers as an emancipation "from oppression by officers." As to the officers, it unfairly took from them the right to exercise influence over their subordinates. Misunderstandings have occurred. Some of the older commanders, I admit, have not been without guilt. But, when the Revolution became a fact, everyone did his best to reconcile himself to it. The difficulties that arose were due to outside influences. Order No. 1 worked confusion in the army. Order No. 2 cancelled it so far as the front was concerned. But in the minds of the soldiers the idea had taken root that their commanders were concealing something, that some were granting certain rights and others taking them away.

The officers welcomed the Revolution. Had we not given the Revolution so friendly a reception, it might not have been brought about so easily. But it turned out that liberty meant liberty only for the private soldier. The officer had to be content to be a pariah of liberty. The granting of liberty has stupefied the masses who have little understood what has really taken place. Everyone knows that important rights have been granted, but not what those rights are, nor are the masses interested in doing their duty. The officers are in a difficult position. About 15 or 20 per cent of them, those who are in sympathy with the new order of things, have quickly adapted themselves; the soldiers trusted them before and trust them now. Some have begun to flatter the soldiers, to indulge them, and to incite them against others. But the majority, about 75 per cent, have been unable to change and have become moody; they have shut themselves up in their shells, and don't know how to act. We are taking measures to get them out of their shells, and bring them and their men together, for we have no officers now. Many officers have no political experience, and many more do not know how to talk to their men. All this keeps them from reaching a mutual understanding. It is necessary to explain things and to show the common soldier that liberty has been granted to all. I have known him for forty-five years, I like him and will try to bring him closer to our officers. But the Provisional Government, the Duma, and especially the Soviet of Soldiers' and Workers'

Deputies, should spare no effort to assist us. They must do it without delay, for the sake of the country.

That assistance is also necessary because a peculiar interpretation has been put on the slogan "without annexations and contributions." One regiment declared that not only would it not advance, but it would leave the front and return home. The committees opposed this, but they were told that they would be replaced by others. I tried persuasion on the mutineers, and for a long time. But when I asked them whether they agreed with me, they asked leave to give me a written answer, and in a few minutes they put before my eyes a poster reading, "Peace at any price, down with the war!" When we began to talk again, one of them declared: "Since 'without annexations and contributions' is to be the word, what value for us has that hill over there?" I replied: "That hill is worth nothing to me either. But we have got to fight the enemy who is holding it." Finally, they gave me their word that they would not withdraw. But they refused to advance. "Our enemies are good fellows," they said, "They told us they would not advance if we did not. We want to go home, to enjoy our liberty and use our land. Why should we get ourselves crippled?"

Fraternization, the newspaper *Pravda*, widely circulated, and the proclamations of the enemy, written in good Russian—all alike result in depriving the officers of all influence, although they themselves are willing to fight.

Upon my recent appointment as Commander on the Rumanian front [testified General Shcherbachev], I made a tour of inspection of the armies under my control, and the impression I received of the morale of the troops and their fitness to fight were identical with those which have just been put before you in detail. . . . Without piling up examples, I will simply cite the case of one of the best divisions in the army, one which in earlier days won the name of the iron division, and which in the present war brilliantly maintained its reputation. That division, on a section of the front where an offensive had been planned, refused to do the needed preliminary trench work, and gave as a reason its unwillingness to advance. A similar case occurred recently in another very fine division. Work begun by it was discontinued. The elected committees made an inspection and decided to stop it, because it was the preparatory step for an advance.

Changes in the Command

On May 1 Guchkov resigned. He explained the "democratization" of the army which he had been trying to bring about in this way: "We wanted to mould the awakened spirit of independence, initiative and liberty which filled everyone, and to direct it into proper channels. But there is a certain limit, at which the disintegration of that powerful living organism, the army, must begin."

There is no doubt that that limit had been passed before May 1. That is, Guchkov himself had gone beyond it. However, we should remember that except at the very beginning, as Minister of War in the Provisional Government of Prince Lvov, Guchkov had no power at all. He could only follow the course set by the Soviet of Workers' and Soldiers' Deputies, and try to block what clearly was leading to the ruin of the army. In his letter to General Kornilov of June, 1917, shortly after he resigned, he explained his course. "My task was," he said, "to seek to prevent that complete destruction with which the army was menaced by the Socialists, and especially by the Soviet of Workers' and Soldiers' Deputies, and to afford the healthy elements a chance to regain strength by giving the disease time to reach its end."

Guchkov was followed by Kerensky, whose first steps were marked by many measures that had a demagogic appeal, for instance his promulgation of the "Soldier's Declaration of Rights." And on May 22, on his demand, the Provisional Government removed General Alexeev and made General Brusilov Commander-in-Chief.

The Offensive of June, 1917

The main attack in the summer campaign of 1917 was to be launched by the southwestern front in the direction of Lemberg. The attacks on the northern, western, and Rumanian fronts were to be only of a subsidiary nature. On June 18, the Eleventh and the Seventh Armies began the offensive. An excellent plan had been worked out. Artillery and technical equipment in quantities previously unknown to Russia's forces were concentrated to prepare the infantry assault. All enemy works were literally leveled with the ground. Then and only then did the infantry advance in the zone of the enemy's fire; for the most part the picked shock units headed the advance. But the rest of the infantry followed with reluctance. Some regiments, having reached the enemy's lines, turned back on the pretext that the trenches had been so completely destroyed that it would be impossible to occupy them overnight. Nevertheless, thanks to the excellent artillery preparation and the heroic action of the picked units, the enemy positions were taken in the first two days. After that the Eleventh and Seventh Armies only marked time, inasmuch as the infantry was unwilling to advance further.

> I feel in duty bound to report [wrote the commander of the Eleventh Army] that, despite the victory won on June 18 and 19 which should have strengthened the spirit and increased the zeal of the troops, no such effect could be seen in most regiments, while in some the conviction prevails that they have done their work and must go no further.

In the meantime, on June 23, the Eighth Army, on the left flank of the southwestern front, went into action. General Kornilov, commanding, had concentrated all his best units for a break through. But the same thing happened. The attack was successful, and even more so than in the center; for the Austro-Hungarian divisions facing the Eighth Army were of inferior quality. On the first day 7,000 prisoners and 48 guns were taken, and the Russian troops penetrated far into the enemy zone. But, as the advance progressed, the picked units, having suffered heavy losses, melted away, while the remaining infantry in their rear became so disorganized that a slight center attack from the enemy caused the entire army to fall back in the greatest confusion.

By July 2 this offensive on the southwestern front was at an end. The losses in the three armies amounted to 1,222 officers and 37,500 men. Such figures, compared with the losses before the Revolution, were small. But they were suffered solely by the picked units and the few regiments not yet in disintegration. Thus they were heavy indeed, for they meant the loss of all elements imbued with a sense of duty, and available for preserving some sort of order among the troops. As they no longer existed, the three armies became nothing but tumultuous crowds, which any first pressure by the enemy could put to flight. Such pressure was brought to bear on the left flank of the Eleventh Army where at that time there had been concentrated 7 army corps* or 20 divisions—a total of 240 battalions, 40 squadrons, 100 heavy and 475 field guns and howitzers. The opposing enemy had only 9 divisions, or some 83 battalions, with about 60 heavy and 400 field guns and howitzers. Despite such enormous numerical

---

* Five corps on the front and two corps in reserve.

superiority, the detachments of the Eleventh Army began to retreat
of their own accord. Soon the whole army was following in a
panic. And the rest of the story may show how completely unfit
it was to fight. On July 9 it reached the line of the Seret. An attack
by three German companies put to flight the One Hundred and
Twenty-sixth and the Second Finnish Divisions. Resistance to
the advancing enemy was offered only by cavalry and infantry
officers and non-commissioned officers supported by single soldiers. The rest of the infantry was fleeing, while crowds of deserters
blocked every road. To tell how many there were it is enough to say
that 12,000 were arrested in the neighborhood of Volochisk by a
single battalion of picked men, who had been posted in the rear.
And these fleeing mobs committed every act of violence. They
murdered officers, robbed the people, and assaulted women and
children.

On July 9 the committees and commissars of the Eleventh Army
sent the Provisional Government the following telegram:

> The German offensive, which began on our front on July 6, is turning
> into an immense catastrophe which perhaps threatens revolutionary
> Russia with ruin. A sudden and disastrous change occurred in the atti-
> tude of the troops, who had recently advanced under the heroic leader-
> ship of a few units. Their zeal soon spent itself. The majority are in a
> state of growing disintegration. Authority and obedience exist no longer.
> Persuasion and admonition produce no effect. Threats and sometimes
> shots are the answer. . . . For hundreds of miles one can see lines of
> deserters, armed and unarmed, in good health and in high spirits, cer-
> tain they will not be punished. The situation calls for strong mea-
> sures. . . . An order to fire upon them was issued today by the Com-
> mander-in-Chief, with the approval of the commissars and committees.
> And all Russia should be told the truth. . . . Though she shudder at it,
> it will give her the necessary determination to deal with those who by
> their cowardice are ruining and betraying both their country and the
> Revolution.

Attempts at an offensive on the northern front ended as soon as
they began. They were made on July 8–10.

> Only two divisions out of six [Headquarters reported] could take
> part. The Thirty-sixth, after seizing two lines of enemy trenches and
> advancing against the third, turned back because shouts from behind
> called it to a halt. The Hundred and Eighty-second, compelled to by
> force of arms, took its position. But, when the enemy opened fire upon

it, it began firing crazily at our own troops. In the Hundred and Twentieth only one battalion advanced to attack. The Neishlotsky regiment of infantry not only refused to attack, but kept others from advancing by seizing the field kitchens of the front line units.

The same thing happened on the western front. General Denikin was then in command. At the Headquarters conference of July 16 he thus described the unsuccessful attempt of his front to attack:

> The troops went forward, passed two or three lines of enemy trenches as if on parade, and . . . then went back to their own trenches. On a section of nineteen versts I had concentrated 184 battalions and 900 guns; the enemy had 17 battalions in the first line and 12 battalions in reserve, with 300 guns. For the attack 138 battalions were moved against 17, and 900 guns were used against 300.

The offensive on the Rumanian front began on July 10. It differed from the offensives undertaken on the other fronts in that not only Russian but also Rumanian troops took part. The example of the latter unquestionably produced a sobering effect. Headquarters, taking advantage of this, organized the attacks so that Russian and Rumanian troops might carry them out jointly. Besides, the shock units were not used as they were on the other fronts; they were regarded as infantry assigned the work of suppressing mutinies in corrupted army units. The offensive made good progress. The German line was broken, prisoners and more than 100 guns being taken. But on July 13 a telegram was received from Kerensky, which, in the name of the Provisional Government, ordered the advance to be stopped. The telegram was sent in accordance with the request of General Kornilov who, following the defeat of the armies of the southwestern front in Galicia, had replaced General Brusilov as Commander-in-Chief.

General Kornilov

The appointment of General Kornilov meant that measures to restore discipline would be taken at once. Before consenting to act he placed before the Provisional Government very definite demands for its restoration; he categorically refused to serve unless those demands were granted. They included the re-establishment of courts-martial, abolished at the beginning of the Revolution, and capital punishment.

On July 12 the Provisional Government issued a decree beginning:

> The shameful conduct, both in the rear and at the front, of certain regiments which had forgotten their duty to Russia, has brought her, and brought the Revolution, to the very verge of ruin, and forces the Provisional Government to take extraordinary measures for the purpose of restoring order and discipline in the army. Fully conscious of the heavy responsibility for the future of the country that weighs upon it, the Provisional Government has found it necessary: (1) to restore capital punishment for the duration of the War, in the case of certain very grave crimes if committed by men in uniform, and (2) to establish courts-martial of the Revolution, to be made up of men and officers, for the immediate trial of those guilty of such crimes.

But it should be borne in mind that defeat was not the sole reason of the change of attitude of the Provisional Government, no longer headed by Prince Lvov, but by Kerensky. Between July 3 and July 5, the Bolsheviks made an attempt to seize power in Petrograd. This first attempt failed because the majority of the number of the Soviet of Soldiers' and Workers' Deputies were opposed to it. It was soon ended by a cadet battalion and Cossack regiments, after a few shots had been fired from a two-gun battery of horse artillery.*

The defeats at the front had a sobering effect on those elements that still retained a sense of duty. The right wing delegates in the military committees began to realize that for the army further to play with revolution must surely bring the country to ruin. But the great mass of the troops were as reluctant to fight as before.

General Kornilov was doing his utmost to bring his forces back to what they should be. But his heroic efforts were meeting immense difficulties. The elements that had remained faithful had been destroyed in the abortive offensives. Such elements had to be created anew, and to do that it was necessary to take advantage of the change for the better taking place in the loyal sections of the army and people. But, without the fullest co-operation of the Government, no lasting results could be obtained. Instead of assistance, General Kornilov was soon meeting with opposition from Kerensky. Such an attitude on the part of the head of the Government was bound to precipitate a crisis, inasmuch as there could no longer be any doubt that the vast majority of the troops

* Polovtsev, *Dni zatmneniia (The Eclipse),* Paris, 1928, pp. 120–130.

and the people did not want the war to go on. Kerensky did not have the courage to tell the Allies this frankly, and at the same time he was anxious not to break with the Left. How afraid he was of such a break can easily be shown. After the Bolshevik uprising in July, General Polovtsev, commanding the troops of the Petrograd district, succeeded in getting the Government to give him a warrant for the arrest of the principal Bolshevik leaders.

> It was not without pleasure [General Polovtsev writes]* that I received from Kerensky a list comprising the names of more than twenty Bolsheviks, headed by the names of Lenin and Trotsky, who had been set down for arrest. . . . But, no sooner had the cars been sent upon the mission, than Kerensky came back to my office and told me that the arrest of Trotsky and Steklov must be cancelled, for they were members of the Soviet. . . . Kerensky hurriedly left my office and rushed off somewhere in a car. The next day Balabin† reported to me that the officer who had come to Trotsky's apartment to arrest him, found Kerensky ahead of him, and he then cancelled the order. Such was the practical application of his fiery speeches on the necessity of a strong government. . . .

The Officers' Corps

In fact, his hesitation resulted in his playing a double role. It was inevitable that such an attitude should lead to that crisis in the army known as "the Kornilov affair." And to understand its psychological side, what had been developing in the officers' corps must first be known.

Even before the war it was a corps that was not really a distinct caste. Men of humble origin were to be found even among the generals occupying high positions. General Kornilov himself was the son of a Cossack farmer. The conditions of service, the sense of honor uniting the officers as a class, the existence of the Guard, all that gave it the outward features of a caste; and they were misunderstood and misinterpreted by those who did not know the army. The corps was fundamentally very democratic. Traditions which had taken root in the army were often at variance with the regulations which had been drawn up under strong German influences. Not only were the latter modified by the power of tradition, but even in spirit the army regulations became Russian as time went

* *Ibid.,* p. 143.
† Chief of Staff of the Petrograd military district.

on. That the democratic spirit was inherent in the whole structure of Cossack life is well known, but even in the regular army also the elective principle in certain questions had been given legal sanction. In the case of the rank and file, that principle had developed in "artel" arrangements, whether of companies, squadrons, or batteries. And among the officers it showed itself in the "courts of honor," established to investigate and pass on cases in which the conduct of an officer was involved.

By the end of 1915 a large proportion of the permanent officers had been killed, and their places had been taken by officers of a new or war-time type. The latter came from the common people. During the winter of 1915–1916, when, following the catastrophe of the summer campaign, the military authorities were at work re-establishing the fighting strength of the army, special attention was paid to the question of filling vacancies in the command. In view of the fact that the war-time junior officers arriving from the interior, were inadequately trained, the following measure was put in force by the present author, as Chief of Staff of the Seventh Army. All such junior officers had to take a six-weeks course in tactics, for which purpose a special school was established in the immediate rear. According to reports made by it, 70 per cent of the men trained there belonged to the peasant class and only 4 per cent to the nobility.

It was with the help of these war-time junior officers that the Galician victories in the summer campaign of 1916 were won. With their blood, shed in torrents, did the new officers cement their union with the remnants of the officers of the regular army. For the strength of that union there were social and psychological reasons. At the beginning of 1916 the following situation existed: the war-time officers then drawn in came from the educated youth of the country. The enthusiasm which marked the initial stage of the war had faded away. In the future one could only look for hardships. Those with a sense of patriotism little developed were seeking safe positions and settling themselves in the rear. As has been said, for the educated in Russia to avoid military service was easy. But all those who were patriotic and courageous had gone to the front, and were serving there. From the social standpoint a certain selection was taking place, and it was for the good of the army. This accounts for the fact that the newly promoted juniors and the older officers of experience were soon undergoing a kind of spiritual welding.

Such was the officers' corps at the outbreak of the Revolution. Systematic persecutions, to which the personnel of the command had been subjected by Guchkov, and especially by Kerensky, had been driving the officers into the ranks of those opposing the Provisional Government. For the time the officers had been suppressing their feelings of protest; but they were growing and certain to burst forth sooner or later, the more so since it would not be a protest from regular officers, in defense of some professional or class interest, but a protest from those who were patriots. This, in their party short-sightedness, neither Kerensky nor his close associates were able to understand. Instead of taking advantage of what was theirs to use, they turned it against themselves. For such a course they had only recently been blaming the Government of the Tsar. Now, having come into power themselves, they repeated the self-same error.

The Kornilov Affair

The circumstances of the Kornilov incident, in which that protest found its first expression, are well known. In Petrograd a Bolshevik uprising was expected. To preserve order loyal troops, under an agreement between Kerensky and Kornilov, were to be sent to Petrograd. Simultaneously it was intended to put an end to the control over the Government exercised by the Petrograd garrison which, under the pretext of "defending the Revolution," had refused to go to the front and, in fact had made the position of Kerensky and his Government virtually that of prisoners. At the last moment Kerensky took fright and, referring to a conversation between his representative, V. Lvov,* and Kornilov regarding the need of strengthening the Government, he sent a telegram to Kornilov removing him. Kornilov refused to obey, and appealed to the army to rise against the Provisional Government. Kerensky, on his part, sent telegrams to all military committees denouncing Kornilov as a rebel.

Kornilov was backed by a small group of officers at General Headquarters, who were ardent patriots but had no real strength; all other officers in sympathy with Kornilov were scattered among the troops and were completely in their power. As for the mass of

* V. N. Lvov, not to be confused with Prince George E. Lvov, head of the first Provisional Government.

the rank and file, it was clearly against Kornilov. On the Rumanian front Kornilov's appeal to rise against the Provisional Government was received about midnight; an hour later there arrived the telegram from Kerensky which proclaimed Kornilov a traitor. The following day, about noon, all the committees in every army on the front wired to the Provisional Government begging it to court-martial Kornilov. In the evening of the same day General Denikin, commanding the southwestern front, his Chief of Staff, as also the generals commanding the armies on that front, were put under arrest by their troops. And they began to massacre the best officers, under the pretext that they were "Kornilov's supporters."

Kornilov's appeal was worse than premature. It was the doom of the flower of the army and the intelligentsia. To save the situation General Alexeev was forced to oppose Kornilov. By taking such an attitude, he showed that he placed the salvation of Russia above his political and personal sympathies. Having the mind of a statesman, he saw that Kornilov must submit to Kerensky, hard though it was. Alexeev persuaded Kornilov to abandon further resistance. Alexeev, that man of sterling honesty, had to hear Kornilov answer in his excitement; "You are following the course which marks the division between the gentleman and the man without honor. . . ."

The Final Breakdown

After Kornilov surrendered Kerensky himself became Commander-in-Chief. The break-up of the army was proceeding at full speed. The existing military committees were considered by the soldiers to be too reactionary. Everywhere self-styled "revolutionary tribunals" sprang up, which soon changed that name to "military revolutionary committees"; their personnel was made up chiefly of men of the extreme Left and, even to a greater extent, of adventurers anxious to fish in troubled waters, and bent on using the Revolution for their personal advantage.

As a result of the Kornilov incident a complete and final break between officers and private soldiers took place. The bulk of the men now looked upon the officers not only as "counter-revolutionists," but as chief obstacles to an immediate ending of the war. The Bolsheviks and the Germans were making full use of the situation. "The attitude of the troops," Zhdanov, Commissar of the western front reported, "is growing worse under the influence of the defeatist propaganda which the papers *Burevestnik,* and *Tovarishch,* and the German paper *Russkii Vestnik,* are spreading. . . ."

What the attitude of the army was on the eve of the Bolshevik *coup d'état* one may judge from the following report of General Headquarters, based on information received between October 15 and 30, 1917.

> The general feeling of the army continues to be, as in the first half of the month, one of highly nervous expectancy. Now as before, an irresistible thirst for peace, a universal desire to leave the front, and end the present situation somehow in the quickest possible manner constitute the main motives on which the attitude of most of our troops is based. . . . The army is simply a huge, weary, shabby, and ill-fed mob of angry men united by their common thirst for peace and by common disappointment. The above holds true, more or less, for the entire front. . . .

On October 25, in Petrograd, the Bolsheviks, supported by the garrison of the capital, overthrew the Provisional Government. A bloody struggle ensued, in which Kerensky had to look for support to those forces which had been undermined by him during his conflict with Kornilov. Anyhow the Bolshevik victory was certain, inasmuch as they had won the masses over to their side by the promise of an immediate cessation of the war.

The Soviet of People's Commissars proclaimed in their wireless message:

> Soldiers, peace, the great peace is in your hands, you will not let the counter-revolutionist generals make peace a failure. . . . Let the regiments, holding the line, immediately select delegates for formal negotiations with the enemy looking to an armistice. The Soviet of People's Commissars authorizes you so to do. . . . Soldiers, peace is in your hands. . . .

This marked the end of Russia's participation in World War I. But the people of Russia did not obtain the promised peace. Simultaneously with the seizure of power by the Bolsheviks civil war began, and one of the cruelest civil wars in history.

ALEXANDER KERENSKY

The Policy of the Provisional Government

A. F. Kerensky describes in the following excerpt, written fifteen years after the Revolution, the difficulties he and the Provisional Government faced in achieving unity of the democratic forces and in mobilizing public confidence and consent.

. . . To prevent a civil war was the whole object of the internal policy of the Provisional Government.

After the collapse of the monarchy the Provisional Government, in the midst of war, was obliged to restore, from top to bottom, the administrative apparatus of the state and to fix the foundations of a new state and social order. Two conditions for the attainment of the two above-mentioned objectives of internal policy prevented the application of a dictatorial or of a so-called "strong" government. First of all to form a "strong" dictatorial government, that is, a government which did not direct and govern, but commanded and punished, it was necessary to have at one's disposal a highly organized and well functioning administration and police. Such a machinery the Provisional Government did not possess. It had to be created anew under the most difficult circumstances. But until it was established, the government had to replace police compulsion

From *The Slavonic and East European Review,* London, vol. 11, no. 31 (July 1932), pp. 12–19. Abridged. Reprinted by courtesy of Oleg A. Kerensky and the editors of *The Slavonic and East European Review.*

by moral persuasion. We know also that Lenin utilized for his counter-revolutionary *coup d'état* the military and administrative apparatus established by the Provisional Government. He planted everywhere among the troops, in government institutions, in the Soviets, and in the town councils, his militant cells.

The second condition which determined the internal policy of the Provisional Government was the war. By its very nature the war demanded the closest national unity, which under existing conditions was hard to achieve.

At the front there was a mass of more than ten million soldiers, highly agitated, recognizing only the Left socialist parties as an authority. It was also necessary to maintain the efficiency of thousands of officers whose position was highly precarious. The great majority of these officers recognized the political authority of the bourgeois parties. Of these parties, the Cadets or Constitutional Democrats, led by Professor Miliukov, was the most influential. Up to the fall of the monarchy this party had represented the liberal-radical wing of the bourgeois opposition. However, at the time of the February Revolution, when the old conservative parties disappeared from the scene, the Cadet Party became the chief spokesman of the Right. The above conditions, I repeat, determined the main lines of the internal policy of the Provisional Government, which did not change throughout the whole time of its existence, in spite of frequent alterations in its composition. Our major purpose was to unite all the creative forces of the country in order (1) to re-establish the functioning of the state apparatus, (2) to create the basis of a new post-revolutionary political and social order, and (3) to continue the defense of the country. The only way of opposing the forces of disruption which were driving the country into chaos and civil war, was to draw into the government the leading representatives of all political parties without exception, whether bourgeois or socialist, which recognized the new order and the supreme authority of the Constituent Assembly. It was clear that the latter had to be summoned, in spite of the war, at the earliest possible date.

It must be said that the collapse of the monarchy came about so unexpectedly for the socialist parties that their leaders did not at once understand their own role in the new political conditions. Suddenly the masses of the people—workers, peasants and soldiers—had obtained an overwhelming power in the life of the state.

In the first days of the Revolution it seemed to the leaders of the Left that the deciding role in the administration of the state had already passed into the hands of the Liberals and that the socialist parties, although not part of the government, ought to help the government but only in so far as it did not act against the interests of the working class. This so-called "dualism," the sharing of power between the Soviets and the government, in the first two months of the February Revolution was partly due to the failure of the socialist parties to appreciate their importance and the part they would have to play in the post-revolutionary period. Conscientiously planning the role of a kind of responsible opposition to the government, the Soviets failed to see that their pressures weakened the broken administrative machinery and the bourgeois classes.

In spite of a generally held opinion, it is precisely the strictly bourgeois original composition of the Provisional Government in which, out of eleven ministers, I was the only representative of the non-bourgeois democracy—that was the cause of the greatest "weakness of authority" of that government. Moreover— and here again we have a paradox—it was just this cabinet that carried out all the programmes of the radical political and social reforms for which later, at the time of the psychological preparations of General Kornilov's *coup d'état,* the blame was placed on Kerensky, accusing him for "having finally succumbed to the power of the Soviets."

As a matter of fact, it was precisely the first "capitalist" cabinet of the Provisional Government which issued a number of decrees on freedom of speech, assembly, inviolability of person; worked out the great agrarian reform (abolition of non-laboring land tenure and landed property); prepared the law on self-government of county and town councils on the basis of proportional universal suffrage without distinction of sex; introduced workers' control into factories and workshops; gave wide powers to workers' trade unions; introduced the eight hour working day; laid down the principles of co-operative legislation; formulated the plan of transforming the Empire into a federation of free peoples; drew up the principles of the electoral law for the Constituent Assembly, etc. And all this vast legislative work, which transformed the political and social system of Russia, the Provisional Government carried out without any pressure "from the Soviet democracy." Of its own free will it achieved the social and political ideals of the whole Russian liberation movement, liberal and revolutionary, which had

had the support of many generations from the time of Novikov and Radishchev.

To be sure, the legislative work by way of issuing decrees was the easiest task of all. The hardest was the administration. We had to create the technical machinery and to establish the authority of the government. For this last task the government had to enlist the confidence of the new strata of the population which up to the Revolution were only objects and not subjects of power. The whole administrative apparatus, however, was also restored in the first two months of the Revolution, but more on paper than in reality. For the new government did not know how to give orders and the population did not wish to submit, often demanding the confirmation of this or that Soviet.

Thus, not only the conditions of war, but also the public mood, shaken by the Revolution, demanded the presence in the Provisional Government of representatives of all parties. After some resistance, both from the Petrograd Soviet and from an insignificant minority in the Provisional Government which persisted in believing in the hegemony of the bourgeoisie, and after some disturbances and street fighting, representatives of the Soviets and of the socialist parties finally entered the government. From the beginning of May and right up to the Bolshevik counter-revolution, the Provisional Government was a bourgeois-socialist coalition which included representatives of all parties which, accepting the Revolution, were opposed to all forms of dictatorship, whether personal, party, or class.

A policy of national unity, of softening class antagonism, of averting the civil war, which was always possible in the first months of the Revolution, naturally excluded the need of a "strong authority." A policy of co-operation in the administration of the state by many parties with the most various programmes is, of course, as is well known in Europe, a policy of compromise. But a policy of compromise and of mutual concessions is the most difficult and unpopular; for such a policy is often unpleasant and irritating for the self-esteem of party committees, and for the country or the wide masses of the population it is not always clear and intelligible.

Thus, it may be said that the war conditions imposed on Russia after the Revolution the coalition system of government which is the most difficult of all. We know that even in time of peace in countries with a prolonged experience of parliamentarism, coalitions in the government delay and complicate government work and soon alienate public opinion. The leading members of the Provisional Government who remained in it to the end (there were only two) very clearly saw the negative side of a coalition government in a period of revolution; but to prevent civil war and an immediate separate peace, we had no choice whatsoever.

Usually the history of the February Revolution is told as a continuous collapse at the front and increasing anarchy in the country. In actual fact the history of this Revolution represents a curve of slow rise followed by a sharp fall after the revolt of General Kornilov.

The essence of the government's internal policy was indisputably threatened by the attempt, by way of a *coup d'état,* to replace the coalition authority by the personal dictatorship of a general. As we know, this attempt took place after the Provisional Government had suppressed the July uprising of the Bolsheviks. The summer months which preceded Kornilov's *coup* saw the greatest decline of Bolshevik influence in the Soviets, in the factories, and at the front.

At the front the commanders, together with the commissars of the War Ministry, from the time of the July offensive were able to employ disciplinary measures, including the application of capital punishment. The authority of the commanders, which had fallen after the collapse of the monarchy to almost nil, towards the middle of the summer had been sufficiently re-established for the leaders of the military conspiracy to feel assured that the troops would execute their orders and that the break-up of the Soviets and the overthrow of the Provisional Government would not call forth any serious mutiny in the ranks of the army. As we know, these calculations proved to be very exaggerated. The attempted revolt of the generals once again smashed all discipline in the army and undermined the authority not only of the High Command, but of the Provisional Government itself. But these consequences of their "patriotic exploit," which the reckless generals had not foreseen, in no way weaken my assertion: it was only when they felt again a certain authority in their hands that the adherents of a personal dictatorship at the head of the army and among the liberal and conservative politicians decided on their unhappy adventure. And we know it was just the same in Germany. The famous attempt of

Kapp and Ludendorff to repeat in 1920 Kornilov's march of 1917 also took place only after the German democracy had checked anarchy on the Left, had suppressed the Spartacists, and re-established the military and administrative machinery of the state.

But apart from this similarity there is also positive evidence of the correctness of the coalition policy of the Provisional Government. The anarchy which broke out in March gradually died down toward autumn, to break out again with renewed force just before the Bolshevik *coup d'état.* In the country the number of acts of violence of the peasants who worked the lands of the squires was falling. Transport was in the process of being re-established. The food situation in the towns was improving. Local self-government was reviving everywhere. In mid-August, in most of the towns, town councils elected by universal suffrage were already at work. Rural self-government was being restored, though more slowly than in the towns. The organs of local self-government, based on universal suffrage, were thus weakening the authority of the Soviets and diminishing their part in local life. *Izvestia* itself, then the central organ of the Congress of the Soviets (which were not yet Bolshevik), wrote on October 12: "The Soviet of Workers' and Soldiers' Deputies as a whole . . . is passing through an evident crisis. The Central Executive Committee, at the time of the highest development of the Soviets, reckoned 800 local Soviets. Many of them no longer exist, still more only exist on paper. . . . The Soviets were an excellent organization for struggling against the old regime, but they are quite incapable of taking upon themselves the building up of a new regime; they have no specialists, no experience, no understanding of business, and, finally, no proper organization."

The summoning of the Constituent Assembly, fixed for the month of November, would have finally reduced to nothing the role of the Soviets in the history of post-revolutionary Russia. The slogan of the Bolshevik counter-revolution: "All power to the Soviets," appeared simply as a demagogic cover for the dictatorial plans of Lenin.

I will not enter into a consideration of the economic and financial policy of the Provisional Government. At a time of war and blockade, with profound social changes going on in the country itself, everything in this domain had a temporary and conditional character. But even then the need was felt for a better planned direction of the whole economy of the country. To achieve this we created a Higher Council of National Economy, similar to the one that sprang up in Germany and later in other countries.

What I have written on the policy of the Provisional Government is far from exhausting the subject and in no way pursues the object of self-defense or self-justification. Even now [15 years after the Revolution] I still fail to see by what road other than that of co-operation of the whole nation it would have been possible to save Russia from civil war and a separate peace. It still appears to me that the main lines of military and internal policy of the Provisional Government were correctly traced. I entirely agree, however, that because of limitations of our personal strength and ability, we were not able to carry out this policy properly. But then the implementation of our program was interrupted by those who thought that they knew better than the Provisional Government how to govern Russia. We must further bear in mind that, opposed to dictatorships of all kinds, the Provisional Government, for the whole period of its existence, did actually express the decisions freely adopted by all the political parties, except for the Bolsheviks.

In the course of its eight months' existence, the Provisional Government lived through four cabinet crises. Each time all the members of the government, without exception, agreed to leave the cabinet, if this was the desire of the parties which had entered into the coalition. I personally, the member most responsible for the work of the Provisional Government, offered to resign, both before Kornilov's attempt of a *coup d'état* and before the October counter-revolution. Each time I proposed this to those persons and parties which considered themselves better equipped than I to govern the nation, I urged them to assume the responsibility for the future of the country and for forming a new cabinet. Neither the politicians responsible for the tragic escapade of General Kornilov nor the adherents of a Bolshevik dictatorship responded to this appeal. They knew that the organized and free public opinion of Russia was against any form of dictatorship and opposed any drastic changes of the system of government until the convocation of the Constituent Assembly. Only through a conspiracy and a treacherous armed insurrection was it possible to overthrow the Provisional Government and thus to prevent the establishment of a democratic system in Russia. Unfortunately, apart from the path chosen by the Provisional Government, no one seemed to have seen any other alternative but the terrible road of the civil war.

What can we conclude from this? I believe that it is only the establishing a national government, only by making the government subject to the free will of the people, only by returning to the fundamental ideas of the February Revolution, that Russia will recover internal peace and will become a source of peace for the rest of the world.

COUNT VALENTIN ZUBOV

Gatchina—October 1917, Reminiscences

Count Valentin P. Zubov (1884?–1969), art historian, was director of the museum in Gatchina in 1917 and, subsequently, founder and director of the Institute of Art History in Leningrad. He left Soviet Russia in 1925 and has since been residing in the West. His book of reminiscences, *Stradnye gody Rossii. Vospominaniia o revolutsii 1917–1925 (Russia's Years of Suffering. Reminiscences of the Revolution, 1917–1925),* was published by Wilhelm Fink Verlag, Munich, 1968.

The following selection, which describes Kerensky's arrival at Gatchina Palace on the night of the October insurrection, is an eyewitness account of the events that took place in Gatchina following the Bolshevik seizure of power in Petrograd.

The end of October was approaching and everybody knew that the Bolsheviks had chosen October 25 for the seizure of power. It seemed as though the Provisional Government alone had no suspicions. The supreme council on the preservation of the arts, formed by F. Golovin,* of which I was a member, met in the Winter

---

* Feodor Alexandrovich Golovin (1867-?) was president of the Second Duma and was a prominent member of the Constitutional Democratic Party. After the February Revolution he was asked by the Provisional Government to take charge of the preservation of the imperial palaces and their art treasures [Ed.].

From *The Russian Review,* vol. 28, no. 3 (July 1969), pp. 289–302.

Palace once a week. On October 18, I believe it was a Friday, a meeting took place; we were almost certain that it would be the last one and at the closing we decided to meet a week later if. . . .

Mikhail Ivanovich Rostovtsev* and I stepped out on the Palace Quay. We were discussing how long the Bolshevik government could possible remain in power if the coup succeeded. Some people said three weeks, others three months, but none gave them more than that. Mikhail Ivanovich, however, predicted: "The Bolsheviks will gain power and remain in power for a very long time causing much harm."

A week later, on October 25, I was about to have lunch in my apartment in the kitchen quarters of the Gatchina Palace when an automobile, flying a small British flag, drove into the courtyard. Expecting grave events on that date, I was not unduly astonished when I learned that the occupant of the car was Kerensky, who had fled the capital. He went to the commandant of the Gatchina garrison, Colonel Svistunov, who occupied several rooms on the ground floor of the palace.

Kerensky's adjutant, an attorney named Boris Ippolitovich Knirsha, was a wartime officer and a friend of mine. He immediately came to see me and informed me about the extraordinary events which had occurred that morning in Petersburg. On the previous evening the unrest in the garrison had reached such a state that the Chairman of the Council of Ministers no longer felt safe in the Winter Palace, where he occupied (in rather bad taste) the private apartment of the former Emperor. He decided to move, for that night, to the adjacent building, situated on the Palace Square on the other side of Millionnaya Street, which was reserved for the staff of the local guard regiment. Here he conceived the plan to go to the front to fetch troops on which he could rely. By morning, however, upon discovering that all telephone lines had been cut and that all spark plugs had been removed from the many military automobiles parked in the square, the Prime Minister and self-proclaimed Supreme Commander realized that he was unable to travel. His sole remaining hope was help from a foreign embassy.

---

* Mikhail Ivanovich Rostovtsev (1870–1952), eminent classical scholar, professor of ancient history and archaeology at Yale University (1925–1944) and author of many works including *Iranians and Greeks in South Russia* (1922), *Dura-Europos and its Art* (1938) and *Social and Economic History of the Hellenistic World* (3 vols., 1941) [Ed.].

I know the details of what happened following this were reported somewhat differently by others, but I am relating them according to what I recall was told me by my friend Knirsha, who participated in these events.

Kerensky was confronted with the problem of getting to one of the embassies. The nearest was the British Embassy on the Palace Quay close to the Mars Field and the Summer Gardens. Kerensky's adjutant Knirsha got there in disguise and by a roundabout way and managed to persuade the embassy to lend Kerensky a car. Thus the Chairman of the Council of Ministers, the comic-opera Supreme Commander, under the protection of the English flag, was enabled to get out of the capital. According to other sources of information, the car belonged to the American Embassy,* but I am certain that I saw the English flag on it. Besides, I had heard from Knirsha that he made his appeal to the British Embassy.

In his memoirs, recently published in English in the United States,† Kerensky says that first the Americans and then the British offered him the use of a car under their respective flags so that he could leave Petersburg but that he thanked them and proudly declined this aid, since, he said, "it is out of place for the head of the Russian government to pass through 'one's own' capital under a foreign flag." This is a boldfaced lie.

The automobile sped to Gatchina where the small garrison was yet comparatively calm. Incidentally, I have the impression that this route was selected by Knirsha, who, for personal reasons, wanted to stop at Gatchina Palace. Thus, minor matters often affect major events.

After a luncheon with Svistunov, Kerensky went toward Pskov

* See Meriel Buchanan, *Ambassador's Daughter,* London, 1958, p. 182: "Kerensky was, however, not with them for earlier in the morning he had borrowed the car of Mr. Whitehouse, one of the Secretaries of the American Embassy, and had driven out of Petrograd leaving the message that he would be back in a few days' time with loyal troops to restore order" [Ed.].

† Alexander Kerensky, *Russia and History's Turning Point,* New York, 1965, p. 438: "At the last moment, just before . . . I left, some officials from the British and United States Embassy arrived on the scene and offered to drive us out of the city under the American flag. I thanked the Allies for their offer, but said that the head of the government could not drive through the Russian capital under the American flag. As I learned later, however, the car turned out to be useful for one of my officers who could not fit into my own car. It drove a distance behind us" [Ed.].

in another automobile. The embassy car returned to Petersburg. Near Pskov stood the Don Cossack cavalry division, the very one which was involved during the conflict between Kornilov and Kerensky. The Cossacks felt that Kerensky had betrayed them and consequently could not have felt too warmly toward him.

It became clear to me that from then on the palace, which was entrusted to my care, was in the orbit of political events. First of all this was due to the fact that, even before our appearance here, the commandant of the garrison had moved into the small place on the ground floor. Therefore, from the moment my friends and I took charge of the safekeeping of the art treasures in the palace, we unsuccessfully wrestled with this problem, foreseeing the possible consequences.

The rest of October 25 passed quietly in Gatchina, but the following day rumors reached us that a Bolshevik coup had occurred in the capital and that the Provisional Government in the absence of its Chairman, had been arrested during a meeting in the Winter Palace. We did not know anything for sure, however.

On October 27, Kerensky returned to Gatchina accompanied by the cavalry division that followed him reluctantly since to them he was the sole representative of order and because it was necessary to struggle against disorder. I can still see Kerensky entering through the gates of the kitchen quarters, leading the top-ranking officers with a very Napoleonic air, his hand thrust between the folds of his military jacket. I watched this scene from a window above. Kerensky went to the apartment of the commandant and I went below to inquire about his wants, since I was still an official of the government which he headed and "the host" of the palace. As I entered he had just begun a game on a small billiard table. Cue in hand he asked that rooms be provided for him and his "suite." At these words I had difficulty in keeping a straight face. Apparently he suffered from megalomania. In his speeches he often presented himself as being endowed with supreme power which in some mystical manner had been passed on to him from the Emperor. Now, while drowning, he still spoke of his "suite."

The prospect of lodging an entire Cossack division in the palace was not a happy one for me; from the museum point of view, to admit an undisciplined crowd into the building was most undesirable.

On that first night I assigned several rooms to Kerensky, Krasnov and to the top-ranking officers, all of them naturally in the kitchen quarters, strictly isolating the central building and the arsenal quarters. The entire balance of the division had encamped under the open sky on the exercise grounds in front of the palace; horses served the Cossacks as pillows. I knew that if the stay of the troops in Gatchina were to continue I would not be able to get off cheaply. And it happened just that way: night after night I was asked for more and more rooms and, night after night, with the aid of my colleagues I had to lug art objects from one room to another. Thank the Lord that, for the time being, the soldiers continued to spend the night outside; only officers tried to penetrate the palace. Thus, as yet, there was not too much disorder although the furniture had already begun to suffer.

Some officers gathered at my table. Fortunately, I could regale them with vodka in spite of the then existing prohibition. Under the excuse of needing alcohol for the restoration of the paintings, I received half a bucketfull of alcohol and personally prepared my own vodka. Half a bucket of alcohol makes more than a full bucket of vodka—four huge bottles; even so my reserve was exhausted in a few days.

Lieutenant Knirsha, promoted from adjutant of Kerensky to the manager of the affairs of the non-existing Provisional Government, was sitting at my desk composing telegraphic messages "to all, to all, to all," announcing that the news from Petersburg regarding the coup by the Communists was a lie, that, outside the capital, the entire country was loyal to the Provisional Government and that tomorrow the gang would be thrown out of the city. Kindly Knirsha was very proud of his literary talents.

I do not recall exactly on which day of Kerensky's stay at the palace I had a telephone conversation with Petersburg, with Makarov, who was then the aid of Golovin. From our talk I concluded that there were many who shared Knirsha's illusions and were waiting for the arrival of the Cossacks. It was amazing that telephone communications between one side of the internal enemy front and the other were still possible, but many of the administrative buildings were not yet in the hands of the Bolsheviks.

On the very first evening Pechenkin, an officer of the Gatchina garrison, came to me with hand grenades draped all over him. He was known to me as a monarchist, a bitter enemy of the revolution (he had urged me to join an organization of monarchists), and was a candidate for an insane asylum. He was determined, at any cost, to explain to me the construction of a hand grenade and to prove that it could not explode without a detonator. I answered that my head and his were of less concern to me than the objects surrounding us, that I believed his words, and I begged him to abstain from a demonstration. Nevertheless, he threw his grenades on the floor and fortunately he was right; they did not explode. Then he informed me that in the morning, when the troops would march against the Bolsheviks, he intended to be near Kerensky and kill him with his grenades or in some other manner. As did many extreme rightists of that time, he saw in the Bolsheviks the means of accomplishing his counterrevolutionary aims.

Regardless of my opinion of Kerensky, an assassination conceived by a half-demented person had to be prevented at all cost. I warned Knirsha, suggesting that he render Pechenkin harmless, without injuring him, pointing out to Knirsha that the latter would be both unnecessary and dangerous at that moment. Knirsha went to get an order of arrest while I involved Pechenkin in a conversation, walking with him through the corridors that surrounded the courtyard of the kitchen quarters. He was astounded when Knirsha appeared and announced that he was under arrest. Later, when the die was cast and the victorious Bolsheviks had liberated Pechenkin and rewarded him with some sort of office, he told me that he could not imagine who could have divulged his secret. Fortunately for me, he had probably blabbed to others about his plans.

At daybreak, the "army" marched off for battle. At that point Krasnov was still able to compel Kerensky, who was gulping tranquilizers, to take part in the venture. Our day passed quietly. If the situation had been as clear to me at that moment as it became forty-eight hours later, I would probably have taken different precautionary measures. Unfortunately my hands were tied. The palace servants were so exhausted by so many guests that I could not enlist their help. Thus I could count only on my scholarly colleagues. Of course, I expected to be asked for more and more space, but I had not foreseen to just what extent.

When the troops returned by night, yesterday's assurance had considerably weakened. Apparently at Tsarskoe Selo, where the meeting with the Bolshevik forces took place, the resistance of the latter had exceeded expectations. Almost the entire garrison of Petersburg fought on their side. Artillery shells criss-crossed over the roof of the palace but fortunately did not hit it. The battle-wearied and somewhat disenchanted officers did not want to sleep outside any longer and I had to give them a larger portion of the palace than I expected. How could I explain to them that in this palace, with its hundreds of rooms, I could not accommodate them? The central section and the arsenal quarters I considered inviolate and I was able to maintain this stand till the end but in the kitchen quarters I had to yield room after room. I put four or five officers in each and they had to fit as best they could, sleeping on divans, armchairs, or what have you.

Among the people surrounding Kerensky, a personality suddenly appeared about whom much was said in the past and much was to be said still later—Boris Savinkov. On October 29, Kerensky flatly refused to accompany the troops who were fighting for him; he remained in his room, lying on the couch, swallowing tranquilizers. How he spent the time was told to me by Knirsha who was much amused at the expense of his chief. The latter aroused in me such revulsion that I avoided closer contact with him. Krasnov and his officers were incensed by his behavior and many of them remarked that he had betrayed the cavalry division before and that now he had misled them again. A spirit of separatism began to spread among the Cossacks. "What do we have to do with Russia, Kerensky and the Bolsheviks? Let us go to the Don, the Bolsheviks will not go there!" The Don began to have an hypnotic attraction for them.

The evening brought bad news. Everyone began to feel that the enemy had superior forces at his disposal. At night a soldier who was standing guard in the corridor ran into the room of one of my associates, Princess Shakhovskoi, announcing that the Bolsheviks were surrounding the palace and would shell it with artillery: "We are all in danger of perishing," he exclaimed. I was awakened at once. My first concern was the art objects; the second, my associates whom I urged to leave the palace at once and to seek shelter for the night somewhere in the town. I did not have to repeat this request, for in a moment they all disappeared—with the exception of Princess Shakhovskoi, a brave woman, who delighted in excitement. She refused to follow my advice and insisted upon remaining in the palace.

Earlier, I had made a list of the most valuable objects, which in the imminence of danger, had to be removed to a safe place. Among these were several paintings including the Holy Family by Watteau, a rare subject for that painter. Later, that canvas was transferred to the Hermitage. Of the porcelains, there were several statuettes of the first years of the Imperial ceramic works. The military authorities put an automobile at my disposal. I loaded it to the hilt, and, with the aid of Princess Shakhovskoi, transported these masterpieces to the house of Golovin, the business manager of the palace. He wife greatly resented this, being afraid that the presence of these objects in their house could bring personal danger to them. Then the Princess and I returned to the palace expecting the bombardment to start. We waited but nothing happened. The sun rose without even a shadow of the enemy.

When we tried to find the reason for the false alarm, it became evident that it was brought about by Kerensky himself who had been seized by a sudden panic. For some unknown reason, two sentries who were on duty in the corridor had entered his room. He took them for Bolsheviks who had come to kill him. Trembling, he moaned: "It is starting!" This was the hero of all the young and the old maids of the revolutionary spring, the brilliant orator, the brave commander-in-chief who had promised to lead the army in a new attack against the Germans. The Bolsheviks were right—he was a buffoon, a clown.

The news that reached us the next day from the "theater of war" was depressing. No longer could there be any doubt: the Bolsheviks were getting stronger. Three days earlier no one would have believed this. The game was lost and, as a result of this realization, the discipline among the officers, as well as among the soldiers, was crumbling minute by minute. I lost control of the buildings; people entered them in droves. When there was not enough furniture they used the floors. Soldiers also penetrated the palace. They flooded the corridors, entered rooms and wrote on the paintings with their bayonets: "This picture was viewed by soldier so-and-so." Only the historic rooms remained locked, but this was only a small consolation. In the kitchen quarters there were still many valuable objects prepared for packing. Besides, the last generation of the Tsar's family, lacking all artistic sense whatsoever, had shifted works of fine art to the service quarters while they decorated the walls of their own rooms with picture postcards and portraits of beauties clipped from illustrated magazines.

The only way of saving these art objects would have been to send them back to the historic quarters but this was not easy on account of a shortage of manpower.

The Bolsheviks owned a weapon that was more effective than

rifles and guns—propaganda. The events of the few days that had passed since the first encounter between the Cossacks and the Reds were persuasive enough to start secret negotiations regarding the surrender of Kerensky in exchange for the promise of a fully armed departure to the Don. Rumors about this began to spread and soon became a certainty. Kerensky also learned about them. Knirsha came to me asking whether, in case of necessity, I would agree to hide the "premier" in the palace—knowing that all of its by-ways were familiar to me—or whether I would help him disappear. If I had believed that Kerensky had the slightest chance of playing a political role, I would have refused but, under the existing circumstances, I promised to do whatever possible at the necessary moment. The palace was huge and two-thirds of it still remained under my complete control. The old servants of the Dowager Empress—the last occupant of the palace—were devoted to me, regarding me as the protector of their former master's interests. I could depend upon their silence, if I had to hide Kerensky for a day and then let him slip outside unobserved.

If my memory serves me well, it was October 31. I was having luncheon when Knirsha rushed in, saying: "Come, it is time, Kerensky is being betrayed now. He must flee!" We went to his drawing room; he was not there. I was told he was changing his clothes in the adjoining room. I waited; time passed. Finally I was told that he had already left. A sailor had given him his uniform. Kerensky put on a pair of goggles and, in this guise, walked past the sentry through the gates of the kitchen quarters, got into a car and left. Years later, his notebook was found on a stove in one of the rooms he occupied, thrown there by him in confusion. A Soviet "artist" drew a picture depicting Kerensky's flight from Gatchina: in this version he is changing into the uniform of a female nurse while his adjutants are burning papers in a stove. This is nonsense, for there were no army nurses at Gatchina, and there were no wounded in the palace, a proof that the battles were not very bloody.

However, with the disappearance of Kerensky, my problem was not over. Knirsha appeared with Kuzmin, the chief-of-staff of the Petersburg military region, an old revolutionary who in 1905 was the president of one of the short-lived local republics which were then mushrooming in Siberia. He, like Kerensky, was a Socialist Revolutionary. He had recently been appointed to his present office, replacing Petr Alexandrovich Polovtsev, whose assistant he had been until then. Following these two came the young Lieutenant

Miller, just named adjutant to Kerensky when Knirsha became the
office manager. One or two other officers joined them. They all
begged me, since Kerensky had left, to take care of them, believing
that they would be lost if they fell into the hands of the Bolsheviks.
The most frightened was Knirsha, who the night before had arrested the most prominent Bolsheviks of Gatchina. He had almost
had them hanged, but luckily restrained himself at the last minute.
Knirsha was infected by his chief's megalomania. He already
visualized himself as a minister and even as the Chairman of the
Council of Ministers and quite seriously was offering me the post
of Minister of Education or of Arts in his future cabinet. True, at
that time every third person considered himself of ministerial
stature. Nevertheless, Knirsha was a delightful person.

I told the group of men to follow me. Somehow or other there
also appeared a representative of an already non-existent world:
the former chief of the Tsar's palace police, who still occupied a
room in the palace. I led them through the historic rooms of the
central building to the farthest rooms in the mezzanine of the
arsenal quarters where I could hide them. When I suggested that
they remain there, assuring them that they would not lack food,
I realized how frightened they were and decided to find at once a
way of leading them out of the palace. There was no point in considering the gates or doors which were guarded by Cossack sentries. There remained the windows that faced upon the garden.
I led my wards to the lowest floor of the arsenal quarters and into
the personal apartments of the Dowager Empress. Around the corner to the right was the wall facing the square where the troops
were quartered. A sentry walked to and fro. Upon reaching the
corner, he could see along the wall facing the garden. It was necessary to catch the moment when he would turn and walk back.
I selected a window which was exactly across from a tunnel-like
garden growth. Having jumped out of the window, one had merely
to run the three or four steps that separated if from the "tunnel" —
a matter of seconds. Under the growth we would be invisible. One
more difficulty remained: the windows had been sealed the previous
year. Were I to open one by force, the dry putty would scatter and
it would be obvious that someone had escaped. But I had no choice;
everything had to be done before Kerensky's flight would be discovered at the other end of the palace. I opened the window and encouraged the men to jump. They did not dare. I had to set an example. I

looked out of the window and saw the Cossack at the corner on the point of turning and disappearing behind the building. A jump and I was in the tunnel. I heard someone following me and I turned around. It was Kuzmin; the others were still lined up at the window, pale and with bulging eyes. We could not wait for them.

The two of us hurried to the back of the garden and arrived at the exit which was far away. The gate was locked and the watchman was in his little house. Although we would be able to leave I had to think of the future. The evidence of this escape could be used later in the accusation that I had let Kerensky get away. I placed my hope in the watchman's stupidity, ordered him to open the gate and led Kuzmin to the street that went straight to the railroad station. I never heard of him again.

Afterward, I calmly returned to the palace, passing the sentry near the kitchen quarters and, on the staircase, I heard Knirsha's voice loudly berating "the dog Kerensky" who had fled, betraying all the others. He followed me to my rooms, shook my hand warmly and told me that he did not know how to thank me for my help. "With the post of Minister of Education in your cabinet," I said. He did not seem to have caught the irony.

. . . Later, Princess Shakhovskoi and I were placed under house arrest by the chief-of-staff of the division, on suspicion of having helped Kerensky to flee. A soldier, bearing a rifle, was assigned to Knirsha with the order to keep him under constant surveillance.

The Cossacks' indignation, aroused by Kerensky's disappearance, was tremendous, and he was cursed right and left. In the meantime, the negotiations with the Bolsheviks continued until the evening and ended with the arrival of Communist emissaries at the palace. Together with their friends from Gatchina Soviets, they took over the command. The Cossacks were allowed to return freely to the Don, while the top-ranking officers headed by Krasnov were taken the next morning to Petersburg, to Smolny, from where they were soon freed.*

---

* General Piotr Nikolaevich Krasnov (1869–1947) soon after his release fled to the Don. In May 1918 he was elected Ataman of the Don Cossacks and served in the White Army under General Denikin. After the Civil War he emigrated to Germany where during World War II he helped the Nazi Government to form Cossack units. In the spring of 1945 he was handed over to the Soviets by the British Army command at Linz, Austria. In 1947 he was court-martialled and hanged [Ed.].

N. VALENTINOV

Encounters with Lenin

N. Valentinov (pseudonym of N. V. Volsky, 1879–1964) was an early member of the Bolshevik faction of the Social Democratic Workers' Party. After a year's association with Lenin in Geneva (1904), Valentinov broke with him. The account of their relationship was published under the title of *Vstrechi s Leninym* by the Chekhov Publishing House, New York, 1953. (English version, *Encounters with Lenin,* New York, Oxford University Press, 1968.)

During the NEP (New Economic Policy), in the hope of restoring the ruined Russian economy, Valentinov-Volsky worked for the Supreme Council of National Economy. In 1930 he defected from his post as the assistant to the Soviet trade representative in Paris. Until his death he contributed widely to émigré publications in Europe and the United States. He is the author of several posthumously published volumes, which include books on the young Lenin and on the NEP.

Although the following selection depicts Lenin as an émigré-revolutionary, and chronologically does not belong in this part of the book, it is included here because it gives an unusually incisive portrait, which is relevant to Lenin's role in 1917. The conversations reported here, which took place in March and September 1904 in Geneva, had an influence on Lenin's treatise *Materialism and Empiriocriticism* (1909).

From *The Russian Review,* vol. 13, no. 3 (July 1954), pp. 176–85.

. . . I called on Lenin and gave him, of course, an account of my visit to Plekhanov. Lenin had a high regard for Plekhanov, who impressed him more than anyone else—more, even, than Kautsky or Bebel. Everything Plekhanov said, did, or wrote, excited his keenest interest. "He is a man of colossal stature; he makes one shrink," Lenin once remarked to Lepeshinsky. So now he made me relate in detail what had put the fat in the fire. I had to go far back to the prologue to the story and began with a description of the Kievan group of religious dissenters and the part played in it by Semion Petrovich and his ideas.

I remember Lenin standing by my chair, his thumbs stuck into the armholes of his waistcoat, and listening with obvious curiosity. When I touched on the faith of Semion Petrovich, on his division of people into "the wicked" and "the conscientious," his belief that socialism could be built only by the hands of "righteous people," Lenin made some comment. It might be pertinent to record his words here, but I have forgotten them and, given Lenin's aversion to any kind of moralizing, I suppose that his remarks in this connection were of no particular interest. Otherwise I would surely have remembered them. I have the clearest recollection of everything else Lenin said in the course of that meeting, for it was then that my disagreement with him, which greatly upset and alarmed me, became manifest for the first time. I discovered that much as I admired Lenin as a great man, much as I felt drawn to him and eager to follow him, his attitude towards some most important issues strongly repelled me. I found that Lenin, while at odds with Plekhanov in matters of party politics, did not hesitate to take the latter's side against me in the field of philosophy, and this in a form that affected me most painfully.

"You told Plekhanov that materialism ought to be replaced by a certain variety of bourgeois philosophy. But this is nonsense, pernicious nonsense! Plekhanov was right, utterly right, in taking you to task at once. The Plekhanov who keeps company with opportunists in the editorial office of the new *Iskra* should not be confused with the other Plekhanov, the best authority and the best commentator on Marxist philosophy since Engels. In a few sentences he has given you a trouncing, and it serves you right! But I didn't know; it's a big surprise to me that you too were given to amending Marx."

"Allow me to point out," I answered, "that Plekhanov called the theory of knowledge of Avenarius and Mach 'the cellar of bourgeois philosophy' without having taken the trouble of getting acquainted with it, without having read a single line by its authors. Such an attitude towards the scientific thought of others revolts me. It means passing sentence without trial."

"In the first place," Lenin continued, "I do not believe that Plekhanov actually has no knowledge of your philosophers; he keeps himself informed on philosophy. If he told you he was not acquainted with their writings, he probably did it to stress his contempt for them. In the second place, your indignation is unjustified. We know all too well by now what comes of the attempts to combine Marx with theories alien to him in spirit. Bernstein is an object-lesson, and so are our own Struve and Bulgakov. Struve began with amending Marxism and slid from there into the most vulgar stinking liberalism, and Bulgakov is on his way down to a still fouler pit. Marxism is a monolithic philosophy which does not tolerate dilution or vulgarization through petty additions and insertions. Plekhanov once said to me, in discussing some critic of Marxism, I have forgotten whom: 'First let's stick an ace of diamonds on him; we'll look into the matter later.'* Well, in my opinion we ought to pin an ace of diamonds on all those who attempt to shake Marxism, without even looking into their cases. Such should be the reaction of every sound revolutionary. When you find a stinking heap in your path, you don't have to dig your hands into it to know what it is, your nose will tell you it's dung, and you'll pass it by."

Lenin's words took my breath away.

"Out of Plekhanov's frying-pan I now fall into your fire," I brought out at last. "Plekhanov says that the philosophers Avenarius and Mach, although he has not read them, are 'witches,' and whether their eyes are red or yellow, does not interest him. And now our other theoretician, Lenin, recommends that we pin the badge of infamy on them without so much as attempting to explore their theories. You keep harping on one string—bourgeois philosophy, bourgeois philosophers. Yet the theory of Avenarius and

---

* A diamond-shaped badge sewn to the back of a convict's uniform in tsarist prisons [Ed.].

Mach is anything but a metaphysical conception, it is an attempt
to create a scientific theory of knowledge based on experience alone.
Before stigmatizing it as criminal, make the effort to study and
understand it. There is no such thing as a middle-class or working-
class astronomy, algebra, physics, or chemistry. Nor is there a
bourgeois theory of knowledge. All that matters is whether the
theory of Avenarius and Mach is true or not. Even if it should contain some features typical of bourgeois mentaility, it would be still
inadmissible to brand its authors as criminals without proving them
wrong. You mentioned Bulgakov. As a student at the Polytechnic
I attended the seminar in economics he had organized for the benefit
of students seeking a better acquaintance with social sciences than
that afforded by the regular one-hour lectures in economics. Here
we were given the opportunity to discuss a variety of problems with
complete freedom. Bulgakov would open most of our meetings with
the solemn reminder: 'Truth is attained through the honest, free,
and loyal confrontation of ideas.' Frankly, I find this method more
to my liking than your 'ace of diamonds.'"

"Oh, I see! So you attended Bulgakov's seminar? That's news.
I don't congratulate you, no I don't. Isn't it perchance Bulgakov's
influence that accounts for your inclination to correct the philosophy of Marx? That's a slippery path. The Social Democratic Party
is not a seminar where various ideas are confronted. It is a militant
class organization of the revolutionary proletariat. It has its own
program and philosophy, a system of thought exclusively its own.
Within the Party you cannot expect any particular freedom to
criticize and to compare ideas. He who has joined the Party has to
accept its ideas, has to share them, not tamper with them. If they
don't satisfy him—well, the door is wide open, he is free to make his
exit. We know all too well what lies behind this so-called 'freedom
of criticism,' insisted upon not by the working-class element of the
Party, but by the intellectuals in its ranks, infected with bourgeois
prejudices. I say it again: 'Well done, Plekhanov!' He sensed at
once that you had to be slapped down."

"Vladimir Ilich," I hastened to say, "I assure you that I do not
sympathize with revisionism in the least. The philosophy of Avenarius and Mach attracts me only because it shatters every kind of
metaphysics in the most revolutionary way. Get acquainted with it
and you will agree. But while I reject revisionism, I still do not think
that Marxism is a petrified system given once and for all and not

subject to change. Plekhanov once wrote that Marxism was the absolute truth forever immune to change. What do you think of such a formula? How does it accord with dialectics?"

"I am in complete agreement with Plekhanov," Lenin stated, "Marx and Engels have outlined and said all that was to be said. If Marxism needs further development, it will have to be in the direction pointed out by its founders. Nothing in Marxism is subject to revision. There is only one answer to revisionism—a slap in the face! Neither the Marxist philosophy is subject to revision, nor the materialist conception of history, nor the idea of the inevitability of the social revolution, nor the principle of the dictatorship of the proletariat—not a single one of the basic tenets of Marxism!"

This was my first disagreement with Lenin. The talk took place early in March. However, Lenin did not seem at the time to attach much importance to my outbursts during the encounter; after all, hadn't I protested again and again that I harbored no sympathy for revisionism? I still remained in his good graces. Only three and a half months later, when our differences had become acute and could no longer be overlooked, did he refer to that first dispute and use it as an additional argument for my relegation to the "enemy camp."

On the 16th, or possibly the 17th of September, a fellow Bolshevik who lived in my neighborhood let me know that Lenin wanted me to meet him that same evening at nine "at the usual place," the Quai du Montblanc. I did not know what to make of it. It occurred to me that Lenin, following his philosophical controversy with Bogdanov, might have decided that, after all, this did not justify a break with him. Perhaps he planned to tell me the same thing. A glance at Lenin, when we met that night, dispelled this idea. With a cold spiteful face, scarcely taking time to greet me, he startled me with the question: "Do you *still* belong to our group?"

Oh! I thought, this "still" sounds like a challenge. I am not going to pretend that I don't catch on. I'll give him as good as I get. So I replied: "Yes, I have *not yet* left the majority group."

"So you have not yet left the group. I had to know this, for had you done it, I'd have turned my back on you without wasting another word. I do not ask you why you failed to sign the protest of the 37 Bolsheviks; I have been told that you had some kind of personal trouble just then."

"I lost my son."

"Whether this or something else was the real reason doesn't matter much in this case. I intend to talk about more important matters. While you are still a member of the Bolshevik group, let me tell you that some things you have done are absolutely inadmissible."

What followed was a torrent of words poured forth in a fury, each with the intent of hurting and stinging. Today, after forty-eight years, I am still unable to think of it calmly. My wife who knew all my weaknesses well — my impulsiveness, my unpardonable propensity, when I was young, of having recourse to my fists (even to dueling, in my undergraduate days) — once told me that she was at a loss to understand how on this occasion I managed to refrain from assaulting Lenin or even from hurling him from the quai into Lake Geneva. She observed that it showed how strong was his hypnotic hold on me.

"Many people, and I in particular," Lenin began, "are aware that for a long time you have been planning to return to Russia. For this you need money, a passport, and underground connections in places other than Kiev, where you are too well known to show up. You have neither the one, nor the other, nor the third. And so, in order to get what you need, you started a campaign of wooing first me, then Pavlovich (Krassikov) and Bonch-Bruevich. And now I've got wind that at the same time and for the same end you have been running after the Mensheviks. This is how you reasoned: 'If I fail to get the money and the papers from the Bolsheviks, I'll try to obtain them from the Mensheviks. If in return they ask for any pledges and declarations, well, I'll sign them.' I call this the vilest, foulest double-dealing, this shifting from one camp to another, one foot here, the other there. Such conduct deserves nothing but contempt."

Beside myself, I shouted: "All this is a filthy lie!"

"The whole point is that it is not a lie. You began by making advances to that moron Martynov, who even filched all kinds of documents from *Iskra* for you, and then through him you managed to sneak into the very center of Menshevism and started toadying to Martov: 'Let me have a passport and some dough, and I'm ready to desert Lenin and the Bolsheviks.'"

"It's all a lie, an outrageous fabrication!"

"It's you who are lying. Can you deny that you met Martov?"

"What of it? Is a meeting with Martov, your close comrade of not so long ago, such a disgraceful thing as to be branded 'double-dealing'? I never sought to meet Martov, it happened by accident, and ever since I've had no dealings either with him or with any other Mensheviks. Not a word passed between us regarding Party matters, or a passport, and least of all money."

"And what, if I may ask, did you discuss with Martov—the weather, I suppose?"

"We talked about philosophy, and nothing else."

"And why, having arranged a meeting with Martov (it was not accidental, of that I am sure!), didn't you talk about Party affairs of interest to all? Why did you discuss philosophy instead, in which Martov, as I well know, takes very little interest? Maybe all you wanted was to weep on Martov's shoulder, complaining of that brute of a Lenin who has given your philosophers a whipping? One thing is sure, if indeed you had a philosophical discussion with Martov it was meant only as bait."

Without letting me put in a word, Lenin went on reiterating with variations the same accusations of double-dealing and trying "to wangle a wretched passport and cash" by dubious means. And yet Lenin had always encouraged his followers to go back to Russia. He was aware that many of them would have been glad to settle abroad for good and were by no means in a hurry to exchange the safety of Geneva for the underground in Russia, with a false passport and the constant threat of imprisonment. But now, in my own case, he was giving the matter a strange twist. He spoke of my desire to go back as of something shameful, revealing me in the worst possible light. For some reason it meant duplicity and bad faith. No longer trusting me, he apparently believed that once back in Russia, in possession of papers and money supplied by the Bolsheviks, I would turn my coat and go over to the Mensheviks. He accused me of having repaid the confidence the Bolsheviks had shown me by "spreading slander about them." But when I urged him to tell me what slander, he answered: "You were chummy with Martov; you met him, didn't you? Who can believe that in this nice company you refrained from malicious gossip about the Bolsheviks?"

I was so dumbfounded by the flood of unexpected and undeserved accusations that under their impact I lost all ability to defend myself. This was taken by Lenin as an admission of guilt and spurred him on to ever more virulent attacks. But after a while I recovered and took the offensive myself. I pointed out to him that I had come to Geneva not because it had been my wish but because

Krzyzanovsky on behalf of the Central Committee had ordered me
abroad; and that now it was up to the same Committee to enable
me to go back. "Some minor expenditure incurred in my behalf by
the Bolsheviks does not turn me into their property. It is incon-
ceivable that the group should give me the means to return to Russia only on condition that I remain well-behaved. I have no intention
of being stuck in Geneva to the end of time, and, though up to now
nothing has even been said about it, if you refuse to help me, I shall
appeal to the minority for assistance."

To this Lenin replied: "What you have just said makes it plain
that from the point of view of the majority, the money spent on you
has not paid off."

I reminded Lenin that X, a member of the Bolshevik group, after
having been provided with a passport and funds for his return to
Russia, had, on his way there, squandered the money in drunken
orgies in the brothel of a big city and never reached his destination.
"And what was your attitude then?" I asked. "You declared, I heard
you myself, that since you were not a priest, preaching sermons
was not your business, and you were inclined to wink at the whole
matter. With such a moral sense, or rather lack of it, what right
have you to lecture me about my 'shameful, unworthy' conduct?
Your sermonizing is all the more outrageous because it is based on
trumped-up charges."

"You want to know what right I have?" Lenin asked. "This is
not a question of right as understood by popish morality but a
political right, a right derived from class and party. I'll try to explain to you what is at issue. You, very probably, would never have
gone to that brothel, and certainly you would never spend Party
money on drink. So far as I know, you have no weakness for liquor.
But you are apt to do things that are much worse. You are capable
of intriguing with Martynov, an inveterate enemy of our orthodox
revolutionary old *Iskra.* You are capable of approving the reactionary bourgeois theory of Mach, a foe of materialism. You are capable
of admiring the alleged 'quest for truth' of Bulgakov. All this adds
up to a brothel many times worse than the whorehouse with the
naked tarts visited by X. Your brothel poisons and obscures the
class consciousness of the workers; and if we are to judge your conduct and that of X from this point of view, the only correct one for a
Social Democrat, we shall arrive at different conclusions. You de-
serve to be held up to shame for trying to substitute an obscure

theory for Marxism; while the offense of X may be easily condoned. As a Party man X is a steadfast seasoned revolutionary; he has proved himself a staunch *Iskra* man before the congress, during the congress, after the congress, and this is of primary importance, whatever the Axelrods may babble. If he went to that brothel, it surely was a case of need; and it shows a complete loss of the sense of the ridiculous to sermonize about a matter of physiology. By the way, in dragging in the X story, you are not very original. Consorting with Martov has already had its effect on you, you follow the path trodden by Martov, Zasulich, Potresov, who went into hysterics, about two year ago, on account of some facts concerning the private life of comrade B.* I told them then and there: 'B is a highly useful man, devoted to the revolution and the Party, and as to the rest, I don't give a damn.'"

"It follows from your words," I observed, "that no infamy is to be condemned if it is committed by a man useful to the Party. From this it is one step to Raskolnikov's 'all is allowed.'"

"What Raskolnikov?"

"The hero of Dostoevsky's *Crime and Punishment.*"

Lenin stopped short, pushed his thumbs behind the lapels of his waistcoat and gave me a look of undisguised contempt. "'All is allowed!' Sooner or later we were bound to come upon them, the mawkish sentiments and pet formulas of flabby intellectuals, ever ready to drown the issues of party and revolution in sanctimonious vomit. Well, which Raskolnikov do you have in mind, the one who butchered the vile old pawnbroker hag, or the one who later banged his head against the ground in a fit of penitential hysteria? Maybe you, as one who attended Bulgakov's seminar, have a preference for the latter?"

His persistent sneering at my relations with Bulgakov made me lose my temper. "After what you have said," I shouted, "it is easy to guess that it was you who started the slanderous gossip about my alleged adherence to the views of Bulgakov. The method you are using to discredit me is utterly dishonest. I have told you again and again that I do not subscribe to any of Bulgakov's religious, philosophical, or sociological opinions. And yet in complete disregard of this you unscrupulously persist in representing me as a follower

---

* Lenin named him, but I do not wish to cite the name. The facts Lenin referred to are not known to me.

of Bulgakov." I pointed out to Lenin that he was making a political crime out of a friendly relationship based upon the gratitude of a university student to a talented teacher, to whom all his listeners owed a great deal. In pronouncing the words "Bulgakov's seminar," Lenin used a special tone, as though making them mean some kind of religious seminary affiliated with a theological academy and devoted to the study of canonical problems, instead of a group of students writing and hearing papers on Marx, Kautsky, Mikhailovsky, Kant, Spencer, and so on. Lenin's habit, I told him, of indiscriminately sticking labels on people whose thinking differed from his own, linking them with the name now of Voroshilov, now of Akimov, Bulgakov, or Martynov, was beginning to nauseate me. For the last six years I had lived in close association with various revolutionary circles, and never yet had I anywhere observed such unsavory ways of settling accounts, such sickening polemical methods, such foul play, as were rampant in the Party milieu of Geneva. Here all was considered fair in a fight. "And you, Comrade Lenin, instead of trying to check this evil, encourage it by your own example."

Lenin exclaimed: "Until now I thought I was dealing with an adult, but now looking at you I ask myself, are you really a child, or are you pretending to be one for some reasons of your own, probably of a highly moral kind? So you find it sickening that the tone within the Party is less refined than that of a young ladies' finishing school? That's an old song, dear to those who would like to turn revolutionary fighters into milksops. God forbid that you offend Ivan Ivanovich by some rash word! For heaven's sake don't hurt the feelings of Piotr Petrovich! Kowtow to each other even when you disagree! Well, if we Social Democrats were to use only toothless inoffensive words in our politics, propaganda, agitation, polemics, we should be no better than those dreary pastors who preach futile sermons every Sunday."

Lenin went on, relating with great gusto what a master of invective Marx had been, how effectively the latter's son-in-law, Lafargue, used abusive language, how French politicians in general excelled in this field—they knew "how to smear an opponent's mug in such a way that he couldn't wash it clean for a long time."

"No," I said, "we have nothing to learn from the French in this respect. To crush a political opponent, and be it an old Party comrade, we have the ace of diamonds. I have not forgotten how swiftly

I was relegated by you to the category of your worst enemies and what a flood of abuse you poured upon my head as soon as you learned that I did not share all your views in the field of philosophy."

"You're right in this, you're absolutely right. All those who give up Marxism are my enemies, I refuse to shake hands with them, and I do not sit down at the same table with the Philistines."

The reference to "giving up Marxism" led to a renewed philosophical argument, almost a repetition of the scene at the rue du Foyer in March; but I shall not dwell on this. From nine to eleven that evening we were pacing up and down the Quai du Montblanc. "It is time to part," I was thinking. "There is nothing to talk about any more," Lenin anticipated me. "I break off the discussion and am going home. The argument has not been altogether fruitless, it has made many things clear to me. It goes without saying that you will not stay in our organization, but even if you should, do not count on my cooperation in any way, in particular in the matter of your return to Russia."

Without shaking hands, Lenin turned his back on me and walked away.

I soon left the Bolshevik organization.

V. I. LENIN

Call to Action

V. I. Lenin (pseudonym of V. I. Ulianov, 1870–1924). A capital event in the development of the Russian Revolution was Lenin's arrival in Petrograd on April 3/April 16, 1917. It determined the subsequent course of the Revolution. Gradually, Lenin took over full control of the Bolshevik Party, set its goals and strategy (the April Theses), and determined the time for action—thus changing the course of history.

Primarily a man of action, Lenin left no real interpretation of the Russian Revolution. As he once remarked, in 1917, while writing his theoretical treatise on the dictatorship of the proletariat, *State and Revolution* (often reprinted and readily available): "It is more pleasant and more useful to live through the experience of a revolution than to write about it" (N. Riasanovsky, *A History of Russia,* 1969, New York, Oxford University Press, pp. 526–27).

After the unsuccessful "July uprising," Lenin went into hiding in Finland to escape arrest. From there he kept constantly in touch with his followers in the capital. Convinced that the Provisional Government was decidedly weakened, partly as a result of the Kornilov affair, Lenin urged immediate seizure of power and overthrow of the Provisional Government.

The following documents record his strategy in 1917: (1) Lenin's two letters to the Bolshevik Central Committee, one written September 12–14/September 25–27, the other, on October 24/November 6, the literal eve of the *coup d'état;* (2) a proclamation from the Revolutionary Military Committee of the Petrograd Soviet of Workers' and

The documents that follow are from the fourth English edition of Lenin's *Collected Works,* Moscow, Progress Publishers, 1964, vol. 26, pp. 19–21, 234–36, 239–40. A few stylistic changes were made by the editor.

Soldiers' Deputies to the people of Russia announcing the overthrow of the Provisional Government, written at 10 a.m., October 25/November 7, while the insurrection was still in progress; (3) Lenin's speech at the meeting of the Petrograd Soviet of Workers' and Soldiers' Deputies on the tasks of the newly established Soviet power, delivered the day of the insurrection, October 25/November 7, 1917.

The Bolsheviks Must Assume Power

A LETTER TO THE CENTRAL COMMITTEE
AND THE PETROGRAD AND MOSCOW COMMITTEES
OF THE R.S.D.L.P.(B.)

Having obtained a majority in the Soviets of Workers' and Soldiers' Deputies of both capitals, the Bolsheviks can and *must* take state power into their own hands.

They can do so because the active majority of revolutionary elements in the two chief cities is large enough to carry the people with it, to overcome the resistance of our adversaries to smash them, and to gain and retain power. For the Bolsheviks, by immediately proposing a democratic peace, by immediately giving the land to the peasants and by re-establishing the democratic institutions and liberties which have been distorted and shattered by Kerensky, will form a government which *nobody* will be able to overthrow.

The majority of the people side with us. This was proved by the long and painful course of events from May 6 to August 31 and to September 12. We gained a majority in the Soviets of the metropolitan cities because the people came over *to our side.* The wavering of the Socialist Revolutionaries and Mensheviks and the increase in the number of internationalists within their ranks prove the same thing.

The Democratic Conference* represents *not* a majority of the revolutionary people, but *only the compromising upper strata of the petty bourgeoisie.* Let us not be deceived by the election figures; elections prove nothing. Compare the elections to the city councils

---

* The Democratic Conference was convened by Kerensky in a desperate attempt to rally support for his government. It took place in Petrograd, September 14–22/September 27–October 5, 1917.

of Petrograd and Moscow with the elections to the Soviets. Compare the elections in Moscow with the Moscow strike of August 12. Those are objective facts regarding that majority of revolutionary elements that are leading the people.

The Democratic Conference is deceiving the peasants; it is giving them neither peace nor land.

A Bolshevik government *alone* will satisfy the peasants' demands.

Why must the Bolsheviks assume power *at this very moment?*

Because the impending surrender of Petrograd will diminish our chances a hundred times.

And it is *not in our power* to prevent the surrender of Petrograd while the army is headed by Kerensky and Co.

Nor can we "wait" for the Constituent Assembly, for by surrendering Petrograd Kerensky and Co. *can* always obstruct its convocation. Our Party alone, by seizing power, can secure the Constituent Assembly's convocation; it will then accuse the other parties of procrastination and will be able to substantiate its accusations.

A separate peace between the British and German imperialists must and can be prevented, but only if we act immediately.

The people are tired of the vacillations of the Mensheviks and Socialist Revolutionaries. It is only our victory in the metropolitan cities that will carry the peasants with us.

We are concerned now not with the "day," or "moment" of insurrection in the narrow sense of the word. That will be only decided by the common voice of those who are *in contact* with the workers and soldiers, with *the masses.*

The point is that now, at the Democratic Conference, our Party has virtually *its own congress,* and this congress (whether it wishes to or not) *will* decide the *fate of the revolution.*

The point is to make the *task* clear to the Party. The present task is an *armed uprising* in Petrograd and Moscow (with its region), the seizing of power and the overthrow of the government. We must consider *how* to bring this about without expressly spelling it out in the press.

We must remember and weigh Marx's words about insurrection, *"Insurrection is an art,"* etc.

It would be naïve to wait until the Bolsheviks achieve a "formal" majority. No revolution ever waits for *that*. Kerensky and Co. are not waiting either, and are preparing to surrender Petrograd. It is the wretched waverings of the Democratic Conference that are bound to exhaust the patience of the workers of Petrograd and Moscow! History will not forgive us if we do not assume power now.

There is no apparatus? There is an apparatus—the Soviets and the democratic organisations. The international situation *right* now, on *the eve* of the conclusion of a separate peace between the British and the Germans, is *in our favour*. To propose peace to the nations right now means *to win*.

By seizing power both in Moscow and in Petrograd *at once* (it doesn't matter which comes first, possibly Moscow), we shall win *absolutely and unquestionably*.

N. Lenin

Letter to Central Committee Members

Comrades:

I am writing these lines on the evening of the 24th. [October 24/ November 6]. The situation is critical in the extreme. In fact it is absolutely clear that to delay the uprising now would be fatal.

I exhort my comrades with all my might to realize that everything now hangs by a thread; that we are confronted by problems which can not be solved by conferences or congresses (even congresses of Soviets), but exclusively by peoples, by the masses, by the struggle of the armed masses.

The bourgeois onslaught of the Kornilovites and the removal of Verkhovsky* show that we must not wait. We must at all costs, this very evening, this very night, arrest the government, first disarming the officer cadets (defeating them, if they resist), and so forth.

We must not wait! We may lose everything!

The value of the immediate seizure of power will be the defence

---

*A. I. Verkhovsky (1886–1941) was Minister of War in the last Provisional Government. He resigned his post on October 19/November 1.

of the *people* (not of the congress, but of the people, the army and the peasants in the first place) from the Kornilovite government, which has driven out Verkhovsky and has hatched a second Kornilov plot.

Who must take power?

That is not important at the moment. Let the Revolutionary Military Committee* seize it, or "some other institution" which will declare that it will relinquish power only to those who truly represent the interests of the people, the interests of the army (the immediate proposal of peace), the interests of the peasants (land to be taken immediately and private property abolished), the interests of the starving.

All districts, all regiments, and forces must be mobilised at once and must immediately send their delegations to the Revolutionary Military Committee and to the Central Committee of the Bolsheviks with the insistent demand that under no circumstances should power be left in the hands of Kerensky and Co. until the 25th—not under any circumstances; the matter must be decided without fail this very evening, or this very night.

History will not forgive revolutionaries for procrastinating when they could be victorious today (and they certainly will be victorious today), while they risk losing much, tomorrow, in fact, everything.

If we seize power today, we seize it not in opposition to the Soviets but on their behalf.

The seizure of power is the goal of the insurrection; its political purpose will become clear after the seizure.

It would be a disaster, or a sheer formality, to await the wavering vote of October 25. The people have the right and the duty to decide such questions not by a vote, but by force; in critical moments of revolution, the people have the right and the duty to instruct their representatives, even their best representatives, and not to wait for them.

This is proved by the history of all revolutions; and it would be an infinite crime on the part of the revolutionaries were they to let the chance slip, knowing that upon them depends the *salvation of*

---

* The Revolutionary Military Committee of the Petrograd Soviet was set up on October 12/October 25, 1917, according to instructions from the Central Committee of the Bolshevik Party. Its main task was to prepare the armed uprising. It was dissolved on December 5/December 18, 1917.

the revolution, the offer of peace, the salvation of Petrograd, salvation from famine, the transfer of the land to the peasants.

The government is tottering. It must be *dealt the final blow* at all costs.

To delay action is fatal.

To the Citizens of Russia!

The Provisional Government has been overthrown. State power has passed into the hands of the organ of the Petrograd Soviet of Workers' and Soldiers' Deputies—the Revolutionary Military Committee, which heads the Petrograd proletariat and the garrison.

The cause for which the people have fought: the immediate proposal of a democratic peace, the abolition of landlordism, workers' control over production, and the establishment of Soviet power—this cause has been secured.

Long live the revolution of workers, soldiers and peasants!

> *Revolutionary Military Committee*
> *of the Petrograd Soviet of Workers'*
> *and Soldiers' Deputies*

10 a.m., October 25, 1917

Meeting of the Petrograd Soviet of Workers' and Soldiers' Deputies October 25 (November 7), 1917*

Report on the Tasks of the Soviet Power
Press Release

Comrades, the workers' and peasants' revolution, which the Bolsheviks have always aimed for, has been accomplished.

What is the significance of this workers' and peasants' revolution? Its significance is, first and foremost, that we shall have a

---

* The meeting of Petrograd Soviet of Workers' and Soldiers' Deputies opened at 2:35 p.m. on October 25/November 7. It heard the report of the Military Revolutionary Committee on the overthrow of the Provisional Government. Lenin defined at this meeting the tasks facing the Soviet power.

Soviet government, our own government, in which the bourgeoisie will have no part whatsoever. The oppressed masses themselves constitute a power. The old state apparatus will be shattered to its foundations and will be replaced by a new administrative apparatus set up in the form of the Soviet organisations.

This is the beginning of a new phase in the history of Russia and this, the third Russian revolution, should in the end lead to the victory of socialism.

One of our urgent tasks is to put an immediate end to the war. It is clear to everybody that in order to end this war, which is closely bound up with the present capitalist system, capitalism itself must be fought.

The international working-class movement, which is already beginning to develop in Italy, Britain and Germany, will help us accomplish our objective.

The proposal we make to international democracy for a just and immediate peace will everywhere awaken an ardent response among the proletarian masses. All secret treaties must be immediately made public in order to strengthen the confidence of the proletariat.

Within Russia a huge section of the peasantry is tired of going along with the capitalists, and will now march with the workers. A single decree putting an end to landed proprietorship will win the peasants' confidence for they will understand that the salvation of the peasantry lies only in an alliance with the workers. We shall institute genuine workers' control over production.

We have now learned to make a concerted effort. The revolution that has just been accomplished is proof of this. We possess the strength of mass organisation, which will overcome everything and lead the proletariat to the world revolution.

We must now proceed to build a proletarian socialist state in Russia.

Long live the world socialist revolution! *(Stormy applause.)*

LEON TROTSKY

An Analysis of the Bolshevik Revolution

L. D. Trotsky (pseudonym of Leon Bronstein, 1877–1940), major participant in the October Revolution. Upon his arrival in Russia in May 1917, he became Lenin's closest associate and was instrumental in establishing Bolshevik control over the Petrograd Soviet. As the head of the Military Revolutionary Committee, he was in charge of preparing and effecting the Bolshevik seizure of power. His brilliant, though polemic and one-sided, account *The History of the Russian Revolution* occupies an important place in the memoir literature of 1917. First published in Russian in 1932–33, it was translated into English and edited by Max Eastman (3 vols., New York, Simon and Schuster, 1932). Among Trotsky's prolific writings in exile is *My Life,* a vivid account of his career prior to the Revolution, his role in the Revolution, and his struggle with Stalin. The book was published by Charles Scribner's Sons, New York, 1930.

What distinguished our party almost from the very first stage of the Revolution was the firm conviction that the logic of events would eventually place it in power. I am not speaking here of the theoreticians of our party, who, many years before the Revolution, even before the Revolution of 1905, had come to the conclusion, from a

The excerpts below, presenting Trotsky's analysis of the Bolshevik Revolution, are reprinted from *Readings in Russian History,* compiled and ed. by Warren B. Walsh, Syracuse, Syracuse University Press, 1963, vol. 3. pp. 717–24. Copyright © 1948, 1950, 1959, 1963. Dates are according to the "new style." Reprinted by courtesy of the editor and publisher.

close analysis of the class relations in Russia, that the victorious course of a revolution would inevitably place the power of the State in the hands of the proletariat, supported by the wide masses of the poorest peasantry. The main foundation for this belief was the insignificance of the Russian middle-class democracy and the concentrated character of Russian industry, and, therefore, the immense social importance of the Russian working class. The insignificance of the Russian middle-class democracy is but the obverse side of the power and importance of the proletariat. True, the war temporarily deceived many people on this point, and, above all, it deceived the leading sections of middle-class democracy itself. The war assigned the decisive role in the Revolution to the army, and the old army was the peasantry.

Had the Revolution developed more normally, that is, in conditions of peace-time, such as prevailed in 1912, when it really began, the proletariat would inevitably have taken the leading role throughout, whilst the peasant masses would have been gradually towed along by the proletariat into the revolutionary whirlpool. But the war imparted an entirely different logic to the course of events. The army had organized the peasantry, not on a political, but on a military basis. Before the peasant masses found themselves united on a common platform of definite revolutionary demands and ideas, they had already become united in regiments, divisions, corps, and armies. The lower middle-class democrats, scattered throughout this army, and playing a leading part in it both in a military and intellectual sense, were almost entirely imbued with middle-class revolutionary sentiments. The deep social discontent of the masses grew ever deeper and strove for expression, particularly owing to the military debacle of Tsardom. Immediately the Revolution broke out, the advanced sections of the proletariat revived the traditions of 1905 by calling upon the popular masses to organize in representative bodies, *viz.* the "councils" of delegates (Soviets).

The army thus had to send representatives to revolutionary bodies before its political consciousness in any way corresponded to the level of the rapidly developing revolutionary events. Whom could the soldiers send as their representatives? Naturally, only those intellectuals and semi-intellectuals who were to be found in their midst and who possessed at least a minimum amount of political knowledge, and were capable of giving utterance to it. In this way, by the will of the awakening army, the lower middle-class intellectuals found themselves suddenly raised to a position of enormous influence. Doctors, engineers, lawyers, journalists, who in pre-war days had led a humdrum private life and laid no claim of any sort to political influence, became, overnight, representatives of whole corps and armies, and discovered that they were the "leaders" of the Revolution. The haziness of their political ideas fully corresponded to the formless state of the revolutionary consciousness of the masses themselves. They contemptuously looked upon us as mere sectarians because we were urging the social demands of the working class and the peasants in a most resolute and uncompromising fashion. At the same time these lower middle-class democrats, in spite of their proud demeanour of revolutionary upstarts, felt a profound diffidence both in their own capacities and in the masses who had raised them to such an unexpectedly high place. Calling themselves socialists and really regarding themselves as such, these intellectuals looked up to the political authority of the liberal bourgeoisie, to its knowledge and its methods, with all ill-concealed respect. Hence the endeavour of the lower middle-class leaders to obtain, at all costs, the cooperation of the liberal middle-class by way of an alliance or coalition. The programme of the party of Socialist Revolutionaries, based as it all is on vague humanitarian formulae, and employing general sentiments and moral constructions in the place of class-war methods, was the most suitable spiritual dress that could have been found for these improvised leaders. Their political helplessness in the impressive political and scientific knowledge of the bourgeoisie found a theoretical sanction in the teaching of the Mensheviks, who argued that the present Revolution was a bourgeois revolution, and could not, therefore, be carried through without the participation of the bourgeoisie in the government. A natural *bloc* was thus formed between the Socialist Revolutionaries and Mensheviks, expressing both the timid and hesitating political mind of the middle-class intellectuals and its vassal attitude towards imperialist liberalism.

To us, it was perfectly clear that the logic of the class struggle would sooner or later destroy this temporary combination and fling aside the leaders of this period of transition. The hegemony of the lower middle-class intellectuals was at bottom the expression of the fact that the peasantry, suddenly called to take part in organized political life through the machinery of the army, had by sheer weight of numbers pushed aside and overwhelmed the proletariat for the time being. Even more, in so far as the middle-class leaders had been raised to a dizzy height by the powerful mass of the army, the working class itself, with the exception of its advanced sections, could not become imbued with a certain political respect for them and try to maintain political contact with them for fear of finding themselves divorced from the peasantry. And this was a very serious matter, for the older generation still remembered the lesson of 1905, when the proletariat was crushed, just because the massive peasant reserves had not come up in time for the decisive battles. That is why in the first phase of the new Revolution also the proletarian masses showed themselves highly accessible to the political ideology of the Socialist Revolutionaries and the Mensheviks — especially as the Revolution had aroused the hitherto slumbering backward masses of workers, and thus made the hazy radicalism of the intellectuals a sort of preparatory school for them. The Council of Workers', Soldiers', and Peasants' Delegates meant in these conditions the predominance of peasant amorphousness over proletarian socialism, and predominance of intellectual radicalism over the peasant amorphousness.

The structure of Soviets rose so rapidly to a gigantic height mainly because of the leading part played in their labors by the intellectuals, with their technical knowledge and middle-class connections. But to us it was perfectly clear that this grand structure was built on deep internal contradictions and would inevitably collapse at the next stage of the Revolution.

• • •

It was during the first All-Russian Congress of the Soviets that the first alarming crash of thunder occurred, which warned of the coming storm. Our party had projected an armed demonstration at Petrograd for June 23rd. Its proximate object was to bring pressure to bear upon the Congress. "Take over the power in the State" — this it was that the Petrograd workers wanted to tell the Socialist Revolutionaries and Mensheviks who had come from all parts of the country. "Spurn the bourgeoisie! Have done with the idea of coalition, and take the reins of power into your own hands!" We were quite certain that if the Socialist Revolutionaries and Mensheviks broke with the liberal bourgeoisie, they would be compelled to seek support from the most energetic and most advanced elements of the proletariat, which would thus obtain the leading role in the Revolution. But that was just what frightened the lower middle-class leaders. In conjunction with the government, in which they had their own representatives, and shoulder to shoulder with the liberal and counter-revolutionary bourgeoisie they opened a truly savage campaign against the projected demonstration as soon as they got wind of it. Everything possible was set in motion against us. We were at that time a small minority at the Congress, and we gave way; the demonstration did not take place. But all the same it left a very deep mark in the minds of the two contending parties, and made the gulf between them deeper and their mutual antagonism more acute. At the closed sitting of the Presidential Bureau of the Congress, in which also representatives of the various parties took part, Tseretelli, then a member of the coalition government, speaking with all the resoluteness of a narrow-minded lower middle-class doctrinaire, declared that the only danger threatening the Revolution was the Bolsheviks and the Petrograd workers who had been armed by them. He therefore argued that the people "who did not know how to use arms" must be disarmed. Of course he had in mind the Petrograd workers and that portion of the Petrograd garrison which supported our party. However, no disarming took place, as the political and psychological conditions were not yet ripe enough for such an extreme measure.

To compensate the masses for the loss of their demonstration, the Congress of the Soviets itself organized an unarmed demonstration, on July 1st. And that day became the day of our political triumph. The masses turned out in overwhelming numbers, but although they came out in answer to the call of the official Soviet authority — a sort of counterblast to the miscarried demonstration of June 23rd — the workers and soldiers had inscribed on their banners and placards the demands and battle-cries of *our* party: "Down with the secret treaties!" "Down with the policy of strategical offensives!" "Long live an honorable peace!" "Down with the ten capitalist ministers!" "All power to the Soviets!" There were only three placards with expressions of confidence in the coalition government: one from a Cossack regiment, another from the Plekhanov group, and a third from the Petrograd "Bund," an organization consisting largely of non-proletarian elements. This demonstration proved not only to our opponents, but also to ourselves, that we were far stronger in Petrograd than had been imagined.

•   •   •

The correlation of forces inside the Soviets at the time was such that a Soviet government would have meant, from a party point of view, the concentration of power in the hands of the Socialist Revolutionaries and Mensheviks. We were deliberately aiming at such a result, since the constant re-elections to the Soviets provided the necessary machinery for securing a sufficiently faithful reflection of the growing radicalization of the masses of the workers and soldiers. We foresaw that after the break of the coalition with the bourgeoisie the radical tendencies would necessarily gain the upper hand in the Soviets. In such conditions the struggle of the proletariat for power would naturally shift to the floor of the Soviet organizations, and would proceed in a painless fashion. On their part, having broken with the bourgeoisie, the lower middle-class democrats would themselves become the target for its attacks, and would, therefore, be compelled to seek a closer alliance with the socialist working class, and sooner or later their political amorphousness and irresolution would be overcome by the laboring masses under the influence of our criticism. This is why we urged the two leading Soviet parties to take the reins of power into their own hands, although we ourselves had no confidence in them, and frankly said so.

But even after the ministerial crisis of July 15th, Tseretelli and those who agreed with him did not give up their pet idea of a coalition. They explained to the Executive Committee that the chief Cadet leaders were, it was true, demoralized by doctrinairism and even by counter-revolutionary sympathies, but that in the provinces there were many bourgeois elements who would march side by side with the revolutionary democracy and whose cooperation would be secured by the co-option of some representatives of the upper middle-class in the new ministry. Dan was already placing high hopes on a new radical-democratic party which had been concocted about that time by a few doubtful politicians. The news that the coalition had broken to pieces only to give rise to a new coalition spread rapidly throughout Petrograd, and created a wave of dismay and indignation in the workers' and soldiers' quarters. This was the origin of the events of July 16th–18th.

• • •

There was still some hope that a demonstration of the revolutionary masses might break down the obstinate doctrinairism of the coalitionists and compel them to realize at last that they could only maintain themselves in power if they completely broke with the bourgeoisie. Contrary to what was said and written at the time in the bourgeois press, there was no intention whatever in our party of seizing the reins of power by means of an armed rising. It was only a revolutionary demonstration which broke out spontaneously, though guided by us politically.

* * *

The movement of July 16th–18th showed with perfect clearness that the leading parties of the Soviet lived in Petrograd in a complete political vacuum. It is true that the garrison was by no means entirely with us at that time. There were among it units which still hesitated, were still undecided and passive. But apart from the ensigns, there was not a single unit among the garrison, which was willing to fight against us in defence of the government or the leading parties in the Soviet. It was from the front that troops had to be fetched. The entire strategy of Tseretelli, Chernov, and others, during those July days was to gain time so as to enable Kerensky to draw "reliable" troops into Petrograd. Delegation after delegation entered the Tauride Palace, which was surrounded by a huge crowd, and demanded a complete break with the bourgeoisie, energetic measures of social reform, and the commencement of peace negotiations. We, Bolsheviks, met every new detachment of demonstrators, either in the street or in the Palace, with harangues, calling on them to be calm, and assuring them that with the masses in their present mood the compromise-mongers would be unable to form a new coalition ministry. The men of Kronstadt were particularly determined, and it was only with difficulty that we could keep them within the bounds of a bare demonstration. On July 17th the demonstration assumed a still more formidable character — this time under the direct leadership of our party. . . . Meanwhile the internal situation was deteriorating and becoming more and more complicated. The war was dragging along without aim, without sense, without any perspective. The government was taking no steps to extricate itself from the vicious circle.

* * *

At the front the state of affairs was going from bad to worse. A cold autumn, wet and muddy, was drawing near. There was the prospect of a fourth winter campaign. The food supply was becoming worse every day. In the rear they had forgotten about the front. There were no reliefs, no reinforcements, and no warm clothing. The number of deserters was increasing daily. The old army committees, elected at the beginning of the Revolution, still remained in their places and supported Kerensky's policy. Re-elections were prohibited. An abyss was formed between the army committees and the masses of the army, and finally the soldiers began to detest the committees. Again and again delegates from the trenches would arrive at Petrograd and ask point-blank, at the sittings of the Soviet: "What are we to do now? Who will end the war, and how shall it be done? Why is the Petrograd Soviet silent?"

The Petrograd Soviet was not silent. It demanded the immediate assumption of authority by the central and local Soviets, the immediate transference of the land to the peasants, the establishment of control by the workers over industry, and the immediate initiation of peace negotiations. So long as we had been in opposition, the cry "All power to the Soviets!" was a battle-cry of propaganda, but since we became a majority on all the chief Soviets it imposed upon us the duty of taking up an immediate and direct struggle for power.

In the villages the situation had become complicated and confused to the last degree. The Revolution had promised the land to the peasants, but had forbidden the latter to touch the land till the meeting of the Constituent Assembly. The peasants at first waited patiently, but when they began to lose patience the coalition government resorted to measures of repression. In the meantime the prospect of the meeting of the Constituent Assembly was becoming dimmer and dimmer. The bourgeoisie was insisting that the Constituent Assembly should not be summoned until after the conclusion of peace. The peasant masses, on the other hand, were becoming more and more impatient, and what we had predicted at the beginning of the Revolution was now coming true. The peasant masses began to grab the land on their own authority. Reprisals became more frequent and severe, and the revolutionary land committees began to be arrested—here and there. In some districts Kerensky even proclaimed martial law. Delegates from the villages began to stream to Petograd, and complained to the Soviet that they were being arrested while trying to carry out the programme of the Soviets and handing over the estates of the private landowners to the peasants' committees. The peasants demanded our protection. We replied that we could only help them if the government power were in our hands. Hence it followed that if the Soviets did not want to become mere talking-shops they were bound to make an effort to get the power into their own hands.

• • •

All power to the Soviets: such was the demand of our party. In the preceding period this meant, in terms of party divisions, complete authority for the Socialist Revolutionaries and Mensheviks as against the coalition with the liberal bourgeoisie. Now, however, in November 1917, this demand meant the complete supremacy of the revolutionary proletariat, headed now by the Bolshevik Party. The question at issue was the dictatorship of the working class, which was leading, or, to be more correct, was capable of leading, the millions of the poorest peasantry. This was the historical meaning of the November rising.

Everything conspired to lead the party along this path. From the very first days of the Revolution we had insisted on the need and the inevitability of the assumption of the entire government authority by the Soviets. The majority of the Soviets, after an intense internal struggle, adopted our standpoint and took up this demand. We were getting ready for the second All-Russian Congress of the Soviets, at which we expected a complete victory for our party. The Central Executive Committee, on the other hand, under the direction of Dan (the cautious Chkheidze left for the Caucasus in good time) did everything possible to hinder the meeting of the Soviet Congress. After great efforts, supported by the Soviet group at the Democratic Conference, we at last obtained the fixing of a definite date for the Congress: November 7th. This date has now become the greatest date in Russian history. As a preliminary, we called together in Petrograd a conference of the Soviets of the Northern Provinces, including also the Baltic Fleet and the Moscow Soviet. We had a definite majority at this conference. We also obtained some protection on the right flank from the left wing of the Socialist Revolutionaries, and laid the foundation for the business-like organization of the November rising.

• • •

And so the whole conflict in Petrograd was coming to an issue over the question of the fate of its garrison. In the first place, of course, it affected the soldiers, but the workers, too, evinced the liveliest interest in it, as they feared that on the removal of the troops they might be crushed by the military cadets and Cossacks. The conflict was thus assuming a very acute character, and the question over which it was tending to an issue was very unfavorable to the Kerensky government.

Parallel with this struggle over the garrison was also going on the previously mentioned struggle for the summoning of the Soviet Congress, in connection with which we were proclaiming openly, in the name of the Petrograd Soviet and the conference of the Soviets of the Northern District, that the Second Soviet Congress must dismiss the Kerensky government and become the real master of Russia. Practically the rising was already proceeding, and was developing in the face of the whole country.

During October the question of the rising played also an important part in the internal life of our party. Lenin, who was in hiding in Finland, wrote numerous letters insisting on more energetic tactics. Amongst the rank and file there was great fermentation and growing discontent, because the Bolshevik Party, now in a majority in the Soviets, was not putting its own battle-cries into practice. On October 28th a secret meeting of the Central Committee of our party took place, at which Lenin was present. On the order of the day was the question of the rising. With only two dissentients it was unanimously decided that the only means of saving the Revolution and the country from complete destruction was an armed rising, which must have for its object the conquest of supreme government authority by the Soviets.

VICTOR CHERNOV

Russia's One-Day Parliament

V. M. Chernov (1873–1952) was the founder and principal theoretician of the SR party, which represented the peasants. In 1917 he became Minister of Agriculture in the Provisional Government and was elected chairman of the Constituent Assembly on January 5/ January 18, 1918. He left Russia in 1920 and came to the United States in 1941.

In 1931 Chernov wrote a brief account of the fatal one-day session of the Assembly on the occasion of the thirteenth anniversary of the Constituent Assembly's dissolution by the Bolsheviks, which is presented below. His memoirs appeared in an abridged English translation edited by Philip E. Mosely under the title *The Great Russian Revolution,* New Haven, Conn., Yale University Press, 1936.

When we, the newly elected members of the Constituent Assembly, entered the Tauride Palace, the seat of the Assembly in Petrograd, on January 18, 1918, we found that the corridors were full of armed guards. They were masters of the building, crude and brazen. At first they did not address us directly, and only exchanged casual observations to the effect that "this guy should get a bayonet between his ribs" or "it wouldn't be bad to put some lead into this one." When we entered the large hall, it was still empty. The Bolshevik deputies had not yet appeared.

From *The New Leader,* January 31, 1948. Copyright © the American Labor Conference on International Affairs, Inc. Reprinted with permission of *The New Leader.*

A tank division billeted in Petrograd remained faithful to the Assembly. It intended to demonstrate this faithfulness by participating in the march to the Palace which was to pass on its way the barracks of the Preobrazhensky and Semenovsky Regiments, the two best units of the Petrograd garrison. At the meetings held by these regiments, resolutions were invariably adopted demanding the transfer of state power to the Constituent Assembly. Thus a prospect was open for the consolidation of democratic forces.

But the Bolsheviks were not caught off guard. They attacked the columns of demonstrators converging on the Tauride Palace from various parts of Petrograd. Whenever the unarmed crowd could not be dispersed immediately, the street was blocked by troops or Bolshevik units would shoot into the crowd. The demonstrators threw themselves on the pavement and waited until the rattle of machine guns quieted down; then they would jump up and continue their march, leaving behind the dead and wounded until they were stopped by a new volley. Or the crowd would be bayoneted by enraged Bolshevik outfits, which would get hold of the banners and placards carried by the demonstrators and tear them into scraps.

The Assembly hall was gradually filled by the deputies. Near the dais were placed armed guards. The public gallery was crowded to overflowing. Here and there glittered rifle muzzles. Admission tickets for the public were distributed by the notorious Uritsky. He did his job well.

● ● ●

At last all the deputies had gathered in a tense atmosphere. The left sector was evidently waiting for something. From our benches rose Deputy Lordkipanidze, who said in a calm, businesslike voice that, according to an old parliamentary custom, the first sitting should be presided over by the senior deputy. The senior was S. P. Shvetsov, an old Socialist Revolutionary (SR).

As soon as Shvetsov's imposing figure appeared on the dais, somebody gave a signal, and a deafening uproar broke out. The stamping of feet, hammering on the desks and howling made an infernal noise. The public in the gallery and the Bolshevik allies, the Left Socialist Revolutionaries, joined in the tumult. The guards clapped their rifle butts on the floor. From various sides guns were trained on Shvetsov. He took the President's bell, but the tinkling was drowned in the noise. He put it back on the table, and some-body immediately grabbed it and handed it over, like a trophy, to the representative of the Sovnarkom (Soviet of Commissars), Sverdlov. Taking advantage of a moment of comparative silence, Shvetsov managed to pronounce the sacramental phrase: "The session of the Constituent Assembly is open." These words evoked a new din of protest. Shvetsov slowly left the dais and joined us. He was replaced by Sverdlov, who opened the session for the second time, but now in the name of the Soviets, and presented its "platform." This was an ultimatum: we had just to vote Aye or No.

In the election of the Assembly's President, the Bolsheviks presented no candidate of their own. They voted for Maria Spiridonova, nominated by the Left SRs. Later they threw Spiridonova into jail and tormented her until she was on the verge of insanity. But at this moment they wanted to take full advantage of her popularity and reputation as a martyr in the struggle against Tsarism. My nomination as candidate for the Presidency received even greater support than had been expected. Some leftist peasants evidently could not bring themselves to oppose their own "muzhik minister." I obtained 244 votes against 150.

I delivered my inauguration address, making vigorous efforts to keep self-control. Every sentence of my speech was met with outcries, some ironical, others spiteful, often buttressed by the brandishing of guns. Bolshevik deputies surged forward to the dais. Conscious that the stronger nerves would win, I was determined not to yield to provocation. I said that the nation had made its choice, that the composition of the Assembly was a living testimony to the people's yearning for Socialism, and that its convention marked the end of the hazy transition period. Land reform, I went on, was a foregone conclusion: the land would be equally accessible to all who wished to till it. The Assembly, I said, would inaugurate an era of active foreign policy directed toward peace.

•   •   •

I finished my speech amidst a cross-fire of interruptions and cries. It was now the turn of the Bolshevik speakers—Skvortsov and Bukharin. During their delivery, our sector was a model of restraint and self-discipline. We maintained a cold, dignified silence. The Bolshevik speeches, as usual, were shrill, clamorous, provocative and rude, but they could not break the icy silence of our majority. As President, I was bound in duty to call them to order for abusive statements. But I know that this was precisely what they expected. Since the armed guards were under their orders, they wanted clashes, incidents and perhaps a brawl. So I remained silent.

The Social Democrat Tseretelli rose to answer the Bolsheviks. They tried to "scare" him by levelling at him a rifle from the gallery and brandishing a gun in front of his face. I had to restore order— but how? Appeals to maintain the dignity of the Constituent Assembly evoked an even greater noise, at times turning into a raving fury. Dybenko and other demagogues called for more and more assaults. Lenin, in the government box, demonstrated his contempt for the Assembly by lounging in his chair and putting on the air of a man who was bored to death. I threatened to clear the gallery of the yelling public. Though this was an empty threat, since the guards were only waiting for the order to "clear" us out of the hall, it proved temporarily effective. Tseretelli's calm and dignified manner helped to restore peace.

There was a grim significance in the outburst that broke loose when a middle-of-the-road deputy, Severtsov-Odoievsky, started to speak Ukrainian. In the Assembly the Bolsheviks did not want to hear any language except Russian. I was compelled to state emphatically that in the new Russia, each nationality had the right to use its own language whenever it pleased.

When it appeared that we refused to vote the Soviet "platform" without discussion, the Bolsheviks walked out of the sitting in a body. They returned to read a declaration charging us with counter-revolution and stating that our fate would be decided by organs which were in charge of such things. Soon after that the Left SRs also made up their minds. Just before the discussion of the land reform started, their representative, I. Z. Steinberg, declared that they were in disagreement with the majority, and left the Assembly.

• • •

We knew that the Bolsheviks were in conference, discussing what to do next. I felt sure that we would be arrested. But it was of utmost importance for us to have a chance to say the last word. I declared that the next point on the agenda was the land reform. At this moment somebody pulled at my sleeve.

"You have to finish now. There are orders from the People's Commissar."

Behind me stood a stocky sailor, accompanied by his armed comrades.

"What People's Commissar?"

"We have orders. Anyway, you cannot stay here any longer. The lights will be turned out in a minute. And the guards are tired."

"The members of the Assembly are also tired but cannot rest until they have fulfilled the task entrusted to them by the people — to decide on the land reform and the future form of government."

And leaving the guards no time to collect themselves, I proceeded to read the main paragraphs of the Land Bill, which our party had prepared long ago. But time was running short. Reports and debates had to be omitted. Upon my proposal, the Assembly voted six basic points of the bill. It provided that all land was to be turned into common property, with every tiller possessing equal rights to use it. Amidst incessant shouts: "That's enough! Stop it now! Clear the hall!" the other points of the bill were voted.

Fearing that the lights would be extinguished, somebody managed to procure candles. It was essential that the future form of government be voted upon immediately. Otherwise the Bolsheviks would not fail to charge the Assembly with having left the door open for the restoration of the monarchy. The motion for a republican form of government was carried unanimously.

In the dawn of a foggy and murky morning I declared a recess until noon.

At the exit a palefaced man pushed his way to me and beseeched me in a trembling voice not to use my official car. A bunch of murderers, he said, was waiting for me. He admitted that he was a Bolshevik, but his conscience revolted against this plot.

I left the building, surrounded by a few friends. We saw several men in sailor's uniforms loitering near my car. We decided to walk. We had a long distance to go, and when I arrived home I learned that rumors were in circulation that the Constituent Assembly had dispersed, and that Chernov and Tseretelli had been shot.

At noon several members of the Assembly were sent on reconnaissance. They reported that the door of the Tauride Palace was sealed and guarded by a patrol with machine guns and two pieces of field artillery. Later in the day a decree of the Sovnarkom was published by which the Constituent Assembly was "dissolved."

Thus ended Russia's first and last democratic parliament.

PETER N. WRANGEL

The White Armies

General Baron Peter N. Wrangel (1878–1928) took command of the White Army in the south of Russia after General Denikin's defeat in the spring of 1920.

The selection below represents General Wrangel's account of the White Army's victories and defeats, covering the whole course of the Civil War. It was written seven years after the debacle of the White Army.

At the end of the year 1917 the government of Kerensky could no longer retain the executive power. It was seized by a group of people who appealed to the lowest sentiments of the populace, promising peace and plenty without work. None of these promises were kept. That, however, did not matter to the Bolshevik leaders. Russia as a national State was of no concern to them. What they sought was a base whence to spread their influence over the whole world.

The moment that the Bolsheviks laid hands on the executive power, Russia, as a national entity, ceased to exist. Even the name which served to describe it disappeared. All the interests of Russia were sacrificed to those of the Communist International. Everywhere this International waged determined war against every element of the national spirit, aggravated class conflicts, and destroyed all the foundations of morality, religion, the fatherland, the family.

Yet, in spite of all, Russia still exists as a nation. Immediately after the Bolsheviks seized the reins of power, a few men, stirred

From Wrangel's memoirs *Always with Honour,* New York, R. Speller & Sons, 1957, pp. 331–37, 348. Reprinted by courtesy of the publisher.

by love for their country—its greatness and glory—raised the national flag that had been dragged through the mud. They started in the south of Russia an implacable struggle against the oppressors of their country.

Their appeal was heard; officers, soldiers, students, intellectuals, politicians, workers, and peasants flocked to the Don. All these courageous men whose hearts were in the right place and who could not admit that Russia was dead, gathered under the national flag. There were men of every class and walk of life, of all ages and political views. Enrolling in the ranks of the National Army, they forgot all political or social differences. They were all united by the same warm love of their country, and the same desire to sacrifice themselves for her.

Thus, in November 1917, the White Army was born. It was the incarnation of the national sentiment and Russian patriotism. United under the tricolor banner, they fought for the national cause. This Army, loyal to all the obligations taken over by previous national governments, still continues the struggle for the honor of its country's name, for the resurrection of Russia as a Nation. Its way of fighting has changed; the outward forms which properly belong to armies have gone, but the idea which inspired it has remained unchanged.

What is this idea? It is life devoted to the fatherland, eagerness to save her at all expense, a passionate desire to tear down the red flag from the Kremlin and hoist in its place the national flag.

The struggle which began in the south of Russia soon raised echoes elsewhere, in the north, the north-west, and Siberia. I will not pause here to talk about past history; I will only recall the brilliant successes with which the White Armies began. The troops of General Denikin occupied a third of Russia and advanced within a short distance of Moscow. In the north-west General Yudenich was already in sight of St. Petersburg. In the west, Admiral Kolchak had almost reached the Volga.

Yet victory was not in store for the White Armies. The troops of the north were driven to the sea and forced to give up the territory they occupied. Some of them perished, while others were obliged to take refuge in Norway. In the north-west the Army of General Yudenich had to retreat to Estonian territory where it was interned. The army of Admiral Kolchak in Siberia was finally defeated and had to disperse. In the south of Russia the troops of

General Denikin retreated to Novorossiisk. What was left of them made a stand in the Crimea. After a year of heroic struggle this last strip of Russian soil was abandoned.

The failure of the White Armies was due to a number of reasons, which I will not examine in detail. I will confine myself to mentioning some of them.

A major reason is due to the political and strategic errors of the leaders who misjudged the psychology of the masses. They exaggerated the importance of their early successes. They did not pay enough attention to securing the territories they occupied, of organizing them, of raising new recruits to fill the gaps in their ranks, and of providing food and munitions.

The political ignorance of the people accounted for a good deal. They had not yet lost their illusions concerning the Bolshevik power; they still went on believing in the false promises of the maximalist agitators. Lastly, the Bolshevik Armies had at their disposal the resources of an immense country, its reserves of food, of arms and munitions.

On the other hand, the White Armies were short of everything. During the first months of the struggle the only arms and munitions we could draw on were those taken from the enemy. Support from outside was indispensable. It could only come from those on whose side the Russian Army had fought during World War I. The White Armies who had refused to recognize the shameful peace of Brest-Litovsk and were loyal to their Allies thought they had the right to count on this support.

But the Western Powers were far from realizing the essence of the Bolshevik idea, the danger it posed to the world. They did not consider the importance of the struggle the White Army was waging. They did not understand that this Army, in fighting for its own country, was also fighting for civilization and Western culture. Not only did the White Armies fail to receive sufficient help in time, on several occasions they even had to surmount obstacles raised by the former Allies of Russia.

It must be noted that the English alone afforded material assistance to the White Armies. But this help was slow in arriving and inadequate. Support in armed forces, to a very small amount, was given only by England and France. Unfortunately, there was never any certainty that this help would not be abruptly withdrawn, and often this happened without any previous warning.

The result was the loss of thousands of lives and immense stores left to plunderers. In the north-west the English, while they supported General Yudenich and promised him their help, were coniving at the same time with his political enemies, thus giving them the chance at the decisive moment to stab General Yudenich in the back.

In the south, the French forces under General d'Anselme, which had occupied the port of Odessa in 1919, gave up the town when the enemy approached. This action without any warning made the position of the Russian troops and the civil population desperate. Finally, there can be no excuse for the handing over of Admiral Kolchak to the Bolsheviks by General Janin. The Admiral had put himself under General Janin's protection; soon after he was handed over, he was shot.

In the spring of 1920 the White Armies of the north, north-west, and Siberia had to admit defeat. In the south the troops of General Denikin were pushed to the Black Sea. The British government had up to this point lent assistance to General Denikin in the shape of arms and munitions. Foreseeing the success of the Bolsheviks, and judging that the time had come to switch from the armed struggle to rapprochement with the enemy of yesterday, it now requested the head of the White Army to cease hostilities.

The government of Mr. Lloyd George took it upon itself to enter into negotiations with the Bolshevik government concerning the amnesty to be granted to the White Army and the peoples of the Crimea. Our Army was threatened to be deprived of all assistance if we refused to abide by their decisions.

At this moment our situation seemed desperate. The remains of the Armies which had fought in the south of Russia, after evacuating Novorossiisk, numbering about thirty-five thousand, had withdrawn into the Crimea. It was no longer an Army, but a disorderly crowd which had grown slack in its discipline and was morally and physically exhausted after a retreat of hundreds of miles in the midst of winter, and a series of defeats. Munitions, artillery stores, and cavalry had been abandoned at Novorossiisk for want of sufficient ships to carry them. In the north, the Crimean peninsula was covered on the Isthmus of Perekop by weak detachments of no more than five thousand five hundred men. The Army found itself pinned to the sea, on a scrap of ground, without a chance to get supplies and replace its losses in men. The Commander-in-

Chief, General Denikin, was heartbroken and relinquished his command. The post of Commander devolved on me. Fate had reserved for me a hard task. While I fully understood the weight of responsibility that I was taking on, and was aware of the difficulties of continuing the struggle under these desperate conditions, I judged that I could not decline the post. I could not promise the Army a victory; all I could do was to promise that it would acquit itself in this hopeless position without the loss of honor.

In the answer I sent to the British government I made clear that I would not accept to enter into direct negotiations with the enemy. I left the initiative to Mr. Lloyd George, and held Great Britain responsible for its decisions.

Meanwhile I worked feverishly to restore the morale of the army and increase its fighting power. I wrote to King Alexander of Serbia, then heir to the throne and Regent, and begged him to give my Army shelter in case of need. I arranged at the same time that measures should be taken to facilitate evacuation, if that course became inevitable. As might have been easily foreseen, the negotiations between the English and the Bolsheviks led to no result. The Soviet government was evasive and demanded a number of political concessions. The British government informed me of this and insisted that I should enter into direct negotiations. They warned me that a continuation of the struggle might have fatal results, and that in any case I could not count on any assistance from them. It was clear that the British government, which sought closer relations with the Bolshevik government, wished above all to see hostilities come to an end. It did not apparently consider that the result would be the sacrifice of thousands of lives.

The Army was already pretty well reorganized, and I answered these threats in May 1920 by ordering an offensive. The troops by this time were rested and showed their old bravery, and the first encounters with the Bolsheviks brought victory back to our ranks. The British government responded by recalling their representatives and military mission from the Crimea. Between the two parties in the struggle, Mr. Lloyd George did not hesitate to choose our enemy. The future course of events showed how unsound his calculations were. Very different was the attitude of the French government. It declared its disapproval of any approach to the Bolsheviks and expressed its sympathy with my action. Unfortunately this attitude did not lead to a true understanding of the international danger presented by Bolshevism. France wished to create a strong Polish state as a means of support against Germany. At the time when hostilities began between Poland and the Soviet government, France thought it necessary to support the White Armies, which might divert a part of the Red forces. Later, M. Millerand, the French president, publicly acknowledged that the help which had been lent to the White Armies had no other aim but the saving of Poland. It was said, particularly in an article that appeared in the official newspaper, *Le Temps,* that France had used every means to save Poland, and that one of these means "was the establishment of a threat to the rear of the Bolshevik Armies. . . . The pressure brought to bear by General Wrangel's forces helped to save Warsaw."

Led by these considerations the French government recognized in June 1920, my *de facto* government. This recognition had a strong moral effect, but France had not the time to give us much material aid. However, it was this official recognition that enabled the Army to receive a part of the Russian supplies which had been available since the Great War in various countries.

Fighting continued successfully in the south of Russia during summer and autumn of 1920. All the exertions of the Bolsheviks proved futile. But after the defeated Soviet armies were at Warsaw, the short-sighted policy of Mr. Lloyd George, then the leading influence on European policies, scored again. Hostilities were prematurely suspended on the Polish front, and once more the Bolsheviks were saved.

Our Army was abandoned.

It was evident that after the armistice and the conclusion of the peace with the Poles the Bolsheviks would direct their forces against the Crimea, and the White Army could not struggle against such odds. What happened was that the Soviet government concentrated more than five hundred thousand men with all their cavalry on the front occupied by my troops. Exhausted by long months of incessant fighting, and weakened by all sorts of privations, the White Army was overwhelmed. To save the remnants of the troops and the people who had put themselves under their protection, I gave the order for retreat in October 1920. The troops retreated by forced marches to the seaports and embarked according to a plan previously arranged. The civilian population, those who served in the rear, the sick and wounded, women and children, were the first to be put on board. The evacuation took place in perfect order. I inspected personally on the cruiser *Kornilov* the ports of evacuation, and I was able to assure myself that all who wished to leave Russian soil found it possible to do so.

Three years of determined struggle, of fighting and suffering, of heroism, victory, and defeat, followed by fresh victory, then had come to an end.

In my order of the day concerning the evacuation [to Constantinople] I did not conceal the fact that our future fate was unknown to me, that we had no longer any Russian territory to move on, and that we had no resources left. I gave everyone full freedom to decide on his own destiny. This order of the day, which warned everyone of an uncertain future, stopped nobody from leaving. From October 31st to November 3rd one hundred and twenty-six ships left the ports of the Crimea, carrying one hundred and fifty thousand men who refused to live under the Bolshevik yoke. We left our country for the unknown—for privations, sorrow, and suffering.

The number of those evacuated was 100,000 officers and soldiers and 50,000 civilians; included in these were 30,000 women and 7,000 children. Of the 100,000 officers and soldiers, 50,000 belonged to the fighting troops, 40,000 to those who served in the rear. There were 3,000 students from the military schools. More than 6,000 were ill or wounded. The 50,000 civilians included all walks of life, among them peasants and workers. It was not an emigration of the privileged and professional classes alone. It was the exodus of National Russia with all its elements, its civilian organizations and its Army. These exiles cherished in their hearts profound faith in a victorious return to the land of their fathers. Of these émigrés the Army was the only group organized and consolidated by the blood all had shed and the ideas they shared. Its new existence [in exile] showed that the fight for the honor of the country and the remaking of Russia as a nation was not yet ended. . . .

. . . History, which knows no favoritism, will record the importance of our struggle and the extent of our sacrifices. One day it will be recognized that the fight which we carried on for the love of our country and the resurrection of Russia as a nation, was also a struggle to safeguard the culture of Europe and its age-old civilization. On that day the nations of Europe will salute the Russian Army, paying homage to its valor, its sufferings, and its agony.

J. V. STALIN

The International Character of the October Revolution

J. V. Stalin (pseudonym of J. V. Dzhugashvili, 1879–1953). A conspirator by training and temperament, he directed the revolutionary struggle of Transcaucasian Bolsheviks early in this century. He played a relatively minor role between February and October 1917 as a member of the Petrograd Committee of the Bolshevik Party and editor of *Pravda*. Sukhanov, in his memoirs, refers to him as a "gray blur." As general secretary of the party he gained, through skillful machinations, control of the party apparatus. At the Fifteenth All-Union Congress of the Communist Party, on December 27, 1927, he won his struggle for power, and for twenty-five years directed the destinies of the country and of the world communist movement.

The following address by Stalin, given on the occasion of the Tenth Anniversary of the October Revolution (published in *Pravda,* November 6–7, 1927) elaborates on the international significance of the October Revolution, particularly for the colonial and dependent countries and stresses the importance of the Soviet Union as a base for the world revolutionary movement.

From J. V. Stalin: *Works,* Moscow, Foreign Language Publishing House, 1954, vol. 10, pp. 244–55.

The October Revolution is not merely a revolution "within national bounds." It is, above all, a revolution of an international, "world-embracing" order, for it denotes a radical turn in the universal history of mankind, away from the old, capitalist world to the new, socialist world.

Revolutions in the past usually ended in changing one group of exploiters at the helm of the ship of state for another such group. The exploiters would change, while exploitation remained. Such was the case during the emancipatory movements of the slaves. Such was the case during the period of the rebellions of the serfs. Such was the case during the period of the well-known "great" revolutions in England, France and Germany. I do not refer to the Paris Commune which was the first glorious, heroic and yet unsuccessful attempt on the part of the proletariat to turn history against capitalism.

The October Revolution differs from these revolutions *in point of principle*. It sets as its aims not the replacement of one form of exploitation by another form of exploitation, of one group of exploiters by another group of exploiters, but the abolition of all exploitation of man by man, the abolition of any and every exploiting group, the establishment of the dictatorship of the proletariat, the establishment of the power of the most revolutionary class of all oppressed classes hitherto existing, the organization of a new, classless, socialist society.

It is precisely for this reason that the *victory* of the October Revolution means a radical change in the history of mankind, a radical change in the historical destinies of world capitalism, a radical change in the movement for the emancipation of the world proletariat, a radical change in the methods of struggle and the forms of organization, in the everyday life and traditions, in the culture and ideology of exploited masses throughout the world.

Upon this is based the fact that the October Revolution is a revolution of an international, universal order.

This constitutes also the root cause of that profound sympathy which the oppressed classes of all countries cherish for the October Revolution, since they regard it as a pledge of their own deliverance.

It would be possible to note a number of fundamental questions indicating the line along which the October Revolution exercises its influence over the development of the revolutionary movement throughout the world.

1. The October Revolution is remarkable, first of all, for having broken through the front of world imperialism, deposed the imperialist bourgeoisie in one of the biggest capitalist countries and put the socialist proletariat in power.

The class of the wage workers, the class of the driven, the oppressed and exploited, has risen *for the first time* in the history of mankind to the position of a *ruling* class, setting a contagious example to the proletarians of all countries.

This means that the October Revolution *has opened up* a new epoch, an epoch of *proletarian* revolutions in the countries of *imperialism.*

It took the tools and means of production away from the landlords and capitalists and turned them into collective property, thus opposing socialist property to bourgeois property. It thereby exposed the lie of the capitalists that bourgeois property is inviolable, sacred, eternal.

It has wrested the power from the bourgeoisie, deprived the bourgeoisie of political rights, destroyed the bourgeois state machinery and transferred the power to the soviets, thus opposing the socialist rule of the soviets, as a *proletarian* democracy, to bourgeois parliamentarism, as *capitalist* democracy. Lafargue was right when he stated, as far back as 1887, that the very next day after the revolution "all former capitalists would be deprived of the elective franchise." By that very means the October Revolution has exposed the lie of the Social Democrats about the possibility of a peaceful transition now to socialism through bourgeois parliamentarism.

However, the October Revolution did not, and could not, stop there. Having destroyed the old, the bourgeois world, it began to build a new, a socialist world. The ten years of October Revolution are years of construction of the Party, the trade unions, the soviets, the co-operatives, cultural organizations, transport, industry, the Red Army. The undoubted successes of socialism in the U.S.S.R. on the construction front have visibly shown that the proletariat *can* successfully govern the country *without* the bourgeoisie and *against* the bourgeoisie, that it *can* successfully build industry *without* the bourgeoisie and *against* the bourgeoisie, that it *can* successfully guide the whole of the national economy *without* the bourgeoisie and *against* the bourgeoisie, that it *can* successfully build socialism in spite of the capitalist encirclement. The old "theory" to the effect that the exploited cannot do without the exploiters, just as the head or other parts of the body cannot get along without a stomach, is not only the idea of Menenius Agrippa, the famous Roman senator of ancient history. This "theory" is now the cornerstone of the political "philosophy" of social-democracy in general, of the social-democratic policy of *coalition* with the imperialist bourgeoisie — in particular. This "theory" which has acquired the character of a prejudice, now presents one of the greatest obstacles on the path of the revolutionization of the proletariat in the capitalist countries. One of the most important results of the October Revolution is the fact that it dealt that false "theory" a mortal blow.

Is there still any need to prove that such similar results of the October Revolution could not, and cannot, remain without serious effect on the revolutionary movement of the working class in capitalist countries?

Such generally known facts as the progressive growth of communism in the capitalist countries, the growth of the sympathy of the proletarians of all countries with the working class of the U.S.S.R.; finally, the influx of the workers' delegations into the land of the Soviets, prove beyond a doubt that the seeds sown by the October Revolution already begin to bear fruit.

2. The October Revolution had shaken imperialism not only in the centres of its domination, not only in the "mother countries." It also dealt blows at the rear of imperialism, its periphery, by having undermined the domination of imperialism in the colonial and dependent countries.

Having overthrown the landlords and the capitalists, the October Revolution has broken the chains of national-colonial oppression and freed from it without exception all the oppressed nations of a vast state. The proletariat cannot free itself without liberating the oppressed nations. It is a characteristic trait of the October Revolution that it carried out these national-colonial revolutions in the U.S.S.R. not under the flag of national animosities and international conflicts, but under the flag of mutual trust and fraternal *rapprochement* between the workers and peasants of the various nationalities in the U.S.S.R.; not in the name of *nationalism,* but in the name of *internationalism.*

It is precisely because the national-colonial revolution took place in our country under the leadership of the proletariat and under the banner of internationalism, that the pariah nations, the slave nations, for the *first time* in the history of mankind have risen to the position of nations which are *really* free and *really* equal, thereby setting a contagious example to the nations of the whole world.

This means that the October Revolution has *ushered in* a new epoch, an epoch of *colonial* revolutions, which are carried out in the *oppressed countries* of the world in *alliance* with the proletariat and *under the leadership of the proletariat.*

Formerly it was the "accepted idea" that from time immemorial the world has been divided into inferior and superior races, into blacks and whites, that the former are incapable of assimilating civilization and are doomed to be objects of exploitation, and that the latter are the only exponents of civilization, whose mission it is to exploit the former. Now this legend must be regarded as shattered to pieces and rejected. One of the most important results of the October Revolution is that it dealt that legend a mortal blow, having shown in practice that the liberated non-European nations, drawn into the channel of Soviet progress, are capable of promoting a *really* progressive culture and a *really* progressive civilization no less than the European nations.

Formerly it was the "accepted idea" that the only method of liberating the oppressed nations was the method of *bourgeois nationalism,* a method of nations seceding one from the other, a method of disuniting them, a method of intensifying national animosities between the toiling masses of various nations. Now this legend must be regarded as disproved. One of the most important results of the October Revolution is the fact that it dealt that legend a mortal blow, having shown in practice the possibility and expediency of the *proletarian, international* method of liberating the oppressed nations as the only correct method, having shown in practice the possibility and expendiency of a *fraternal alliance* between the workers and peasants of the most diverse nations on the principles of *voluntariness* and *internationalism.* The existence of the Union of Soviet Socialist Republics, which is the prototype of the future amalgamation of the toilers of all countries in a single world economy, cannot but serve as direct proof of this.

Beyond question these and similar results of the October Revolution could not and cannot remain without serious effect on the revolutionary movement in the colonial and dependent countries. Facts like the growth of the revolutionary movement of the oppressed nations, in China, in Indonesia, in India, etc., and the growth of sympathy with the U.S.S.R. among these nations undoubtedly bear this out.

The era of undisturbed exploitation and oppression of the colonies and dependent countries *is gone.*

The era of emancipatory revolutions in the colonies and dependent countries, the era of the awakening of the *proletariat* in these countries, the era of its *hegemony* in the revolution, *has begun.*

3. By sowing the seeds of revolution, both in the centers of imperialism and in its rear, by weakening the power of imperialism in the "mother countries" and undermining its domination in the colonies, the October Revolution has jeopardized the very existence of world capitalism *as a whole.*

While the spontaneous development of capitalism in the conditions of imperialism has grown over—owing to its unevenness, owing to the inevitability of conflicts and armed clashes, owing, finally, to the unprecedented imperialist slaughter—into the process of the "decay" and the "withering away" of capitalism, the October Revolution and the resultant secession of an enormous country from the world system of capitalism could not but accelerate this process, washing away, bit by bit, the very foundations of world imperialism.

More than that. In undermining imperialism, the October Revolution concomitantly established a powerful and open *base* for the world revolutionary movement, represented by the first proletarian dictatorship, a base which it *never had before* and on which it can now rely. It created that powerful and open center of the world revolutionary movement which it *never possessed* before and around which it now can rally and organize a *united revolutionary front of the proletarians and of the oppressed nations of all countries against imperialism.*

This means, first of all, that the October Revolution inflicted a mortal wound on world capitalism, a wound from which it will never recover. It is precisely for this reason that capitalism will never recover the "equilibrium," the "stability" that it possessed prior to October. Capitalism may become partly stabilized, it may rationalize its production, turn over the administration of the country to fascism, hold the working class down for a while, but it will never recover the "tranquillity," the "assurance," the "equilibrium" and the "stability" that it flaunted before, for the crisis of world capitalism has reached the stage of development where the flames of revolution are bound to break through, now in the centers of imperialism, now in the periphery, reducing to naught the capitalist patchwork and daily bringing the fall of capitalism nearer. Exactly as we find it in the famous fable: "Pull the donkey's tale out of the mire and his nose will be stuck in it, pull out the nose and his tail will be in it."

This means, in the second place, that the October Revolution raised the force, the relative importance, the courage and the preparedness to fight for the oppressed classes of the whole world to a certain level, forcing the ruling classes to reckon with them as a *new,* an important factor. Now it is no longer possible to look upon the toiling masses of the world as a "blind mob," groping in the dark, devoid of all prospects, for the October Revolution raised a beacon for them which illumines their path and gives them prospects. Whereas formerly there was no *world-embracing* open forum where the aspirations and ambitions of the oppressed classes could be expounded and formulated, now such a forum exists in the form of the first proletarian dictatorship.

There is hardly room for doubt that the destruction of this forum would cast the gloom of unbridled dark reaction for a long time to come over the social and political life of the "progressive countries." It is impossible to deny that the mere fact of the existence of a "bolshevik state" exercises a restraining influence on the dark forces of reaction, thus facilitating the struggle of the oppressed classes for their liberation. This, properly speaking, explains the brutal hatred which the exploiters of all countries feel for the Bolsheviks. History repeats itself, though on a new basis. Just as formerly, during the period of the fall of *feudalism* the word "Jacobin" evoked horror and loathing among the aristocrats of all countries, so now in the period of the fall of *capitalism,* the word "Bolshevik" evokes horror and loathing in bourgeois countries. And *vice versa,* just as formerly Paris was a place of refuge and school for the revolutionary representatives of the rising *bourgeoisie,* so now Moscow is the place of refuge and school for the revolutionary representatives of the rising *proletariat.* Hatred for the Jacobins did not save feudalism from foundering. Can there be any doubt that hatred for the Bolsheviks will not save capitalism from inevitable perdition?

The era of the "stabilization" of capitalism *has gone,* taking along with it the legend of the unshakable character of the bourgeois order.

The era of the downfall of capitalism *has begun.*

The October Revolution is not only a revolution in the domain of economic and social-political relations. It is at the same time a revolution in the minds, a revolution in the ideology, of the working class. The October Revolution was born and strengthened under the flag of Marxism, under the banner of the idea of the dictatorship of the proletariat, under the flag of Leninism, which is the Marxism of the epoch of imperialism and of proletarian revolutions. It marks, therefore, the victory of Marxism over reformism, the victory of Leninism over social-democracy, the victory of the Third International over the Second International.

The October Revolution erected an impassable barrier between Marxism and social-democracy, between the policy of Leninism and the policy of social-democracy. Formerly, *prior to the victory of the dictatorship of the proletariat,* social-democracy could disport the flag of Marxism without openly repudiating the idea of the dictatorship of the proletariat, but at the same time without doing anything whatsoever to bring the realization of this idea nearer, for such behavior on the part of social-democracy did not jeopardize capitalism in the least. Then, in that period, social-democracy was formally merged, or almost merged, with Marxism. Now, *after the victory of the dictatorship of the proletariat,* when it became patent to all *whither* Marxism leads, *what* its victory could mean, social-democracy was no longer able to disport the flag of Marxism, could no longer flirt with the idea of the dictatorship of the proletariat without putting capitalism in jeopardy to a certain extent. Having long ago broken with the spirit of Marxism, it found itself forced to break also with the flag of Marxism, it openly and unambiguously took the stand against the October Revolution, the offspring of Marxism, against the first dictatorship of the proletariat in the world. Now it had to, and really did, dissociate itself from Marxism, for under present conditions it is impossible to call oneself a Marxist without openly and self-sacrificingly supporting the first proletarian dictatorship in the world, without conducting a revolutionary struggle against one's own bourgeoisie, without creating the conditions for the victory of the dictatorship of the proletariat in one's own country. A chasm opened up between social-democracy and Marxism. Henceforth, the *only* exponent and bulwark of Marxism will be Leninism, communism.

However, matters did not rest there. After dissociating social-democracy from Marxism, the October Revolution went further, by throwing off social-democrary into the camp of the outright defenders of capitalism, *against* the first proletarian dictatorship in the world. When the Adlers and Bauers, the Wellses and Levys, the Longuets and Blums abuse the "Soviet regime" and extol parliamentary "democracy," these gentlemen mean by this that they fight and will fight *for* the re-establishment of the capitalist order in the U.S.S.R., *for* the preservation of capitalist slavery in the "civilized" states. The present social-democracy is the *ideological prop* of capitalism. Lenin was absolutely right when he said that the present social-democratic politicians are "real agents of the bourgeoisie in the labor movement, the labor lieutenants of the capitalist class," that in the "civil war between the proletariat and the bourgeoisie" they will inevitably range themselves "on the side of the Versailles people against the Communards." *It is impossible to put an end to capitalism without putting an end to social-democracy in the labor movement.* Therefore, the era of the dying off of capitalism is at the same time the era of the dying off of social-democracy in the labor movement. The great importance of the October Revolution lies, incidentally, in the fact that it marks the inevitable victory of Leninism over social-democracy in the world labor movement.

The era of the domination of the Second International and of social-democracy in the labor movement *has come to an end.*

The era of the domination of Leninism and of the Third International *has begun.*

EPILOGUE

R. V. IVANOV-RAZUMNIK

After Twenty Years

R. V. Ivanov-Razumnik (1878–1946) was a prominent literary scholar and critic before 1917. A lifelong Populist, he was in sympathy with the Left SRs at the time of the Revolution, and in 1918 edited two of their periodicals. After the October Revolution he became a spokesman of revolutionary messianism then in vogue. Almost from the inception of the Soviet regime he was considered an enemy, a "subjective idealist," and an "ideologist of the petty bourgeoisie." He spent many years in prison and in exile—the most harrowing of his experiences was his imprisonment during the terror of the NKVD chief, Ezhov, in 1937–38.

His reminiscences *Tiurmy i ssylki (Prisons and Exile)* were published in 1953 by the Chekhov Publishing House, New York. An English edition entitled *The Memoirs of Ivanov-Razumnik* appeared in London in 1965 under the imprint of Oxford University Press. A human and historical document of unusual interest, his book is an honest record of what thousands of Russian writers and thinkers had to endure for deviating from the official ideology of the party. A typical representative of prerevolutionary intelligentsia, Ivanov-Razumnik was a man of courage and a gifted chronicler.

The following excerpt is a factual and dispassionate account of his arrests and imprisonments under the Soviet regime. We are printing his testimony as the epilogue to the "living documents" of the Revolution of 1917.

From *The Russian Review,* vol. 10, no. 2 (April 1951), pp. 146–54, reprinted by courtesy of G. Jankovsky; vol. 10, no. 4 (October 1951), pp. 301–3, 307–10; vol. 11, no. 1 (January 1952), pp. 51, 52, 53–55; vol. 11, no. 2 (April 1952), pp. 106–12.

"The days' upheaval is completed. . . ."—Alexander Blok

Long ago, in my early youth, I used to forget the world over the foolish but fascinating novel by Alexander Dumas *Vingt ans après*. I have borrowed my title from it, straining a point, however, since there was an interval not of twenty but of nineteen years between my first and my second imprisonment. Later I shall outline the principal landmarks of my personal history; here I shall only note that the events of 1901–02 altered the direction of my whole life.

At the university I studied mathematics and physics with great enthusiasm. Professor O. D. Khvolson, the physicist, took an interest in me and had a fellowship in mind for me for post-graduate studies in his special field; I wrote several papers for him. At the same time I followed courses of the historical-philological faculty, devoting special attention to the lectures and seminars of our eminent sociologist Lappo-Danilevsky; studied the history of literature with Professor Zhdanov, psychology and the history of philosophy with Professor A. I. Vedensky, Greek literature with F. F. Zelinsky, and attended various other courses. Where did I find the time and strength, I wonder?

Then came my deportation to Simferopol in 1902. In that town I found no facilities whatever for laboratory research in physics; but I was able to pursue my literary studies without hindrance; and I had the good luck to make the acquaintance of the owner of an excellent library on Russian literature of the eighteenth and nineteenth centuries. I began collecting the material for a long-planned book, a history of the Russian intelligentsia. I started with what was to be the last chapter, an essay on the "Attitude of Maxim Gorky towards Contemporary Culture and Intelligentsia."

After a year in Simferopol, I was allowed to settle in a remote part of the province of Vladimir, on the estate of the parents of my fiancée who became my wife in 1903. Here I worked hard on a book that was published in 1906 in two volumes, under the title *A History of Russian Social Thought*. This determined my future career as a writer. Were it not for my exile in 1902, I would have never found the time for such an extensive work and probably would have remained faithful to physics, with literature as a hobby; I might have ended up as a venerable professor in such a politically harmless field as physics, and presumably would have escaped all the deportations and imprisonments that were in store for me. Whenever I met Professor Khvolson in later years, he would chide me for having betrayed the queen of sciences—physics—for such foolishness as literature. But, after all, the choice had been made for me by circumstances. My fate had been decided by the "kind solicitude" of the government and by my long exile.

Here I shall not go into details concerning my further literary and public life. One thing I wish to make clear; in the controversy between Marxism and Populism *(narodnichestvo)* I took the side of the latter, writing against Marxism and crossing swords with its cleverest exponent, Plekhanov, and its most light-minded one, Lunacharsky. All this was brought up and held against me a quarter of a century later, during my examinations by GPU and NKVD.

Although I shared the "populist" ideology, I never joined the party which represented it politically, that of the SR (Socialist Revolutionaries). I "walked alone," like the cat in Kipling's tale. However, I took an active part in the literary undertakings of that party and became the literary editor of its review *Zavety* (Bequests) and, after the Revolution, its daily paper *Dielo Naroda* (The People's Cause). When, in the autumn of 1917, the SRs split into a right and a left wing, I sympathized with the latter and took charge of the literary section of its daily—*Znamya Truda* (Labor's Banner) and its review *Nash Put* (Our Way). All this was duly entered into the black books of the Cheka and the GPU, and I was destined to pay for it sooner or later.

In July, 1918, a year and a half after the Revolution, the left SRs organized the assassination of the German ambassador von Mirbach in Moscow and an uprising against the Bolsheviks which was ruthlessly crushed. *Znamya Truda* and *Nash Put* were closed. All non-Marxist, non-Communist literary activities became impossible. At that time, V. E. Meyerhold organized the TEO, Theatrical Department, and asked me to work in the Theoretical or Repertory section of that Department. The latter was headed by Alexander Blok. I was active in these sections throughout 1918-19. During the same period, together with Alexander Blok, Andrey Biely and others, I was busy organizing the Free Philosophical Association ("Wolfila"), which actually came into being at the end of 1919, and existed for five years. All these activities were far removed from politics and confined to the fields of culture, philosophy, literature, art; nevertheless, the Bolsheviks had not forgotten me.

The terror of the era of War Communism was then in full swing. Every day "hostages" were arrested and shot; real and imaginary plots were exposed one after another. In February, 1919, a conspiracy of Left SRs was uncovered which in reality never existed but, nevertheless, resulted in a series of severe repressions. The day came when I, too, as so many others, was engulfed in the wave of arrests.

In January, 1919, I fell ill with pneumonia. By the middle of February, I had sufficiently recovered to get up and walk around my room. On February 16, at 6 p.m. I was peacefully sitting in my study at Tsarskoye. The doorbell rang; V.N. (my wife) went to open it; a little man of Oriental type (an Armenian) in civilian clothes rushed in, brandishing a gun; he was followed by a soldier with a rifle. The Armenian, an agent of Cheka, presented a search warrant, put away the unnecessary weapon, forbade me to move, and got ready to start the search. However, at the sight of book cases with thousands of volumes, of a filing cabinet overflowing with papers, of a desk loaded with letters and manuscripts, he was taken aback and visibly lost heart. He collected at random a package of letters, a manuscript, a thick notebook with material for a book I had just begun: *The Vindication of Man* (it was then entitled "Anthropodicy" and this word obviously aroused his suspicion). For two hours he helplessly fumbled around the bookcases, picked out a few volumes dealing with anarchism, made up a small parcel, and by 8 o'clock the search was over. It all seemed rather funny. Then he told me to get ready; he was taking me to Petersburg. I packed a few things in a small suitcase—a towel, soap, a change of underwear, a mug. Those were hungry days; and all the food V.N. was able to give me was a lump of bread and a small box of sugar-candy. And since we were short of money, too, I could take with me only two "kerenkas" at 20 rubles each. I took leave of my family, arranged with V.N. that she would notify Meyerhold of my arrest, and walked to the station, escorted by the two men, a wearisome walk for one so recently recovered from illness. The train was nearly empty; my escorts paid no attention to me; I sat in silence, remembering my journey to prison some twenty years before.

We reached Petersburg at 9 in the evening, and, in a car of the Cheka, were driven to "Gorokhova 2," the notorious center of the

Bolshevik secret police and simultaneously a transit prison for all arrested persons. I was ushered into the registry where I had to fill out a form with preliminary biographical data, and then was taken up an endless staircase, up and up skywards. Soon I was to get acquainted with the cellars of the Cheka, but I began with the attic. My convoy turned me over to a gloomy warden who, with much jangling of keys, opened the door of this subcelestial prison before me and shouted: "Starosta! Number 195!" The starosta (foreman), a prisoner, came up to me, welcomed me with a grin, registered my name, and we went together in search of a place for me to sleep.

The attic consisted of two large rooms connected by an open door and dimly lit by a few naked bulbs overhead. Some 200 men crowded the rooms, most of them asleep, and it was by no means easy to find a vacant bunk. At last, a group of prisoners, sitting on their bunks, took me in as their "fifth." They explained that the prisoners were divided into "fives," each group of five forming an independent "dinner unit." At mealtimes, they were given a separate bowl of food for the group. The prison population was fluctuating, and new lists were made up and new "fives" were formed every day.

Tired out, I stretched myself out on the bare boards of my bunk, listened to my companions, and wondered what had brought me here.

Two prisoners from the other room came up to me and called me by name. I recognized them—they were workingmen, belonging to the Left SRs who had often called at the office of *Znamya Truda*. They told me that for the last three days arrests had been going on among members of the Left SRs on the charge of participation in a conspiracy of which not one of them had the slightest knowledge. They supposed that my arrest had some connection with this matter. They proved to be right.

Slowly the attic quieted down. Despite my fatigue, I could not sleep. The boards were too hard, and the foul air of the overcrowded room was stifling. Swarms of bedbugs added to the discomfort. At every moment the warden would throw the door open and call out some name: "For examination!" The starosta had to look for the owner of the name among the sleeping crowd, arousing every time dozens of others. I was dozing off when towards 3 a.m. I heard my own name called up.

I was taken down to the second floor, into a brightly lit room.

Behind a desk sat a young man in military uniform—the examining magistrate. I recognized him at once. About a year before, he had been a member of the Left SRs and I had often seen him hanging around the office of the party's Central Committee which was next to the editorial room of *Znamya Truda*. We were not acquainted, and he had every reason to believe that I did not know him. Shortly before the assassination of von Mirbach he had vanished from our horizon, had gone over to the Communists and now had emerged as a Cheka examiner charged with the task to investigate, or rather to cook up, a case implicating his former party comrades in a nonexisting conspiracy.

He made me fill out the usual questionnaire. After a glance at it, he said:

"You have made a false statement. To the question 'Were you a member of any political party?' you reply: 'No party membership.' Now cross it out and write the truth: 'was a member of the Left SR party.'"

"This I cannot do," I said, "because it would not be true. I never was a member of that party."

"And yet you were often seen at the Central Committee; you were a member of it, weren't you?"

"What if I was seen there? After all, you were constantly dropping in at the Central Committee yourself; does that mean you were a member?"

He reddened. All at once his manner became rude.

"Your lies won't help you! I'll bring all your doings to light! Member or no member, you certainly played a part, probably a leading part, in the conspiracy that has just been uncovered. You better come out with it! A frank confession will make things easier for you. Here"—he pointed at the paper—"write here the truth."

In the spot he indicated I wrote that I had for the first time heard of the alleged conspiracy from the examiner himself, and therefore could have had no part in it.

"You are going to regret it," he said. "I advise you to think it over."

He turned his attention to the parcel of books and papers taken from my study. The word "Anthropodicy" puzzled him and he asked for its meaning. He closely studied my little notebook with addresses, and copied out the names and addresses, each on a separate piece of paper. I did not like this at all, and, as it turned out, with good reason. For a whole hour he busied himself with my papers, while I was left in peace "to think it over." At last he finished, tied up the parcel again and said:

"Well? Have you changed your mind?"

"No, I have not."

"A pity! We both are educated people, aren't we? We ought to understand each other. But you refuse to understand that your stubbornness will aggravate your fate. Now sign here, and expect the worst." "I shall hope for the best," I said, putting my signature to the paper, and then was led back to the attic. It was 4 a.m.

An hour after this, at 5 a.m., cars of the Cheka, as I learned later, were dashing off to various parts of the city, seeking out my friends whose addresses I had so imprudently jotted down in my notebook (I never repeated that mistake). The following persons were arrested: the poet Alexander Blok; the writer Alexey Remizov; the historian M. K. Lemke; the writer Yevgeny Zamiatin; professor S. A. Vengerov, and some others, all living far apart from each other. What brisk activity was being displayed by the Soviet organs of vigilance!

All my arrested friends were brought to "Gorokhova 2." Instead of being sent up to the attic, where they might have conspired with me, they were locked up elsewhere. One after another they were summoned for questioning, and each in turn was surprised to learn that he was charged with participation in a conspiracy of Left SRs. Each one reacted to the absurd accusation according to his temperament. The aged Professor Vengerov remarked calmly, "I have heard many absurdities in my life, but this one tops them all." Zamiatin burst out laughing, which greatly shocked the examiner—after all, it was a serious matter, wasn't it? But all his efforts failed to convince the arrested men that they were conspirators and members of the subversive party. Then he made them write down their answers to the following questions: "How long have you known the writer Ivanov-Razumnik? On what terms are you with him at present? Have you talked to him lately, and what about?" After having answered these extra questions, the dangerous political criminals were dismissed, to be released in the course of the day and allowed to return to their homes after a detention of less than 24 hours.

There were two exceptions: Zamiatin who was released immediately after the examination, and Alexander Blok who was held longer than the others and sent up to the attic.

Zamiatin later recounted his dialogue with the examiner as follows: In answer to the question: "Did you ever belong to a political party?" he had written: "Yes, I did."

"Which party?" asked the examiner, anticipating a major political charge.

"The Bolshevik Party."

Many years before, as an undergraduate, Zamiatin had indeed joined the Bolshevik Party whose rabid enemy he became after the Revolution. The examiner was taken aback.

"How's that! Then you are still a Bolshevik?

"No, I am not."

"When and why did you leave the Party?"

"Long ago, for ideological reasons."

"But now, after the Party's triumph, you surely regret your desertion?"

"I do not."

"Explain, I don't understand."

"Why, it's simple. Are you a Communist? A Marxist?"

"Of course."

"Then you are a bad Communist, a bad Marxist. A good Marxist knows that the stratum of petty-bourgeois fellow-travellers tends to disintegrate and that the workers alone provide a reliable class basis for Communism. Since I belong to the petty-bourgeois intelligentsia, I fail to understand why you are so surprised at my defection."

The examining magistrate was so impressed with this ironic argumentation that he set Zamiatin free on the spot.

The case of Alexander Blok was different. He was obviously connected with the Left SRs. His poem "The Twelve" first appeared in *Znamya Truda* and so did his cycle of articles "Revolution and Intelligentsia," which was also published by the party as a separate pamphlet. Blok's poem "The Scythians" appeared in the review *Nash Put* and was issued by the party separately with my introduction. Clearly he was a Left SR! For that reason he was subjected to a lengthy examination and while the others were allowed to go home, he was transferred to the attic. By then I was no longer there. A. S. Steinberg, our future "Wolfila" secretary, was

brought in at the same time and occupied the bunk next to Blok. A
year after Blok's death, Steinberg's vivid reminiscences of that
night of February 14 spent by the poet of "The Twelve," who had
saluted "triumphant freedom," in the attic of the Cheka, appeared
in the "Wolfila" symposium dedicated to the poet's memory. On the
following day Blok was released.

Back in my bunk after the interrogation, I tried to go to sleep,
but by seven the whole attic was already astir. Now in daylight I
had a good look at my fellow-prisoners. What a motley of races,
tongues, social classes, of faces and clothes! Russians, Germans,
Finns, Estonians, Jews, Latvians, even several Chinese; former
army officers, working men, students, soldiers, civil servants (some
of the highest rank); non-party men and members of various parties,
mostly socialists of every denomination; political offenders and
common criminals; clad in ragged sheepskin coats, business suits,
worker's jackets, Russian blouses, uniforms — a cross-section of the
nation. . . .

I approached several groups. They were all discussing the same
subject: the possibility of an "intervention" by mythical "allies"
and in that case the inevitable evacuation of Petersburg by the
Bolsheviks. Throughout the night, the distant roar of artillery had
been heard. . . . And if the Bolsheviks have to get out, what will
they do with us? Set us free? Shoot all and sundry? Divide the
sheep from the goats? The overwhelming majority had the answer
ready: all would be shot!

Early in the morning, huge kettles were brought in with a hot
liquid that passed for tea, and every prisoner was given an eighth
pound of bread. The hot liquid, whatever it was, cheered me up.
But the general mood of the attic was one of utter dejection. What
a difference from the prison of my student days twenty years ago!
No jokes, no laughter, no loud discussions. Crowded as it was, the
room was strangely quiet; even the common criminals, even the
anarchists were subdued and shared in the mood of anxious waiting. They all regarded themselves as hostages doomed to be shot as
a measure of "social defense" — a measure so freely applied by the
Cheka in that period of War Communism. Moreover, those who
had already spent a few days in the attic suffered acutely from
hunger.

The midday meal, called "dinner," was indeed appalling. Every
"five" were given a bowl filled with some brown mush, strongly

smelling of herring. Armed with wooden spoons, we sat down around the bowl, each waiting for his turn to take up a spoonful. It is impossible to give an idea of the look and taste of this nauseating concoction. Five bits of a half-rotten herring floated in the bowl. I took out my lump of bread brought from home and divided it into five parts. Supper, they said, would be exactly like "dinner." But by then I was no longer there. Little did I suspect that I would have my next meal five days later!

Shortly after "dinner," there was a stir outside, the sound of footsteps, the clatter of arms. Several Cheka men entered, one of them holding a list. He called out names, and those called up stepped forth with their belongings and took position by the door. Soon I heard my own name. There were some sixty of us. We were taken down to the prison yard and told that our destination was the prison on Shpalernaya Street. The gate swung open, we marched out into the street, convoyed by some twenty men. It was a cold and sunny day, the streets were filled with people who gloomily watched our procession, without giving any sign of emotion, everyone knew he might become a unit in such a column any day.

We reached Shpalernaya without incident. There was the prison (House of Preliminary Detention); we were turned over to the administration. The usual procedure of registering began. The heavily whiskered warden, apparently a veteran of tsarist times, was rude but efficient.

After the registration the newcomers were distributed among different wards. I was placed in solitary confinement in cell No. 163. Years later, I was to spend many months in that same cell, so I postpone its description until I come to that period. To be alone was pleasant after the crowded noisy attic. It was 2 p.m. At six they brought in "supper," a bowlful of some hogwash which I left untouched; it looked even worse than the attic soup. I ate some bits of candy and drank water from the faucet. At 8 o'clock I was summoned "with belongings" to the registry. The same whiskered oldtimer examined me, checking my answers with the questionnaire I had filled out on arrival. Then he turned me over to my convoy, three young Red Army men with rifles and tightly packed haversacks. A car was waiting in the street, we got in and were rapidly driven through the dark streets to the Nikolayevsky station.

They were taking me to Moscow.

. . . There had been an interval of nearly twenty years between my first and my second imprisonment; fifteen years were to pass until the third. And if my first was a gay introduction, my second—a by no means gay interlude, my third might be characterized by the old Russian saying: "Those were only blossoms—the berries were still coming."

It should be kept in mind that the incidents recorded below all happened during the grim period when Ezhov—a mentally unbalanced man and possibly an *agent provocateur*—headed the NKVD. Under him, a wave of arrests swept the country; their number went into the hundreds of thousands and the millions; the prisons in Moscow and the provinces were filled to overflowing; emergency barracks to receive the ever growing droves of new prisoners were being hastily erected all over the country. . . . I was engulfed in the wave of the September mass arrests and was well aware that this time it was in earnest and for long. . . . I proved right: I spent 21 months in prison.

It was late in October of 1937. Still a "greenhorn," after only one month at the Butyrki prison, I used to sleep in the so-called "subway," the space under the bunks (spending the nights not so much sleeping as gasping for breath, since the air under the bunks, to one still unaccustomed to it, was stifling). We were just getting ready for the night; it was rather warm outside and the *framooga* (upper part of the window) was open. All of a sudden a hush fell on the ward; everybody listened intently: from somewhere through the window came stifled screams:

"Comrades, comrades, help! You devils, what are you doing to me? Comrades, murder, help!"

And after a brief silence, a long inarticulate wail:

"Oh-oh-oh!"

Again a moment of sinister silence—and then renewed frantic screams.

"Help, help, they're killing me!"

This went on for several minutes, but to us it seemed like ages. . . .

Professor Kalmanson, our ward-monitor, was the first to recover his wits; he jumped down from his bunk, seized a heavy stool and began furiously battering the heavy metal door. All the prisoners were yelling, the adjoining wards were also storming; guards from

the whole length of the corridor came running. They tried to reassure us, pretending that the screams we had heard had come from
the "mental" ward. By now all was quiet. In silence we went back
to our bunks, but hardly anyone was able to sleep that night.

We were only too well aware that the matter had nothing to do
with the mental ward and that we had witnessed—not *oculis sed
auribus*—a "questioning" by an examining magistrate. I wish to
note here that such a thing happened only once: the magistrate was
doubtlessly reprimanded for his "inept conduct of the examination"
(the fool had forgotten to shut the *framooga!*) and the ensuing
riot among the prisoners. After this, the beatings in the examination
rooms were administered with the windows tightly shut.

Long before being arrested, we had heard rumors about beatings
and even torture in the prisons; now for the first time we had listened with our own ears to the agonized wails of a victim. . . . The
examination rooms were located on the third floor, right above us,
and the screams had reached us through the open window of one of
these rooms.

There can be no doubt that some kinds of torture had been prac-
tised before Ezhov's time by the GPU, but probably as an exception—apart from the notorious "stewing chambers" of the mid-
twenties where arrested bourgeois were "steamed" until they were
ready to surrender any gold and dollars in their possession. It was
also in the twenties that the poet Nikolay Kluev happened to spend
three days and nights at the "cork room" of the GPU, and related
his experience with horror; it is a fact that such a room actually
existed, and it must have been established with some definite purpose. . . . Until now, however, all the rumors and reports of torture
in the prisons had been to us a matter of hearsay. Now we were
destined to become witnesses and often victims of an undisguised
system of torture applied by Ezhov's staff of examiners by order of
their chief.

. . . In ward 45, the bunk next to mine was occupied by Dr. Kurtglass, an army surgeon. I am not quite sure of the name, but it could
be ascertained through reference to the Moscow telephone directory
for 1937—at that time the Doctor held the position of senior medical officer of the Moscow military district.

He was charged with participation in the well-known conspiracy
of General Tukhachevsky. Endless examinations with beatings,
insults, humiliations, had been fruitless—the Doctor stubbornly

refused to "confess." Coming back to the ward after such a "questioning," utterly exhausted in body and mind, he would say to me: "Don't tell me Dostoevsky knew all about cruelty! He was a babe-in-arms, your Feodor Mikhailovich!" Soon he was to suffer an ordeal indeed worthy of Dostoevsky's somber imagination.

At daybreak on Monday, the 3rd of December 1937, he was taken away for an examination that lasted for six hours; all this time he spent standing silently by the wall (not allowed to lean against it), while the examiner busied himself at his desk, remarking now and then:

"So you won't confess, you scoundrel? All right, keep standing there by the wall, we're in no hurry! We'll make you squeal yet!"

At noon the guard led him back to the ward, warning him to be ready again in fifteen minutes; he kept watching the prisoner through the peephole. The Doctor finished his meal in a hurry and was taken away. He was back by 6 p.m. and told us that again they had kept him standing by the wall all the time; but there had been a different examiner behind the desk. This was called a "conveyer" questioning: the examiners relieved each other every six hours, day and night, while their victim was passed along this unusual "running belt."

After a hasty supper in the ward, the Doctor spent the whole night—twelve hours—standing on his feet by the wall. Brought back next morning at six, he tried to lie down on his bunk but was immediately aroused by the special guard who was watching him through the peephole. Within a few minutes he was returned to the examination room for a continuation of his harrowing experience.

Thus Monday, Tuesday, Wednesday went by—the Doctor standing by the wall on his feet, *without a moment of sleep.* Whenever the exhausted man would doze off or sway on his feet (since he was forbidden to lean against the wall), the examiner would spring up from his seat, pull at the Doctor's beard and shower him with threats and abuse. On Friday morning, after four days and nights spent thus without sleep, the Doctor, brought back to the ward for his breakfast, said to me: "My wife—there's a clever woman for you! Somehow she managed to get inside Butyrki and to sneak a pouch of tobacco into my pocket, right under the examiner's nose! But where is it?"—and he feverishly began to search his pockets. Throughout Friday, the fifth day of the "conveyer," he suffered from similar hallucinations; after that they stopped. A medical man, he had found a way to counteract in some measure the effects of insomnia and to keep up his strength: every morning he would fill his pockets with lumps of sugar we collected for him, and throughout the day would surreptitiously put bit after bit into his mouth, the examiner never noticing. This kept him going.

Saturday and Sunday—December 8 and 9—passed in the same way; the Doctor stood the test with amazing fortitude and still would not confess. How long would the cruel experiment go on? On Monday, December 10, the Doctor was brought back to the ward as usual for his breakfast; how he was still able to move, to walk, to speak, passes understanding. The usual fifteen minutes were over and still no one came to fetch him, and there was no eye watching him through the peephole. Apparently, after precisely a week of cruel torture, the "conveyer" had been brought to a stop. We made the Doctor comfortable on a bunk, covered him with a fur coat, put a makeshift pillow under his head—but he was unable to sleep. Only gradually, day by day, did he recover; and he would say again and again: "A babe-in-arms was your Dostoevsky!"

From old-timers among the prisoners we learned that the ordeal by deprivation of sleep required a special authorization by the Chief Prosecutor of the NKVD and was never extended beyond one week—such was the law (the law, indeed!). Very few were able to withstand it; Dr. Kurtglass did. A month later he was called out "with belongings," and we heard after a while that he had been transferred to the most dreaded of all prisons—Lefortovo.

At Lefortovo, according to many accounts, real instruments of torture—iron-tooth scrapers, thumb-screws, and such—were in use; but since those who told me about it had themselves been neither objects nor eyewitnesses of that kind of torture, I shall not dwell upon this aspect. Suffice it to say that a year later, while I was held in ward 113 of Butyrki, one of the inmates of the adjoining ward was the well-known builder of the aircraft named ANT after his initials—A. N. Tupolev. He told me the following: a year before he had been arrested and brought to Lefortovo where he had to share a cell with Muklievich, a former big party boss, who after weeks of examinations at Lefortovo had already signed a confession. Muklievich urged Tupolev to make a confession at the very first questioning and drew up a picture of the unspeakable horrors that awaited him in case of recalcitrance. The picture was apparently so convincing (Tupolev would not go into details) that the unfortunate ANT, unwilling to suffer all that had been done to Muklievich, took the latter's advice and at the very first examination admitted everything the examiner wanted him to admit. In this way he escaped torture and was transferred to Butyrki where he now awaited the decision regarding his further fate.

I also remember a fleeting glimpse I had at the Lubianka "kennel," in November, 1937, of a bearded engineer who had just returned from an examination and was sobbing like a child: they had told him that, since he was unwilling to confess, he would be taken to Lefortovo and would have "to bear the consequences." Within a few hours he was actually taken away from the "kennel."

And so Dr. Kurtglass' fate had brought him to that gruesome Lefortovo. . . . What they did to him there, I do not know; but a year later I learned through a fellow-prisoner who had just come to Butyrki from the Lubianka prison that the Doctor was there in the common ward, that he had confessed and was expecting to be either shot or sent to a concentration camp.

I have told a lot about life in jail, about the affairs of other people. It is time to resume my own story. . . .

. . . It happened on November 2, 1937—a date that has stuck in my memory, for the night of November 2–3 proved one of the culminating points of my prison career. Early in the morning of November 2, I was called out "without belongings." They took me across the yard to the "station," put me into a tiled cubicle and kept me there for three hours. After that, the routine procedure: a guard appeared and made me strip; he examined thoroughly my clothes and underwear, went through the usual ritual: "Get up! Open your mouth! Show your tongue!" . . . and walked away. After another hour of waiting, they led me into the yard to the prison vehicle, the "Black Raven"; it was full, all the iron-walled single stalls were occupied, except one by the entrance whose door stood ajar; I was pushed into it, the Raven croaked, and we jogged along.

We stop. The door of the Black Raven swings open, we are in the yard of the Lubianka inner prison. I am taken down a flight of stairs into a deep cellar flooded with electric light. The place is new to me; it is the notorious "kennel" I have heard so much about from fellow-prisoners who have preceded me here. Opposite the entrance is the commandant's office where they enter me into the list of "kennel" inmates; I fill out a short questionnaire (surname, first name, patronymic, date and place of birth, place of imprisonment).

There follows a cursory search (for some reason they confiscate such a harmless object as my glasses); then I am conducted through a corridor to the kennel number assigned to me. The corridor is not long and ends in a closed wall; to the right are the four kennel wards, to the left—the lavatory and the large examiners' room.

So this is the famous kennel! A cellar about 8 paces long, 5 paces wide; about 14 feet high; a stone cage brightly lit by electric bulbs. No daylight, although there is a small window high up in the wall, under the ceiling; the windowpanes are thickly smeared with white paint to keep the daylight out. The window looks out on the street, the Bolshaya-Lubianka; in the morning when the sunrays hit the panes and after dark when the street lamp opposite the prison is lit, one sees black shadows moving across the windowpanes projected by the legs of free men and women passing by. A stone floor, bare stone walls, neither bunks nor a table nor benches, nothing but the stinking coverless bucket in the corner; a bare empty stone cage—that's the kennel.

I was assigned to ward 4, directly opposite the lavatory. The cellar was nearly full; I was the eighteenth. Six months later I discovered from personal experience that the same room could be made to hold three times as many people. I found a place by the wall, sat down on the floor and started getting acquainted with my neighbors.

At Butyrki, the lavatory and the bathhouse were called "post offices" No. 1 and No. 2, here at Lubianka, the kennel was known as the local "radiotelegraph station." Inmates of all Moscow prisons were brought here together and exchanged information, news, and experiences. On that particular day one half of the prisoners were from Butyrki and the other half from the Taganka prison. The kennel population was fluid, changing all the time; during the twenty-four hours I spent there about half the prisoners were taken back to their respective prisons while several new ones were brought in. When I left, the ward contained about twelve people.

I did not rest long. A guard opened the door and called out my name: "For examination!" I had not far to go—just diagonally across the corridor to the examiners' room. It was large and comfortably furnished: a couch, a few chairs, a file cabinet, a desk with a desk lamp. By the desk stood a tall clean-shaven man of about thirty in military uniform, holding a briefcase. He said: "Lieutenant Sheptalov, your examining magistrate. Sit down!"—and sat down himself behind the desk.

After filling out the routine questionnaire (name, address, profession, family status) he asked with unconcealed irony:

"Of course, like all defendants, you do not know on what grounds
you have been arrested?"

He was obviously taken aback when I replied:

"I do know."

"Is that so? Well, that simplifies matters. On what grounds?"

"For not being a Marxist."

He gave me a searching look and laughed:

"Nonsense! We do not punish for ideology. We have far more
serious reasons to call you to account. Wouldn't you prefer to make
a sincere and honest confession?"

"I should like to submit a written statement to you and your
superior," I replied.

For a moment he looked at me thoughtfully, without speaking;
then he took a sheet of paper from his briefcase, pushed pen and ink
toward me and said curtly:

"You may write."

I wrote out a statement addressed to the supreme investigating
organs of the GPU which were handling my case. It ran about as
follows:

In 1933 I was arrested by the organs of the GPU on the charge—
categorically denied by me—of participation in the "ideological-organi-
zational center of populism." I was forced to give up my literary work
which had been my exclusive occupation; I spent nearly nine months in
the Leningrad House of Preliminary Detention and after that, nearly
three years, in exile at Novosibirsk and Saratov. After completion of
my term of exile, I settled at Kashira where I lived in complete seclusion,
devoting all my attention to an extensive literary work undertaken at the
request of the State Museum for Literature. I have avoided all political
activities and upon my return to Moscow have consorted only with 2–3
writers; so there could have been no new grounds for rearresting me.
Nevertheless, on September 29 of this year I was arrested; and for
over a month now I have been waiting to learn what are the charges
brought against me. The law requires that a prisoner be formally charged
within two weeks after his arrest. Since I regard my arrest as a mis-
understanding and the withholding of a charge as a violation of the law,
I declare herewith: the investigating organs should either recognize their
mistake and set me free without delay, or else inform me about the nature
of the charges brought against me and give me the reasons for my new
arrest—which, convincing as they may appear to those organs, will be
easily refuted by me. Should no reply be forthcoming to this my state-

ment, I shall begin a hunger strike and shall keep it up until one of my
two above-stated requests is fulfilled.

As can be seen, I had decided to take the bull by the horns, without the slightest hope, of course, of proving stronger than this formidable Cheka beast. But I had absolutely nothing to lose—the bull
was already poking his horns into my ribs; I was sure that the end
had come—if not of my life, so at any rate of my freedom, even the
ephemeral freedom of Kashira. I knew that the beast would never
let me go, that they intended to finish me off one way or another. I
figured that my "statement" would neither aggravate nor improve
my situation, yet might speed up the inevitable course. But then
who knows? It was quite possible that the opposite effect would be
achieved of slowing up my case, fortunately for me, as it turned
out. . . . Anyway, I was in a somber mood and did not expect
anything good from any source.

Lieutenant Sheptalov took the paper from me and read it through
without any comment except one remark when he came to the
sentence that "the investigating organs should recognize their mistake," he uttered emphatically:

"The NKVD never makes mistakes!"

How many times have I heard this idiotic formula from my examiners! How many thousands of times did other prisoners as inno-
cent of guilt as myself hear the same assertion! The NKVD had
appropriated to itself most of the attributes of Lord Almighty: it
was infallible, omniscient, omnipresent, all-powerful. Only loving
kindness was completely absent from its make-up.

Lieutenant Sheptalov finished reading my statement. For a
moment he sat in silence, looking thoughtfully, then said brusquely:

"All right. It will be reported. You may go. You will be called."

It would have been naïve to suppose that my written statement
might disconcert the supreme investigating authorities of the
NKVD; nevertheless, by its very rarity, it did cause a kind of sensation, as was shown by the events of that same night.

I was soundly asleep on the bare stone floor, where at least I did
not have to squeeze myself in between two other men, when a
shout coming from the door aroused me and I heard my name called
out. I had lost all sense of time and thought that it was far on into
the night. I got up and was about to cross the corridor to the examiners' room, but instead they led me out of the cellar into the
yard, then through a doorway up a filthy flight of stairs to the

fourth floor. After a long walk through a maze of passages and office rooms crowded with people in Cheka uniforms or civilian clothes, I was ushered into a spacious well-furnished room (the private office of the department chief, as I learned later) where I found Lieutenant Sheptalov. A carpet covered the whole floor, on the walls were the portraits of the leaders and a big clock which had just struck eleven, there was a desk with two telephones, a broad needlework-covered couch, two file cabinets, and between them a solitary chair.

Behind the desk, placed obliquely in a corner, Sheptalov was sitting with his back to the door. When I entered, he turned round and invited me to sit down, not, however, by the desk, as was usual, but on the chair between the file cabinets, some six feet off. This puzzled me; another thing that seemed odd was a row of a dozen chairs along the opposite wall. Still with his back to me, Sheptalov took up the receiver of one of the telephones and said into it laconically: "He's here," then returned to his work without paying any attention to me. I waited, feeling rather hot in my fur coat and fur cap.

About ten minutes went by. A man in Cheka uniform walked briskly in; he was about thirty, short, stocky, clear-shaven (they are all clean-shaven, I never met an examining magistrate with a moustache). Lieutenant Sheptalov got up, pointed at me without a word and resumed his seat, pretending to be engrossed in his work. The newcomer asked, pointing a finger at me, "That's him?"

He took his stand in front of me, one hand in his pocket, the other akimbo, and scrutinized me for a moment. Then he uttered with indescribable contempt,

"A wrrriter? Ivanov-Razumnik?"

I stared back at him in silence. Then, starting at a low pitch and gradually working himself up and raising his voice, he began:

"A writer! Ivanov-Razumnik! So you have the nerve to submit declarations to us? So you dare present demands? You miserable scribbler, you insist on observance of the law? Don't you know, you blockhead, that the law for you—that's us? Don't you know, you scribbling swine, that we can turn you into ground meat, law or no law? This is no longer the year thirty-three when we handled the likes of you with gloves! This minute I'm going to call in our boys, they'll show you what's what, . . . your mother!* You filthy dog,

* An untranslatable obscenity [Ed.].

you ought to tremble before us and confess without much ado, instead of threatening us with hunger strikes! Do you think you scared us? Scared indeed! To hell with you and your brazen demands!"

By now he was screaming like a madman. He yelled:

"Stand up when I talk to you!"

I did not move and tried to keep my composure, but inwardly I was shaking under this shower of obscene abuse. I addressed myself to the back bent over the desk:

"Citizen magistrate Sheptalov, do you countenance this outrageous treatment of a writer in your presence?"

The back replied (Sheptalov did not turn round):

"I have no right to interfere; the department chief is talking to you."

The department chief, now frantic with rage, shook his fists in my face and went on screaming:

"You stand up or I'll smack your ugly mug! Get up or I'll throw you downstairs, you and your chair! . . . your mother! Get up, you hear me?"

Again I addressed myself to the bent back, trying to keep my voice from trembling (without much success, I fear):

"Magistrate Sheptalov, I emphatically protest against this infamous treatment! Tell your chief that he will not draw a single word from me!"

"So, you swine, you won't talk to me? You won't stand up? As you please! I'm not going to soil my hands with you! I'll send in one of our boys and he'll take care of you! A writer, indeed! Ivanov-Razumnik!"

He turned abruptly on his heels and hurried out of the room. I never saw him again. I regret not having asked Sheptalov for the name of this worthy GPU official; I would have enjoyed making it public.

Convinced that I was in for a savage beating, I said to Sheptalov's back:

"Once again I enter an emphatic protest against the vile insults and threats you seem willing to ignore, turning your back on them! If you wish to remain a silent witness of what is going to happen here, it's all right with me, but you should know that after that you won't hear a single word from me. I know what I shall have to do."

The back replied:

"Nothing is going to happen here."

And indeed the minutes passed and no henchman appeared. Later I gathered that my statement had been discussed by those "on the top," and it had been decided, instead of applying violence to an author, to try intimidation instead, which task had been entrusted to the department chief. When the attempt at intimidation failed, they resorted to the usual methods of questioning, without beatings, however. Why? Because a writer might some day bear witness against them in print? I do not know their reasons, but I feel bound, in all fairness, to acknowledge that after this first and last outburst of the department chief, they treated me decently throughout the following eighteen months of continuous questioning. Six months later, while cross-examining one of the witnesses in my case . . . Sheptalov actually told him that he held me "in high esteem." Possibly this was a result of my behavior in the face of his chief's attempt to terrorize me.

All this I came to understand later; at the moment I was waiting for the appearance of a Cheka "tough" and bracing myself for the worst. When I said to the examiner: "I know what I shall have to do," I meant a plan of action conceived a few days previously under the impact of the frenzied screams of a tortured prisoner heard through the open transom of our ward. If worst comes to worst, the best thing is to put an end to one's life, it is the only answer to torture and degradation. This, however, was easier said than done under prison conditions. It seemed to me, nevertheless, that suicide, while difficult, was not impossible. I might break off the handle of the tin tea-mug given to each of us; prisoners taken to the bathhouse were not searched and I might be able to smuggle in the sharp-edged handle; and once there — a small tub of hot water, an opened vein. . . . Who would notice in the dense steam of the bathhouse?

Had it been necessary, I believe that my courage would not have failed me. Whether the attempt would have succeeded is another question. About two months later we learned that the wife of Agranov, Yagoda's well-known assistant in charge of literary affairs, detained in the women's ward of our prison building, after learning of her husband's execution, had opened a vein on her wrist in the bathhouse. This was immediately detected and she was taken to the infirmary which she left with her arm paralyzed. I was spared such an ordeal. However, I was unaware of this as I waited for the

guard who was to show me "what's what." But the moments passed
and still he failed to turn up. Instead, various other people appeared
on the scene, one after another. Soon there were about ten people
in the room.

What had brought them in? Had the roaring of the department
chief aroused all the other examiners on the same floor? Or had they
been told about me beforehand and were now curious to have a look
at the prisoner who had dared to produce such an amazing document? I do not know the answer, but no sooner had the department
chief left than various young men began drifting into the room,
some in uniform, some in civilian clothes, examining magistrates of the secret-political department and their assistants. One
after another they seated themselves on the row of chairs opposite
mine (which seemed to have been placed there for that very purpose) and stared at me with curiosity, apparently waiting for the
show to go on. They were not disappointed. But before the second
act there was a brief interlude.

They were watching me, chuckling and sniggering among themselves, waiting for something to happen. Then one of them, a red-
haired young man in civilian clothes, came up to me and said with a
peculiarly mean and vicious expression:

"So you choose to call yourself a writer, sir?"

I said nothing.

"And why don't you answer, dear sir?"

I kept silent.

"And why, my dear sir, do you keep your pretty cap on your
head?"

"Because you keep your caps on, all of you."

"So! You deign to talk at last! Well, there's quite a difference
between you and us, dear sir. *We* may keep our caps on but *you*
have to take yours off in our presence!"

Gingerly, with two fingers, he lifted my fur cap from my head and
as gingerly put it down on the floor. There was something unspeak-
ably repellent about everything he said or did; I am sure that as an
examiner he was a sadist and torturer.

I picked up my cap, put it on and again addressed Sheptalov's
back:

"Magistrate Sheptalov, I beg you to protect me against the insults of your colleagues. You no longer have the excuse that they
are your superiors."

I do not know what turn things would have taken had not a new actor appeared on the scene. They all rose as he entered; Sheptalov stood to attention by his desk. I recognized the newcomer instantly—the man in yellow! He wore the same clothes as a month before when I had seen him in the orderly officers' room of Lubianka 14—yellow leather leggings, yellow leather breeches, yellow leather jacket of military cut with a decoration attached to it, yellow oil-cloth cap. Later in the night I learned from Sheptalov that the "man in yellow" was Redens, a Latvian, head of the secret-political division for the whole district of Moscow.

He went up to Sheptalov and they exchanged a few sentences, looking sideways at me. Probably they were talking about my case; maybe Sheptalov was reporting to him about the effect on me of the department chief's performance. Redens then came up to me; I was still sitting on my chair with all the others standing about and tensely watching. But no one, and least of all myself, would have guessed the kind of question he asked me:

"Well," he said, "what do you think of our new edition of Saltykov? Fine work, isn't it?"

"Not as fine as it was planned but good enough," I replied in utter amazement. "This is very gratifying to me."

"Gratifying to you? What concern is it of yours, how we edit Saltykov?"

"It means a great deal to me," I said, "since I did all the preparatory work on the edition for the State Publishing House."

Redens stared at me speechless; then he turned on his heels and addressed the group of young magistrates still respectfully standing on their feet.

"Now mark this, comrades, here you have before you a representative of that counter-revolutionary intelligentsia which we, unfortunately, have been unable to weed out completely. A rabid foe of Marxism! Conceals his counter-revolutionary ideas under legal literary forms with which our censorship agencies are often powerless to contend. And that's the very purpose of the ever-watchful eye of the NKVD to detect and expose those hidden counter-revolutionaries! They are longing for the return of capitalism; they would gladly take away the land from the peasantry and return it to the former owners; they would be happy to put some bloody despot back on the throne and to become his ministers! To this species belongs this representative of that hostile Socialist Revolutionary intelligentsia which it is our task to uproot like an evil growth from our Communist field. . . . "

The magistrates listened reverently and nodded assent. I must admit that I found little to object to in the first part of Redens' peroration; but the hints contained in the second part puzzled me and I came to understand their meaning only two months later, in the course of one of my examinations. When Redens finished, I said:

"If in your lectures for examiners you indoctrinate them in such a fashion, I feel sorry for your audiences. Never did the Socialist Revolutionary Party dream of a restoration of the monarchy, of the return of capitalism and landlordism; never did I personally aim at a minister's post. . . . As far as I am concerned, this is all nonsense."

Without honoring me with an answer, Redens again exchanged a few words with Sheptalov and left the room. The magistrates and their assistants, those nurslings of the NKVD, disciples of the man in yellow, followed suit in single file. I was left alone with Sheptalov. The clock showed less than midnight, yet it seemed to me that I had spent ages in this place.

Six months later, in ward No. 79 of Butyrki, we learned through the usual "post office" and "radiotelegraph" channels that Redens was among the inmates of the adjoining ward, transferred there from Lefortovo where he had confessed to espionage in favor of Latvia. I greatly regretted he was not in my ward—it would have been interesting to have a look at him in his new role. . . . Later we learned that he had been returned to Lefortovo, and the last news we heard was that of his execution in the summer of 1938.

Strange, indeed are the ways of the NKVD!

Index